ABOUT THE AUTHOR

James Ladd Thomas, born and raised in Alabama, is the author of the novel *Ardor*. He has published short stories in various literary journals, including *Berkeley Fiction Review, Hawai'i Review, RE:AL, First Class, littledeathlit*, and *Finding the Birds*. For twenty-five years he taught fiction workshops at Valencia College. He currently lives in Florida.

Visit *jamesladdthomas.com* to read more.

PRAISE

"This Lester can lie down wherever he wants to, as far as I'm concerned. And James Ladd Thomas is a hell of a novelist."
TOM FRANKLIN, AUTHOR, *CROOKED LETTER, CROOKED LETTER*

"Deftly written, audacious and probing, *Lester Lies Down* is a memorable piece of work, and James Ladd Thomas writes some of the quirkiest dialogue I've come across in a long time. I'm glad his book found its way to me. I'll be watching for his next one."
STEVE YARBROUGH, AUTHOR, *STAY GONE DAYS*

"When an old girlfriend shows up with stolen money and two goons on her tail, widower Lester Gordon is wrestling with the tricky transition from car wash owner to hospice worker. Lester is already dealing with death and dying all around him and with his three children who are experimenting with junior high porn and bookmaking. Oh, and he's on the spectrum. By turns hilarious and heartbreaking, and with an eccentric cast of secondary characters, *Lester Lies Down* catches the joys and pains of Southern life in bright colors."
JOHN CALVIN HUGHES, AUTHOR, *THE LOST GOSPEL OF DARNELL RABREN*

"Funny, heartbreaking and, at times, thrilling, James Ladd Thomas's *Lester Lies Down* is a more than worthy successor to his earlier and equally unique novel, *Ardor*. Peopled with vividly realized, all-too-human characters, starting with the titular Lester Gordon, a mildly autistic hospice caregiver, you'll often feel as if you're eavesdropping on the most intimate conversations, many occurring on that indefinable border between life and death. *Lester Lies Down* is a remarkably insightful achievement that deserves to be read, discussed, and savored. I thank both Thomas and Lester for introducing me to a world I would never have experienced otherwise. For this I remain sincerely grateful."
MICHAEL LIBLING, AUTHOR, *HOLLYWOOD NORTH: A NOVEL IN SIX REELS*

"*Lester Lies Down* reminds me of why I started reading books in the first place—to be enchanted, to be carried away from my world and dropped into a world more vivid and incandescent. James Ladd Thomas casts his considerable spell with exquisite sentences, unerring and evocative details, and with unforgettable characters, like Lester Gordon, widow, autistic father of three, and hospice nurse who is most alive while caring for the dying. I started reading the book slowly hoping the story wouldn't end and I wouldn't have to say goodbye to Lester and Ardor and Ced and Marlin. Yes, fate may slap us down, but friends and family will us up. Did I mention the bad guys and the enigmatic pack of white dogs that just might haunt your dreams?"

JOHN DUFRESNE, AUTHOR, *I DON'T LIKE WHERE THIS IS GOING*

LESTER LIES DOWN

JAMES LADD THOMAS

www.vineleavespress.com

Lester Lies Down

Print Edition
ISBN: 978-618-86002-4-9
Published by Vine Leaves Press in Greece 2022

Cover design by Jessica Bell
Interior design by Amie McCracken

A catalogue record of this work is available from The National Library of Greece.

For Ron Harris, Patrick Morrow, and Barry Lopez

“If liberty means anything at all, it means the right to tell people what they do not want to hear.”

George Orwell

ANOMALY

THE LATE AFTERNOON SUN soothed Lester Gordon's face, a face tight from the thoughts of the past few weeks. The October grass tickled his neck and something wiggly crawled up his right leg under his pants. Whatever it was didn't sting, so he felt no urgency in its removal; lie on the ground and bugs will find you. Lying face up in his backyard felt good this day, the shaggy overgrown grass providing a cushion of turf in this late fall day bearing a swimming-pool-blue sky, though good wasn't what he had been feeling during these past eventful days.

"Now this is much better," he said to himself. Bending his chin to his chest, he examined his go-to home attire: blue jeans, faded and worn, his favorite pair; a black and blue flannel shirt; and a pair of tan running shoes, worn from use. His arms and legs were so contortedly positioned on the billowy grass that if someone had spray-painted the outline of his body orange, the shape would have matched the misshapen outlines in endless TV dramas. He wasn't dead, just, like everyone else, wounded.

Mary King, the neighbor directly behind his house, saw him lying on his back while she gazed out her kitchen window as she made her husband, Bill, his usual Saturday roast beef, hot peppers, and thick-sliced tomato sandwich for lunch. If anything, it relieved her to see Lester sunk in his six-inch-high grass. Such an odd sight took her back to her youth when her mother drove her to school every morning. Mary remembered the innocence of a neighbor's special needs son who stood most every morning in his driveway waving at the passing cars. She turned to Bill as she spread the mayo on a slice of white bread and remarked, "Sure is good to see Lester lying out there in his backyard. Certainly odd, not what you would call ordinary, but somehow it's reassuring."

Bill, while keeping his eyes on the sports page, replied, "What Lester needs to do is get off his butt and mow the grass."

Mike Alexander, the neighbor to Lester's left, sat at a worktable in his carport where he kept his fishing boat and tackle. He had seen Lester come out and lie down while Mike tinkered with his outboard Mercury motor. After a few minutes Mike had called out, as he had done many times through the four years of living next door, "How's life, Lester?"

Raising his head toward Mike, Lester shouted back, "Sucks, man."

Mike's response, a loud "Don't it, though," made them both laugh, and as usual the conversation had comfortably died there.

Connie Rogers, the neighbor on Lester's right, saw him as she jammed her old '72 blue Beetle into reverse and beeped her horn; she was on her way to the grocery store. When Lester heard the beep he raised his right hand, forming his fingers into the peace sign. Like the others, Connie thought Lester lying on his back in the grass was as natural as if he was sipping a cold beer in a hammock on a hot summer afternoon. Lester was doing, in their view, what Lester did.

One of the constants in Lester Gordon's life involved his capability of just dropping down and lying on his back anytime and anywhere. As a toddler, Lester would suddenly drop down to his knees, roll on his rear, then ease back to "The Lester Position," as his father came to call it. He would do it while playing on the cracked sidewalk in front of his house, while watching cartoons on the den floor, even while eating lunch at his Big Bird table in the kitchen.

A few times his mother found him under his bed looking up at the bottom of the box springs as if contemplating their complexity or perhaps pretending to be a mechanic like one of the workers at his father's car wash who worked on cars in his backyard garage.

To this day his mother tells friends he became nearly obsessed with spread-eagling on his back while accompanying her in the grocery store as a young boy, though he seemed to prefer the dairy aisle where the tiles were refreshingly cool on sweltering summer days. He would pat the floor next to him while looking up at her grinning face. His mother, being the loving mother she was, would drop down and join her son in observing the world from a grounded view (though in stores she'd shake her head and exclaim, "I can't do that here, honey").

His fifth-grade teacher, Mrs. Jordan, said he would stretch out on a worktable at the back of the classroom during morning break and stare intently at the ceiling tiles. In high school Lester enjoyed gazing up at the pine tree branches in Mastin Lake Park while nestled in the copper pine straw. He loved to lie back on the top row of the bleachers during baseball games. His first girlfriend, Donna White, said he loved to lie on her front porch while they talked and smooched, but his place of choice was to lie out in her front yard looking up at the stars and moon.

More than once an employee had stumbled onto Lester while he lay on his back in the storage room of the video store he owned and operated. A couple of his high school workers, in their ignorance, thought that he was crazy. "I'm working for Rain Man," eighteen-year-old Paul Hagan often said.

No one ever understood why he did it, why he would stretch out on his back like he was about to take a nap, though there were all types of explanations. His sister had always said he wanted attention, wanted people to look at him. "When we were little tykes he saw Momma's and Daddy's looks of satisfaction as I rode my bike for the first time without training wheels. Then and there he plopped down on his back in the middle of the street in front of our house. Old Man Daniels from across the street almost ran him over with his Cadillac while pulling out of his driveway."

At first, his parents thought his behavior was just plain cute, as most parents would think of their toddler. However, as the years flowed by they understood there was something unusual about this habit, something that didn't appear to be diminishing as he grew and matured. His mother thought he might have an equilibrium problem and took him to the doctor, only to be told Lester was, physically speaking, fine. His father, ever the man of reason, said the habit was nothing more than a benign eccentricity. "Who is he hurting?" he would always say. "Let the boy have his pleasure. It's not like he's masturbating in public." They knew their son was different, that he was odd, a bit off. And many nights in bed together they reasoned that "some people are just eccentric." Their attitude reflected their love for their son. They helped him in any way they could, but most importantly they loved him for who he was, not for who they wanted him to be.

When asked, "Why do you lie on your back, Lester?" his response, whether as a young boy or a young man, was generally the same: "It makes me feel good. It stops the world from spinning out of control, like everything's okay." Most people nodded their heads at this explanation, but deep down they did not understand what that meant exactly, that he was just playing them off. But that wasn't the case at all. Lester was being honest, as was his way forever and ever. When the world became too much, when too many pitches from the world came at him at one time, Lester would apply the brakes by plopping down and looking at the sky. It baffled Connie, the neighbor, as much as anyone when she first observed these lie-down breaks, but her curiosity hovered at a distance until the day she mentioned Lester's behavior to a special needs teacher friend who told her that such a behavior could be a trait of autistic people.

"They lie down to center themselves, to calm the sensory overloads they can easily experience. They also do it because they are fearful of the world."

"Fearful of the world? What do you mean?" Connie asked.

"Autistic children, even autistic adults, feel alienated when they are around neurotypical people. They are in a world that they find terrifying. Maybe terrifying isn't exactly right. They see a world where they must always try to fit in. It's exhausting for them. Lying down helps them take a little break. A little recharge."

"Huh," said Connie. "I never thought of it like that."

"Most people don't," said her friend.

The immediate cause of Lester Gordon's need to stretch out under this day's soothing sky was from a seed that had been planted a few weeks ago when he had seen Bob Mosely standing in Connie Rogers' front yard. That evening had boiled Lester's blood like the black bubbles in the steaming roofing tar he had used during a stint as a roofer the summer of his first attempt at college. He had been awakened at 2:30 in the morning by a fire truck's siren as it screamed down his street to answer the call of Phil McAllen's house fire. He stood bewildered, the hair on the right side of his head pillow-mashed a side-angle pompadour, on his front porch steps looking left down the street at the flicker of red lights to see whose house was burning. People all along the street poured out of their homes, stood in their yards, on the sidewalks, in the street, and tried to catch a glimpse of the flames and firefighters doing their jobs. He turned right to see who was out of their houses on this particular side of the street and saw Connie, in a white T-shirt and blue sweatpants, standing in her front yard. He had taken a few steps toward her when he saw a barefooted Bob Mosely walk from Connie's front door wearing tan shorts and a black T-shirt with TENNESSEE written in orange across the chest.

Bob Mosely? he thought. He raised his right hand and gave a wave to Connie and Bob. *Must God mock my very existence?* he whispered to himself.

He then noticed Bob's truck sitting in Connie's driveway, a late-model Dodge with a gigantic chrome grill. Lester laughed. "Sorry about your little dick," he softly said to no one.

"Hey, Lester. What's going on? Somebody's cat stuck in a tree?" Bob shouted out with a chuckle.

"I think it's Terry and his crew out for a joy ride. Gets kinda boring at the fire station," Lester called back. He looked at Connie. She waved. He decided to walk over, at least have the pleasure of absorbing her beauty. He walked deliberately across his yard. A cool breeze blew through his shoulder-length hair and across his bare feet. The frosty breath of winter's approach surprised him, though the first intrusion of cold caught many unprepared. Lester could see Connie quite clearly since the moon was full, shining a soft, comforting light, the faint shadows providing a deathly tone.

"It's a wonderful night for a fire, don't you think?" Lester said as he walked up to Connie and Bob. Lester looked at Connie. The shape of her face and the tint of her skin bespoke a Native American quality: high cheekbones narrowing down to a firm chin, rather noble in structure, eyes that glistened with intensity, yet their dark, forest green color made Lester question life's genetic crapshoot. Was the universe this insanely chaotic in its creations? Those deep-set green eyes and skin colored with several drops of carmine pigment caused Lester to pause beyond a polite stutter of focus. Though fully conscious of this brain freeze, the seconds collected into a dab, then a pile, then a small mound until finally provoking Lester to avert his eyes from this "accident" of nature. Lester's social skills were awkward, to be kind, whereas some would call these social burps rude and narcissistic in nature. The more attentive observers, such as Connie, found these odd behaviors endearing.

"That's exactly what I was telling Connie just a few minutes ago as we were sipping glasses of wine in her bed."

Lester searched Bob's face for a smile, a showing of teeth. In Lester's view, Connie should have been physically, intellectually, emotionally, monetarily, culturally, humorously, even musically far beyond Bob's place in the universe. And, it came, of course, the gloating smile, from just a slight lift of the upper lip that revealed his teeth in the light of the moon. When Lester's eyes had finally stopped on Connie's face, he saw her giving Bob a sidelong stare. After a few seconds, Connie turned to Lester and looked him straight in the eye without saying a word. Lester enjoyed the intimacy of her look, but as always, he had no clue as to what it meant. The three of them stood in Connie's front yard under the moon's revealing beam for a few minutes making mild chatter while Lester and Connie exchanged glances. That night, not for the first time, Lester fell asleep picturing his lips kissing Connie's.

The next day, Lester rose at mid-morning, walked into the kitchen to put on a pot of coffee, then made himself pad into the den and take a glance out the window to see if Bob's truck was still parked in Connie's driveway. As he pulled back the curtain, he only saw Connie's blue Beetle in the drive. He walked back through the house and eased out the front door to retrieve the morning paper. He glanced toward Connie's house, considered walking over and placing her paper on her front steps, but he dismissed that thought as rather childish or excessively good-neighborly. He walked back into his home, made a cup of coffee, then went out to his back patio and sat down in one of his two aluminum garden chairs with woven green and white nylon strips. The chairs had been handed down from his parents and dripped with childhood memories, and he loved them far beyond their monetary value.

While reading the paper, as ever full of death and chaos, Lester intermittently chastised himself for not taking the initiative in his relations with Connie. Lester had always been rather clumsy around people, of course, especially women. He masked his awkwardness by imitating his friends and family. Through the years he sharpened his social skills in order to fit in, but when facing impromptu conversations with the feminine world he would become a tongue-tied schoolboy, melting like a salt statue of Thor in a blinding rainstorm of the libido.

"Come on, man, take the dog to the fight, you passive sad sack of dicks," Lester said to himself. "Now or never, man."

"Who you talking to, Lester?" Mike called from the fence while on his way to his carport.

"Just me, myself, and I. We got quite the argument going on."

"Don't let me interrupt y'all. Just keep it peaceful; no fighting. This is a good neighborhood."

"We're all friends enjoying one another's company most times. Except when the other two are drinking. They can get a little ugly and mean."

Mike had rested his arms on the fence while he talked to Lester. He nodded his head. "Okay. I get that. Y'all be cool," then he turned and walked into his carport and began preparing for a fishing excursion to one of the sloughs on the Tennessee River.

By early afternoon, Lester had finished dutifully folding a load of socks and underwear when he heard a knock on his front door. He opened it and was struck almost breathless by the sight of Connie holding a bottle of wine and smiling. Lester smiled back, his eyes gliding over her face. She flickered not a bit, not a smidgen, her eyes piercing his tenuous shield of confidence. Lester glanced away.

"Hey, Connie."

"I thought you might like a little wine with your Saturday afternoon."

"The only thing better with wine than Saturday afternoon is Saturday evening," said Lester as he stepped back and swung his left arm around in a panoramic wave. "Enter, young lass," his words whipped through the air. Connie smiled, then chuckled and shook her head as she walked in, giving the den an overt quick study.

"You know, I've never seen the inside of your house."

"You can't say that now, huh?" Lester walked over to the middle of the room and opened his arms. "At first glance, what do you think? Does it fulfill all your expectations, or are your dreams suddenly dashed? Be honest, I can take it. I'm fully aware I have no taste. My whole life is like driving in a snowstorm."

"To tell you the truth, I didn't know what to expect. You're an anomaly, Lester Gordon. A mystery."

Lester smiled. "A mystery," he repeated. "A mysterious man. I like that. Keep 'em guessing. The less you know, the more you'll like me. That's a fact, Connie."

Connie held Lester's eyes, trying to understand this quirky neighbor with whom she felt an odd attraction. "Oh, it's all a mystery, right?" She held up the bottle of wine. "Shall we?"

They drank the bottle of wine sitting on Lester's aged green leather couch, another relic handed down from his mother. While Connie stroked his right arm with her fingertips, a gesture in its second hour, he took notice of her lips, billowy rims, swollen, deliciously puffy. After they emptied the bottle, he slowly leaned over and kissed her. It was sudden and without thought. He wasn't sure if the kiss was appropriate. He would never know if such a kiss was appropriate.

The kiss lasted several seconds, a delicate meeting of the lips at first, then a slow grind, not his first kiss but one of the few he possessed at this stage of his life, a twisting, turning, mashing of the folds of flesh. Lester kept his eyes closed for the initial touch; but as the kiss intensified, libidinously coiling, tongues probing, dancing, he opened his eyes to her lush forest-green circles surrounded by the bright white.

The next morning, Lester woke to an empty bed and a throbbing head. He quickly closed his eyes, the night a jagged memory. Connie had retrieved a second bottle of wine from her house once they polished off the first one; music played, their laughter intensified. He remembered Connie leaving, but the exact time was out of his reach. He was dozing when she gathered her clothes, kissed him delicately on the lips, then sashayed to the bedroom door; her long look expressed through sleepy eyes and a soft smile. The memory ended and he finally opened his eyes and glanced at the clock radio on the bedside table; the red numbers forced him with their indifference to contemplate the new day. "8:09?" he whispered to himself. He rubbed his eyes with the heels of his hands.

Walk over, say hello, "I enjoyed the evening," no, too soon, let her come, just work in the yard, mow the grass, nope, lawnmower not running, take to the shop, maybe next door, let Mike have a go at it, no, not happening, fishing today, call her, just let her know last night was nice, ohhhhhhhhh, front lobe pounding, need to drink water, down several aspirins, toast, maybe cheese toast, salted grits, get up, gotta get up, come on, raise head, oh my god, down, easy fella, how big of a fool was I last night, blips of scenes, could have been ridiculous, she could be on the phone with friends, relating obnoxious acts of lust, belly-splitting laughter, curled up on her couch, tears streaming down face, living next door to the cable guy, pondering a move? will she ever speak to me again? calm down, settle, everything's fine, remember the look as she left, she'll be back, mentioned a canoe trip, Flint

River? with friends today? declined her invitation, fearing to appear anxious, complete idiot, truly moronic behavior, blew it, a dunghill of pathetic confusion, could be over there now, deliberate sabotage? a paralysis of fear, a toad of masculinity, must force these bullfrog legs to function, get up, even an ape would seek some form of relief, crawl to bathroom, shower, maybe lie low today, watch a football game, a movie or two, nurse head back to health, let the world come to me, check email, ohhhhh, the phone, avoid contact, could be Connie, let machine pick up.

"Hey, Lester, are you there? Hey, man, this is Snook."

Lester grabbed the phone. "Hey."

"Did I wake you?"

"No, just nursing a family-size hangover."

"You tied one on last night? Where'd you go?"

"Nowhere. The abuse took place at home."

"Who came over?"

"Next door neighbor."

"Mike? I didn't think he drank."

"No, not Mike, the other side. Connie."

"Connie? Beautiful Connie came over?"

"Out of the blue, man. The gods decided to reward my worthless ass. But I can't talk right now."

"You mean she's there with you?"

"No, no, she's gone. It's just that I'm in the process of dying. I'm speaking to you through gritted teeth. Let me call you back. I'm still trying to process the night. Are you going to be around this afternoon?"

"I'll be in and out all day. Give me a ring. Maybe I'll drop by later on. I want to hear more about the evening."

"It was a very nice evening. I think completely spontaneous, at least on my end. I don't know where this is going, but I like the first step. I'll talk to you later, okay?"

"All right, man, later."

Lester found himself waiting for Connie's return. He waited the rest of that day. Sunday evening he noticed Connie's bug sitting under her carport. A few times during the week he saw Connie pull out of the driveway. On Friday afternoon, Lester finally made eye contact for the first time since early Sunday morning. He was walking back to his house from the curbside mailbox when Connie pulled into her driveway and came to a stop under her carport. He shuffled his mail as he walked up his driveway. She carried a couple of plastic bags of groceries along with her purse as she walked the few paces from her car to the steps leading up to her side door. She turned and gave him a half-wave with her left hand. Lester returned the wave as he walked toward her but stopped after a few steps.

"Hey, stranger," he said.

"Hey, Lester. What a week. It's been crazy at school. Lots of parent conferences. How ya been?"

"Fine, business has been rather good lately. Thank God some big names have new releases. Most of it is schlock, but, you know, give the people what they want. I was going to come over or call you tonight to see if you wanted to do something this weekend."

Connie smiled, then hesitated. "I've got plans for this weekend, but maybe some other time," she said.

"Oh, sure, some other time."

"Well, I need to get in. I'm expecting a call."

"Okay, I'll see you later," he said, then turned and walked across the yard to his front door. Lester sat down on his bed, bowed his head. He closed his eyes, before allowing himself to fall back and watch the red minutes change on his clock. The light gradually receded from his room, his thoughts still whirled around Connie.

Lester awoke to the slamming of car doors that poured in through the bedroom window next to Connie's house. He quickly popped out of bed and walked over to the window facing her carport. Pulling back the curtain to create a crack of sight he saw Connie loading a sleeping bag into the back end of a blue sports utility vehicle that was parked behind her VW. A young man Lester didn't recognize stood next to her, tickling her belly. They exchanged words and broke into laughter with Connie jovially punching the man on the shoulder, before he closed the rear hatch.

Lester walked into his kitchen and downed a can of beer in a few large gulps, then walked through the house looking for his small cooler before he remembered that he had left it at a party a couple of weekends before. He pulled out a kitchen garbage bag and loaded several cans of beers from the fridge and a few hands of ice from the freezer, then walked back into the bedroom for one more peek out the window. The SUV was gone, and Connie's house was dark besides the front porch light. Carrying the bag of beer and ice he walked back through the house and out his back door, stood on his patio, and looked up at the fall sky. A blustery wind blew across his backyard; a cold front had pushed into North Alabama from the northwest. Feeling the biting approach of the inevitable winter, he walked back inside and retrieved an old Army jacket he wore for the woods.

Adjusting the coat as he returned to the patio, Lester looked over at Connie's house and opened one of the beers from the bag. He chugged a few swallows of the liquid gold and called out into the night, "Kilroy was here!" A non sequitur for everyone but Lester. He looked at the other houses surrounding his backyard for any curiosity seekers, perhaps Mary King giving a stare out her kitchen window or Mike poking his head out of his workshop, but he found no one at a window, no heads poking out of doors. Lester finished the beer and dropped it into the bag, then walked over to Connie's house and sat the bag of beer just behind the carport, turned and walked back over to the rear of his house and retrieved an aluminum extension ladder. He adjusted the ladder so the top would jut up a couple of feet above the carport's flat roof. Tucking the beer under his left arm he slowly climbed the ladder, placing the bag on the roof when he reached the top, then stepped onto the roof himself.

Lester looked around the carport's rock and tar roof, a scattering of a couple of Frisbees, a wine bottle, and what looked like a shirt. He scanned the neighborhood once more, the view from the roof allowing a more-reaching detection. Many lights glowed from the homes, the evening ripe with activity. A group of teenagers climbed out of a sports car four houses down from Connie's front yard. They laughed, two dancing around the yard while the others walked into the house. He spied the Johnsons lying on the couch together watching television through a sliding glass door at the rear of a house, a kind and earnest elderly couple who had always been nice to Lester and lived a couple of houses down on the street behind Lester. He turned to look at his own front yard and suddenly spied what looked like several dogs standing in his yard just out of the street. They were white, which Lester found strange. They were looking right at Lester as he stood on the roof, staring at him almost in rapture as if they had been looking for him, waiting for him, and suddenly there he was, on the roof of the house next door. He didn't see a collar around their necks, and he was positive he had never seen them before. Surely, he would have remembered several white dogs living in his neighborhood.

"What are you looking at, motherfuckers?" he shouted at the dogs.

He heard a crash in the backyard of one of the houses a few lots down from his own. He quickly looked over and eyed a woman bent over on her patio picking up the pieces of a broken flowerpot. And when he looked back at the dogs they were gone, nowhere to be seen, not in his yard, not in Connie's yard, not in the street, no signs of the white canines as Lester quickly panned the neighboring yards. Vanished.

Shuddering, he zipped up his coat and dug his hands into the pockets to look for the gloves he usually kept for hiking during the bitter months of winter. With relief he found the gloves and pulled them on, then turned up the collar to provide another defense against the intruding cold. Low clouds hovered above, blocking the stars and moon. He sat down, crossed his legs, and pulled another beer from the bag. After popping open the can he poured a few more swallows down his throat.

Within twenty minutes, he emptied two more beers from the bag. Without hesitation, he decided to drink one more rather quickly. Why? He wasn't sure, but it made sense to Lester while he sat shivering on his neighbor's carport roof. Two minutes later, the beer can clanged against the other cans as he dropped it in the bag. He leaned back, letting the weight of his head slowly take him down until the touch of his shoulders to the gravel roof allowed him to finally relax. He closed his eyes and listened to the wind play a melody through the surrounding pines and oaks, limbs and trunks creaking and cracking, the rush of air whispering and sighing. The roar of an engine and the peel of rubber on asphalt alerted Lester to an approaching car; and for a brief moment he feared Connie's sudden return, but the car quickly passed. Lester fell asleep for a few seconds but awoke with a start from a loud knock that sounded very close, as if under the carport, but when he sat up he found himself lightheaded and had to use his hands to give himself balance. He waited patiently for another sound, but he heard nothing save the symphony of the cold wind.

Tangled in the haze of the mild acceleration of beer intoxication, he slowly came to his feet and began walking across the many slants and angles of Connie's old home. Stopping and steadying himself a couple of times, he made it to the chimney, the very top and center of the house. With one hand grasping the rim of the chimney for balance, he inspected the nearby houses and unceremoniously dropped an empty can from his bag down the chimney and waited for the clanging that never came. Lester panicked as the can left his grip and then peered down into the open hole, a curious and infinite black. He shook his head, feeling the bitter wind gnaw at his face and neck, unable to comprehend the silence. Again, Lester slowly scanned the neighborhood. He found himself crying without understanding why.

On his walk back to the flat carport roof he stumbled, but this time was unable to right the loss of balance and began tottering down the backside of the roof. Though possessing mind enough to jut his limbs out in an attempt to stop his tumble toward the edge, the combination of beer and the cold wind made the attempt ineffective. As if in a slow-motion replay, he tumbled over the edge, still gripping the bag of beer cans and ice, and began his descent to the grass below. He feared falling on his head, but, luckily, that was not to be. Lester landed on his right thigh and hip, which would have been fine but that his right leg was sticking out like a spider in his attempt to break the fall. The weight of his torso on his limb snapped his thigh bone much like the breaking of a Popsicle stick. The pain from the break, although not a compound fracture, was, of course, excruciating, but only a part of the wound Lester would negotiate for months to come.

After a few seconds of gathering his thoughts, Lester Gordon began to yell for help, a desperate wail that pierced the frigid wind. Mike Alexander, who was in his workshop and had heard "Kilroy was here" earlier, was hunched over one of his fishing lures when he heard the shout and knew immediately that Lester was in pain somewhere. He dropped the plastic bait, then rushed out of the shed and began running toward the direction of the plea. Lester Gordon was lying on his back, drunk, in pain, cold, and confusion in the icy darkness of the approaching winter.

RUBY SWEET

LESTER SAT in his green pickup, hood a lime green; passenger door a dark forest green; driver-side door a white with a smidgen of green; and the rest, roof, quarter panels, and bed a candy apple green. Lester wasn't sure if the color was candy apple green, but he loved to say it, and it reminded him of the candy apple green Honda Mini Trail 70 he road nearly twenty-five years ago. The truck's front tires parked a few inches in the grass off the edge of the driveway. He swung the keys in his right hand then rolled the fingers of his left along the top of the steering wheel as he looked straight ahead at the two plum trees that he and Connie planted six years ago in the backyard. The cool October air felt fresh to Lester, the wind curling the changing seasons as the plum trees' branches danced naked, bereft of the recently harvested first season of tangy fruit. His memory snaked to the Douglas Nursery, how the elderly owner had convinced Connie that plums were worth the risk for the home gardener in North Alabama, the justified danger of early flowering wiped clean by late winter freezes, the old man shaking his head for emphasis as he explained how the high susceptibility of the Japanese plums to diseases limited their longevity.

"I'm of the minority with these plums, but I certainly understand people's trepidation. The percentages ain't gonna work in your favor, but sometimes the really sweet stuff is worth the risk. Same way with women, you know," the man said with a wink to Connie.

"Sweetness can be deceptive," said Connie.

"Whatcha mean?" asked the man.

"In the plant world it's used for bait to help spread the seeds."

"Right," said the man.

"But humans, now correct me if I'm wrong, do use it as bait, just that the purpose can be more than spreading seeds," said Connie.

The old man nodded his head. "Yeah, yeah, you're right about that. Some folks got a hell of a sweet tooth. Sad to see."

"I love the sweet stuff," said Lester.

The old man snickered and then shot a glance at Connie. "I'd recommend the A.U. Roadside and the Ruby Sweet since you need two varieties for cross-pollination. And these two," the owner said as he stroked his gray walrus mustache and gave an exaggerated chef's kiss, "are heaven on Earth. Now I'm gonna be honest with you. The trees probably won't live that long, even if a freeze don't kill 'em you're looking at eight, ten years tops," said the man.

"Just a few years of fruit then you have to start over," said Connie.

"True, you'll only get a few seasons of plums, but those years are really something to behold. A person can buy sturdier varieties that'll live longer, give you more years of fruit, but you'd be hard-pressed to find trees that bear sweeter and juicier plums. Plums you dream about. And that's a fact."

Lester looked down at the keys in his hand. He knew he could still back out, call Jenny Lynn, his supervisor, tell her he was bailing, that he just couldn't do it. That he had made a mistake, fallen prey to chasing that American Dream of believing you could do anything because you had faith, that putting in hard work almost guaranteed success. He believed in the dream, like everyone else, dreams creating hope. Now he realized the dream was a work in progress. He thought of friends who had chased a dream only to realize their aim was a bit too high, not realistic. And even if you committed to the hours of hard work needed to attain the skills to accomplish your dream, success would not always be waiting for you. There was luck, good and bad, and, of course, money, good and bad.

What a fool, he thought. I'm an idiot. Naïve, stupid, foolish, a gaggle of childish dreams. A last-second exit would cause problems, burdens created by no one but himself, shifts added, schedules twisted inside-out. Maybe all this was just routine in the hospice world, people coming to terms with the realities of the fantasy of such an altruistic career. He inhaled a deep breath, wondered if he could actually follow through and make caring for the dying a focus in his life. Talking the talk had been fun, people nodding their approval of this new career choice, admiration glistening in their eyes, the little encouragements of "You have such compassion," "What a noble career," his explanations full of belief and confirmation, his enthusiasm genuine. His doubts, insecurities, and paranoia now hammered his confidence. Was all this training worth the effort, the time, and the money invested? The early goals achieved, earning R.N. certification at a local technical college, logging in a year's experience at the Huntsville Hospital I.C.U., shadowing veteran hospice nurses during his training, chewing through the hospice books and pamphlets to soak up all those ideas about comforting the dying, and chanting the hospice mantras of autonomy and self-determination. Such perseverance, grinding each step of the way, knowing he was plowing the fields for a future harvest. But now the first official day of solo calls brought doubt, or was it fear? Or was the struggle what he wanted all along? His world was spinning and he felt lost.

Lester fought anxiety all during the night, running through the protocols a few more times, checking off the steps for different situations, rehearsing and planning, hoping the stewing anxiety would generate the needed energy for the day. He rose at 4:12 a.m., surrendering to his buzzing mind, no longer able to patiently toss and turn. He had taken a Xanax the night before to help calm his nerves, but that led to a fear of sleeping through his alarm. His first solo visit would be with Toots Richards, a fifty-three-year-old Alabama native Lester had visited with supervisor, Jenny Lynn, a half-dozen times. Sucking cigs for thirty-five years had earned a lung cancer death sentence. He was living his last days with his daughter, Irene, a thirty-four-year-old single mom with three children in elementary school.

An hour before dawn, an armful of minutes before his kids began to stir, his thoughts ran to Connie as if he hadn't told her yet, fearful of owning up to his decision to enter the world of the dying. Lester ached. He hadn't felt comfort since Connie breathed for the last time that Sunday night in June five years ago. Was such a drastic change okay with her? The grief still fogged his world, the days of clarity few at best, like he was walking through a world of Jell-O. He wanted her input, her ability to weigh the costs and benefits, her practicality to harness his creativity, her calm in his world of storms. In his world, her pragmatism was perhaps her greatest strength. He felt stronger with her and appreciative of her love for such an odd soul. Her bewilderment evolved into love, not falling in love, such an emotion impossible when he himself drunkenly tumbled off the edge of her roof. From the moment her friend provided answers to weird behavior, she began connecting the dots, researching, reading articles and books; the information took on weight as she realized other friends and acquaintances dotted the spectrum. She told him more than once that his mystery possessed a charm she found irresistible.

He never saw her, even though he looked for her during those numbing first weeks after the lymphoma pulled her from his world. No face in the window glass, no revenant standing in the kitchen, no phantom keeping him afloat. Never heard a whisper during these dark hours of the morning. Lester fully accepted Connie vanishing from his life. Yet he stalked in these silent moments, not hunting the nodding of her head, nor her smile, he craved her reasoning, wanted to see the gears of her mind as he explained his fear of stepping into the unknown, of risking his family's financial security, the trepidation caused by truly believing he could help another human being face death head on. He knew she would look into his eyes, listen to the distress rattling up his throat, smile, then explain her caution, her support, her practical deliberation, her reasoning assuaging his mushrooming anxieties. That's what he missed. That's what he wanted from his wife who was no longer by his side.

When Lester heard twelve-year-old Jase singing "Get back, Loretta" on his way to the bathroom he found himself wiping sweat from his brow. He held the edge of his desk to steady the sudden dizziness, healing the runaway train beats of his lungs; surely a panic hatched from a firm belief that he had made a bad decision, not only for himself (he wasn't ready to soothe the dying, probably never would be, his true self never possessing such steady behavior), but for his family too: his kids the top priority, their welfare his main purpose in life.

So why did he think selling Rocket City Car Wash, inherited from his daddy, was the right thing to do? The money from Connie's life insurance had been a blessing for the family, bought at her insistence over his cries of foolish choice for a woman her age, paying off the mortgage and credit-card debt as well as creating financial simplicity to his life. The car-wash money he'd put into a low-risk portfolio at the behest of a successful financial manager, a childhood friend. The numbers worked; this was a sound plan, but selling the business his father worked, managed, and owned for over thirty years was the decision he never could quite live down, an act that seemed a betrayal. The investments and hospice income would support his family, but he seemed full of doubt just because he was risking his family's welfare on his own, however calculated and reasoned. When he heard Jase flush the toilet, he whispered to himself, "What the fuck have I done?"

Jase walked into his dad's study/bedroom as a man with a mission. He stopped at the right side of the small secretary desk.

"Daddy?"

"Hey, Jase, what are you doing up so early?"

"The game. We're doomed. Those guys are going to kill us, show us no mercy. It's gonna be ugly, Dad."

"You never know. Teams that are favored to win get beat all the time."

"That's a fantasy, Dad. In the real world, we're gonna get creamed."

"Do you enjoy playing basketball?"

"Yeah, love the game, but there is no pleasure in getting stomped."

"You got a game to play, so go play and enjoy yourself."

"I'm talking of getting embarrassed. We'll be humiliated."

"You'll do fine."

"I also woke up thinking about you."

"Yeah?"

"Today is the day for you to be by yourself in your job."

"Today is the day, Jase."

"I was wondering, will you ever see 'em die, your patients? I mean, while you're trying to help them?"

"There's always the possibility; it's one of the reasons I'm there. To help people accept their death, and, of course, help them live every day they have left with everything they got."

"To help them see the light?" asked Jase.

"See the light?"

"Yeah, you know, people say when you die there's a big light you see at the end of a tunnel with people waving you toward the light, dead relatives telling you to come on down."

"Right, right," said Lester as he tapped the fingers of his right hand on the desk, "well, nobody knows if that's really true, of course. I tend to think that's just what people want to believe is true, that your loved ones will be welcoming you to the next life."

"Life?"

"The afterlife, the next stage. If you believe it then it's true, at least true in your head. Nothing wrong with that. I like to think it's an interesting image. I suppose one way to look at it is that such a belief helps people find peace in their approaching death."

"What do you believe?"

"What do you mean?"

"Do you believe that you'll see Mom after you die?"

This question caught Lester completely off guard. He looked at Jase, then looked at the floor in front of Jase's feet. "Well," he said, but he was unable to finish a sentence.

"Are you gonna be okay, Dad? You know how you can get when you get overloaded."

Lester took a deep breath. "Damn, I'm lucky to have you kids. Just so damn lucky."

Jase walked up to his father and wrapped his arms around his shoulders without saying a word. Lester hugged his son with his right arm. Neither father nor son spoke for a couple of minutes.

"Thank you, Jase. Y'all do help me."

"I think you'll see her. I think we'll all see her again," said Jase.

"I think that's a great image to have, Jase. I was just thinking about Mom. I like thinking that I'll see her again. Not sure if it'll happen, but what a wonderful world it would be if it does. So I guess I'm gonna believe it."

"Me, too," said Jase.

"And really, that's all I'm trying to do with my patients: help them find their own path and peace as they die."

"I guess I understand that."

Jase stepped back and saw Lester nod his head.

"You know, I'm a little afraid of death."

"Of course, kinda scary to think about no longer living here on Earth. But there's no sense in being afraid. What I've learned in training to be a hospice nurse is that one needs to find peace with their death so that they can live their days with some joy. Sounds easy, right? But lots of people struggle with the fear."

"What about heaven? Is there really a heaven?"

"I think it's like believing people are waving to the light. Maybe the idea of heaven is that something good awaits you after you die. Everybody finds their own way. Some people think the veil between Earth and heaven, whatever heaven is to you, is thinnest during death."

The boy looked at his father, turned his head at a siren in the distance and then back to his father, and nodded. "If I were dying, I'd want you by my side. I really would. I think these people will be very lucky to have you helping them."

"Thanks, Jase. That means a lot to me. It really does."

The boy looked at the desk for a moment in silence. "The game," was all he said.

"The game?"

"Yeah, the game this Saturday, it's going to be a disaster, Dad. I'm not kidding, we're gonna get stomped. The kids are so big in this new league, especially the Rockets. They will show no mercy."

"You know all you can do is your best. Take care of your position, what you control."

"I just don't want to get embarrassed."

"I wouldn't worry about getting embarrassed. Who cares what people think? And worrying about it will just make things worse because you won't be able to focus on the things you need to do to play well. Just give your best out there and, above all, have fun. If you get beat, then think about what you can do to improve."

"That sounds like loser talk."

"Embrace the challenge, Jase. Embrace the challenge."

"Like you're doing today?"

Lester looked at Jason, nodded his head a couple of times, then smiled and pointed at his son with his right index finger. "Wow, you are a wise young man, Jason."

"I am?"

"Absolutely. I'll be honest: I had a rough night like you." He placed a hand on his chest. The mad thumping had slowed; the trembling vanished.

"What do you mean?"

"I couldn't sleep all night, tossing and turning, just eat up with worry about today, if I could really do it, really help people who are dying. I've been thinking that maybe I've been wasting my time. I'd made a mistake and I should just go back to running a car wash. Who am I fooling?"

"So worrying like you makes me wise?"

"Realizing that I need to face my challenge just like you will be facing your challenge makes you a very wise fellow."

"I got a feeling I'm gonna get my butt kicked on Saturday. I hope you don't get your butt kicked today," he said with his head down. He turned and walked back to his bedroom.

"'Though I walk through the valley of the shadow of death,'" shouted Lester.

"'I will fear no evil,'" said Jase from the hallway. "And those dudes are huge and they're gonna kill us."

"Let them know they've been in a battle," shouted Lester.

Lester loved thinking about that moment with his son, that the impromptu moments were the sweetest of all. No plan, no rehearsed words of wisdom, just raw reactions to the moment. He sat there in his truck for a few minutes to savor the connection with Jason, how his young son helped him with his own anxiety. He looked into his backyard and squeezed the keys again, stepped out of his truck, and walked to the chain link fence. Georgia, the family's black lab, ran up to Lester. Her tail wagged a chaotic rhythm, bursts of energy caused by any indication of affection from Lester, whether a murmur of kindness or a head stroke.

Music floated from the yard directly behind Lester, the neighbor, Marlin Turnipseed, an old hippie and retired teacher in his mid-sixties. Morning tunes were a tradition in the Turnipseed family, most of them songs from his youth. Marlin had a soft spot for Southern rock. "Early morning Skynyrd with my bowl of bran flakes is the start of a perfect day," Lester whispered Marlin's mantra to himself, then gave a hard look to see if he could see Marlin through one of his den or kitchen windows.

He lifted his right arm in the air and gave a few fist pumps, opened the fence gate located a few feet from the house, and patted Georgia on the head as he walked under the canopy of the nearest plum tree. The faint aroma of marijuana created a slight smile, a surprise since Marlin had explained not long ago that he was switching to edibles now that his source had found a Colorado edibles supply chain, "I like the hard caramels, about 10 mils of THC does me right." He thought of the young couple who had moved into the house next door to Marlin and his wife. "Hipsters," Marlin told Lester one late afternoon as they sat in lawn chairs and drank a beer. "They love their pot. They call it weed. Good folks, a little odd and full of themselves, but still good folks."

Lester looked around the perimeter of the yard, checking to see if anyone was out in their yard before he sat down, as his father always said, "to assume The Lester Position." Georgia stuck her head in his face. "Old gal, Georgia," Lester said then began aggressively rubbing the dog's face and neck. Lester gave her a couple of pats on her ribs as he slowly lay back, the back of his head nestling into the grass, which was several inches overdue for a cut. The dog understood the maneuver and rolled on her side with her back along Lester's side. With his keys still in his right hand, Lester closed his eyes and rubbed Georgia's shoulder.

The guitar riffs caught his attention, Rossington's strokes mingled with Van Zant's brokenhearted wail.

"Oh she's gone, all right. Fuck, she's gone," Lester told Georgia.

After a few moments, he brought up his left hand to his own face and massaged his forehead. Then he massaged his temples. Then his nose. Then his mouth. He finally opened his eyes and eyed the plum tree's canopy. He thought of a young girl he had known in junior high, how much he liked her, how they spent every day together in the history class they shared, how he realized his crush was meaningless since she had a boyfriend in high school. This experience connected to another girl in high school he desperately loved, his obsessive crush on this girl who didn't know he even existed. How the girl became pregnant the next year in high school by her four-years-older-than-her boyfriend. He wondered if he had had a fixation for girls who had boyfriends, older boyfriends.

A cardinal suddenly flew into the branches above him, a male, and began a relentless call to his mate. "Let it go, dude. She'll come back when she's ready. If you love somebody, set them free," he said to the bird. His thoughts shifted to Connie, again, how living without her was so strange and empty; he thought of his mother, now eight years removed from her sudden death in an automobile accident, the woman, like most mothers, always in his corner. The two most important women in his life taken from him, never to return. Those two deaths confronted Lester with his lack of understanding of death, understanding what it meant (which Lester had now accepted as not knowable, not within our limits), and more importantly, how the living dealt with the loss of loved ones, how we soothe our souls when someone we love has been plucked from the world.

When the second death hit, he wondered if dying was cut and dry, just a fact of life, nothing to understand since it came for us all, even his father, mother, and wife. Weaving death, the blackness, the end of all ends, that unknown with embracing life. Lester acknowledged his anger, that rage exploding from the knowledge that he and his three children now fended for themselves at no fault of their own. The very fact that his little family was not responsible for this darkness enveloping their lives provided, perhaps similarly to his friends of faith, a way to endure. The first year after Connie's death nearly took him down. The weight of being a good father to his kids, of fitting in when he didn't fit in, was unbearable. He had felt a complete emotional collapse was just over the horizon.

"What makes you think I can do this?" Lester called out, his eyes now following the cardinal as it hopped through the branches. "I need you," he shouted up to the limbs of the Ruby Sweet. He felt Georgia turn and look at him.

"You need who, Lester?"

Lester blinked a few times then, turned to his left to see Austen, his neighbor, standing at the gate Lester had entered a few minutes before.

"Austen, what's going on, man?"

Austen, a short stocky man in his seventies, claimed to be Native American, a descendant of the Cherokee tribe and named after the great warrior Cherokee Chief Ostenaco. His everyday clothes consisted of khaki pants, a white T-shirt, and black canvas hi-top Chucks. He held a cereal bowl with his right hand and scooped up a spoon of food with his left into his mouth.

"Welcoming another day on this Earth, my friend," said Austen.

"Having you some sausage and grits?"

Austen made his own venison sausage, buying the deer meat from hunters and creating the sausage himself from an old Cherokee recipe, so he claimed. Lester wasn't sure of the validity of the recipe, but he knew this detail helped Austen sell his sausage.

"Yes, you know me well, Lester."

"Austen, you eat venison sausage and grits every morning. Sausage and grits are just part of Austen." Lester quickly rose to his feet.

Austen nodded and scooped up another bite into his mouth. He studied Lester as he chewed and swallowed.

"So who you talking to, Lester?"

"They say talking to yourself is a sign of madness," said Lester.

"Some say it's a sign of higher intelligence," said Austen.

"And some say both."

Austen nodded. "Probably can't have one without some of the other."

"You want to know who I'm talking to?"

"Only if you want to tell me."

"Okay, I was talking to George Washington."

"Good choice. I'm sure he feels shame right now," said Austen.

"You know it."

"Is he still sore about not being on the twenty-dollar bill?"

"He was actually on the back of the $5,000 bill printed in 1918."

"The same picture?"

"No, it's a picture of him when he was General George Washington. It shows him resigning his commission as commander in chief of the Continental Army. I think in the 1780s."

"Who's on the front?"

"James Madison. I'm sure George was pissed off about that."

"And, he can't be happy with the fruits of his labor. Yet, I speak from a native perspective. My view of the father of America is steeped in my people's journey in our homeland covering hundreds of years."

"No doubt. Your dead chiefs have to be in a constant rage. Manifest Destiny ain't looking too hot right now. Killing off your people by the millions and using slave labor, not pretty no matter how much you polish it."

"The truth can be ugly. I believe many people are afraid of their own thoughts; they avoid the truth in their lives, but not you, Lester. You are very comfortable in this world."

"That means I have done a good job of hiding my fear."

"No one escapes that fear. I believe you speak the truth quietly and listen to others with an open mind. I have much admiration for you."

"That all sounds mighty Cherokeeish."

"I know you think I'm faking my heritage," said Austen before he scooped another bite of sausage and grits into his mouth.

"No, you know that's not true. I've never doubted your Cherokee heritage. Just saying you play that card very well. We all do it, learn to use the cards we're dealt to our advantage."

"Hey, Mr. G, good morning. And good morning to you, Mr. Austen," a voice called from the chain-link on the other side of the yard.

"Oh, god, not first thing in the morning," Lester said to Austen.

"Good morning, Kwame," called out Austen.

"Here we go," said Lester.

"Mr. G, can you come over here a minute? I need to ask you a question."

"Okay, okay," said Lester. He turned to Austen and told him, "I'll be right back," then turned and walked to where the teenage young man stood by the fence. "What's up, Kwame? Whatcha got for me?"

"Maybe you can answer this question. No one else can."

"What is it?"

Kwame, a tenth grader at the local high school, wore a bright red robe trimmed in white with MUHAMMAD ALI stenciled in white on the back, a black T-shirt, baggie khaki pants and black penny loafers. He was his parents' only child; his mother was a secretary for an insurance office and his father a mechanic at the local Chevrolet dealership. The mother and father kept to themselves, but Kwame at times explored the neighborhood and enjoyed talking to Lester when the opportunity presented itself. He had been taught not to knock on people's doors.

"I've asked many people, but I have not received an adequate answer."

"What's the question?"

"Why don't we eat dead people? They're dead, so what does it matter?"

"Do you want to eat dead people?" asked Lester.

"I don't know; probably not, because I don't have to. But what about all the people around the world who are starving?"

"Huh. Right. Well." Lester looked over at Austen who was bending over and giving Georgia a piece of sausage. "Austen."

Austen looked over, "Yes?"

"Come over here a minute. I need your knowledge on this." Austen walked over and stood next to Lester. "Kwame wants to know why we don't eat dead human beings."

"Why we're not all cannibals?"

"Yeah."

"There have been cannibals throughout history, but most of the people who practiced cannibalism did it as a ritual, mostly to eat the flesh of enemies they defeated. There's evidence the Aztecs did it. A few native tribes probably did it some. There's the religious practice of some Amazonian tribes who ate pieces of dead family and friends. And all throughout human history there's been instances of cannibalism brought on by people in dire straits, like people trapped in snowstorms who eat the flesh of the ones who have died."

Kwame looked at Austen as if he had flown down from a roof and landed right in front of him.

"Right, right, now lots of animals eat their own, mostly due to starvation and survival. Sometimes it's about male dominance. But I think humans have a natural aversion to eating other humans because—I think this is right—we can transmit disease through eating infected humans. I forget the disease, seems like it causes loss of muscle coordination, trembling, even uncontrollable laughter. So the theory is that our evolution has pushed that out as a possible way to feed ourselves."

Kwame nodded. "So cannibals had uncontrollable laughter?"

"The ones who became infected, I guess. Never really thought of it like that. I guess if you ran into someone with uncontrollable laughter, you would be good to avoid that person."

"Okay, right, thanks, Mr. G., Mr. Austen." Kwame turned around and walked back to his house where he walked up the front steps and into his home.

When Lester saw Kwame enter the home, he turned to Austen and shook his head. "Kwame sure is inquisitive."

"Kwame views life from a very different perspective," said Austen, and then he scooped up another spoonful of sausage and grits.

"That was a shot in the dark, but it would make sense that there is an evolutionary reason why we don't eat each other. I'm almost positive that's right, but I could be wrong. Culture certainly plays a role."

Austen smiled. "Kwame has no boundaries in his curiosity. I find that refreshing."

"He's a different soul," Lester said.

"You think Kwame is a different soul. I find that quite interesting. Quite marvelous, actually."

Lester then looked at the rear of his yard toward the music.

Austen also turned in the direction of a Lynyrd Skynyrd song. "Marlin's enjoyment is much to be admired. He, like the Cherokee, loves life's journey."

"Okay, you're yanking me now."

"As Miles Davis once said, 'a man must learn to play many notes,'" said Austen smiling.

"A Cherokee Miles Davis fan? Why am I finding that odd?"

"Because your stereotyping is deeply rooted," said Austen. "Anyone, maybe everyone, should appreciate Miles Davis. Both Miles and Charlie Parker claimed Native American heritage. And Jimi Hendrix had Cherokee blood."

"Didn't Elvis have Cherokee blood?"

"And Linda Ronstadt is part Mexican."

"So was Ted Williams," said Lester.

"The greatest hitter of them all. And Jim Thorpe's grandmothers were full-blooded American Indians," said Austen. "White America isn't very white. It's the seed of much of the hatred."

"The anger of the self-hatred. And economic reasoning, in their head, that these who are less pure will take my job, will hurt me and mine."

"Truth is truth," Lester said, then he pointed his finger at Austen. "Talking like that, exposing the hatred, will get people around here to call you a liar."

"Yes, facts are almost meaningless today. People hear what they want to hear."

"First, my son schools me about facing my fear, now my Cherokee neighbor explains the origin of willful ignorance."

"Lester, I've observed the many days you lie under these trees. Perhaps you have Indian blood."

Lester laughed. "Hey now, I'm a good American. Money, money, money, money. It's not about race, it's about money. You got money, you good; you're a mover."

"Ah, the one true religion in the land of the free," said Austen.

"Let's bow our heads to the almighty. If you're white and ain't got money, you're a loser," said Lester as he made an "L" with his right hand on his forehead.

"So you were asking George Washington about money?"

"Honestly, I was calling out to Connie. And I guess my mom, too. I'm just battling some insecurities on the day I begin my hospice career."

"Begin?"

"I go solo today."

"Oh, the training is done. Good. I know you are ready."

"I should be, right?"

"'Being ready' is a frame of mind. Once you've trained then you have to believe. These people will see the confidence and the compassion in your eyes. They will know, 'Yes, I am dying, but I am dying with a compassionate man by my side.' You will help them embrace the journey to the other side."

Lester smiled at Austen. "Thank you. Those are very kind words."

"Your actions will comfort many. Such selfless acts create mercy."

Lester smiled. "Hey, let me ask you something."

"Okay."

"Are you ready for the other side?" asked Lester.

Austen returned the smile and scooped up another bite of sausage and grits. He scanned the backyard, looked up at the plum trees, and then looked once again to the music from the home behind Lester.

"Marlin loves to embrace the day with Lynyrd Skynyrd," said Austen.

"'A Simple Man,' indeed."

Austen raised his nose into the air. "And the herb of peace."

"True that. Marlin has a recipe for Marlin."

Austen looked at Lester. "I know ..." he began with his face turned to his right shoulder, then he paused. "I try to enjoy every day, Lester, whatever the day brings. If the journey of my life on Earth ends today, then yes, I am ready."

"You amaze me," said Lester.

Austen grinned again. "I am not an amazing man, Lester."

"Hell, Austen, everybody's amazing."

"Some more than others," said Austen.

"Ha!" Lester slowly stepped up to within a few feet of Austen. "One thing I always remember about you, Austen, is when Doris died. You didn't seem to skip a beat, man. You know? You just carried on. Motherfucking stoic. I remember looking at you through my windows in admiration. You'd be out in the yard cutting grass, washing your truck, grilling burgers, like nothing was wrong. You were able to carry on very quickly."

"But nothing was wrong."

"Are you kidding me? The woman you had lived with for nearly fifty years had died. Yet, there you were, waving hello to me as you turned the burgers. I just couldn't believe your strength. You didn't feel pain?"

"Of course, I felt the loss. As an old friend told me when his wife died, 'Music tastes different and food sounds the same.' Mourning is inescapable. I lived in a haunted house, Lester. Everywhere I turned there were ghosts. Doris's closet was stuffed full of ghosts. I'd open the door and all her dresses and shoes, all those memories, just washed over me. She wore these shoes to this dinner, that dress to this celebration. I was suffocating."

"I felt that, too," said Lester.

"I knew I had to get rid of them, but they seemed to know they had no future, like they were holding their breath, hoping I couldn't stomach the inevitable cleansing. They were goners; the gig was up and they knew it. I was about to explode."

"So how did you do it, man?"

"One night when I couldn't sleep, when the loneliness of those clothes was just too much to bear, the pain just howling, I suddenly sat up and had this powerful desire to bag all of Doris's clothes and drive them to the nearest Goodwill. Extract the source. I grabbed a box of garbage bags and walked into the closet, willing myself to move forward. But I did something very strange when I walked in the closet."

Austen looked into Marlin's backyard and then back at Lester.

"What did you do?" asked Lester.

"I grabbed a dress, one of the ones she wore all the time, a housedress, a dress I'd seen her wear in the kitchen a thousand times. I was just about to rip it to shreds when I suddenly put it on."

Lester paused, twirled the keys in his hand.

"You put on her dress? Over your clothes?"

"I stripped to my underwear and slipped on the dress. We were roughly the same size."

"Yeah, I get that. You fit into it. But you put on her dress?"

"I just did it. There was no thinking about it. Took off my clothes and slipped it on. I stood in the closet for a few minutes with my eyes closed. When I finally opened them I felt famished. I hadn't eaten in days. I walked into the kitchen, made coffee, eggs, sausage, grits, toast, a big country breakfast. Sat down at the kitchen table and ate every bite."

"Wearing Doris's dress."

"Yes."

Lester gave Austen a hard stare. He wanted to know more about Austen wearing his dead wife's dress, but he felt intrusive and nosy about his neighbor mourning his wife. He turned to look at his truck, stroked Georgia's head, and then looked back into Austen's eyes. "That sounds crazy, man," he blurted out. "Were you finally cracking up?"

Austen frowned, then after a few seconds he smiled at Lester.

"I suppose that made you feel closer to Doris. You had this aching need to be with her again. I'm just guessing."

"I don't remember feeling anything. Maybe it was an attempt to get as close as I could to Doris. I remember I cried. Tears ran down my face."

"What time was it?"

"Past midnight, early morning. I seem to recall looking at the stove clock when I was cooking, that it read exactly 3:00."

"Did you just go back to bed after eating?"

"No, I sat on the back porch and smoked a cigar."

"In Doris's dress."

"Yes. And I drank a few shots of tequila."

"Tequila? Wait a minute, you drank shots of tequila after all that. Why? I mean I get the tequila and you being Native American."

Austen shook his head and smiled. "Sometimes, Lester, you are just too much. Here is a truth. When a white man battles alcohol, it is considered an individual battle. When a Native American battles alcohol it is considered a weakness of our people."

"Sure, I apologize for that."

The two men looked at each other for a few seconds in silence.

"Doris loved tequila. She would rather drink tequila than champagne. And as you know, Doris was not a Native American."

"I remember drinking tequila with Doris," said Lester.

"That woman could hold her liquor," said Austen.

"Oh yeah, I remember her holding court in your kitchen, her drinking tequila like ice water. I guess it all makes sense now. The kids still wear a few of Connie's things, which nearly knocks me to my knees," said Lester. "I have a recording of her voice that I still play. I've been toying with the idea of getting rid of it. Move on, right? I just can't make myself. I don't think I'll ever be able to erase it."

"Then don't," said Austen. "Everyone's journey is unique."

"Here is a good stereotype. You are a Native American elder and you are wise as fuck. I mean it."

"I am touched by your flattery."

"From right here, man." Lester patted his heart with his right hand. "So what happened then?"

"When I finished the cigar I walked back in the house to the bedroom, crawled into bed, and fell asleep."

"Still wearing her dress?"

"Yes."

"I don't know what to say to that," said Lester.

"Omniscience is not a goal, nor attainable."

Lester laughed. "You, you, I'm being schooled. Is that the end of the story, you falling asleep in Doris's dress?"

"There's more."

"Did you wear it for a while? I don't remember seeing you grilling with that dress on."

"No, the dress was not worn outside."

"Did you bathe in it?"

"Actually, I had a dream."

"That night?"

"Yes. I dreamed I was in bed. I guess it was a dream. Some might say Doris decided to visit me. I remember waking up and seeing Doris sitting on the side of the bed. She was smiling. I told her I missed her so much. That I wanted to talk to her so bad. She kept smiling, nodded her head and said, 'Austen, I'm right here. You can always talk to me.' I told her I was wearing her dress. She said, 'I know.' 'I hope that doesn't make you mad,' I said. She said, 'No, not at all, Austen. I admire your love. You should wear my dress as much as you want.'"

Lester rubbed Georgia's ears. "What did you say then?"

"Nothing. She walked out of the bedroom, and after a moment I eased out of bed and followed her, but when I walked into the den and kitchen she was gone. I wore her dress all that day and all that next night, never leaving the house. I fell asleep deep into the next night, hoping that she'd come back. But she didn't."

Lester squatted down and began massaging Georgia's neck with both hands. "So you only dreamed about her or saw her that one time?"

"Just that one time."

"What about the dress?"

"I gave away all her clothes. Lots of shoes, dresses, coats, sweaters, but I kept that dress. I give it a glance almost every time I walk into the closet. Sometimes I take it off the rack, give it a hard look, and then place it on the bed, pretend she's in the room with me, standing there and looking at the dress with me. I tell her I love her and I miss her. Then I pick up the dress, walk back in the closet, and place it on the rack in the exact same place."

Lester walked up to Austen. "Just so hard to let go of someone when they die."

"You can never let go of the ones you love, Lester. It's just not possible. Whether they're alive or dead has nothing to do with it. They're always in your heart."

"Yes, I know what you mean," Lester said. "I'm sorry I have to leave, Austen, but this talk, hell man, I feel like taking on the world now." He walked to the gate, opened it, and waited for Austen to pass through before following and closing the gate behind him. Austen stopped in front of Lester's truck.

"You're taking the Green Hornet, huh?"

"Seems fitting. And I feel like a pimp in my mom's car." Facing Austen, Lester smiled and patted him on the shoulder. "I always feel I should let Connie go. Carry on without her and all that. But I can't do it. Just can't do it." He shook his head.

"This is not an affliction, my friend. Holding loved ones in your heart should be encouraged and embraced," said Austen. "You should never let go of that recording of Connie."

"Do you really think you saw Doris that night?"

"You are asking an irrelevant question."

Lester smiled and paused for a minute.

"This was a bountiful year for my Ruby Sweets," Lester said as he pointed to the plum tree.

"Yes, the ones you gave me were sweet indeed."

"They say the Ruby Sweet doesn't live long. A few more years at most for that one."

Austen nodded. "I've not had sweeter."

"You're a good neighbor, Austen. You take care of yourself." Lester walked around Austen and the corner of the truck as he made his way to the driver-side door. He opened the door, then gave a quick glance at Austen's house, not really looking at anything specific. That's when he saw the body. It looked to be a man in jeans and white sneakers lying face down between cedar bushes at the back corner of the house. Lester stopped in his tracks to give the body a closer inspection. Lester was sure the body was a man who seemed to be wearing a dark blue sweatshirt. There was no movement. Then, from the depths of his memory, Lester knew. He turned to Austen who had seen Lester stop and stare at something by Austen's house. The men locked eyes.

"Jamee," Austen stated.

Lester nodded.

Jamee was Austen's son, a construction worker who also built custom wooden canoes. Jamee's only child, Carson, a fifteen-year-old kid, had been killed last year in a boating accident on Guntersville Lake, the biggest lake in Alabama. Always a big drinker, Jamee chose to numb his pain with alcohol. His wife had finally cut him loose after being fired many times for drinking on the job. Even the workmanship required for building the canoes was in tatters from the alcohol. Days of sobriety were few and far between since the accident; the drinking was a rollercoaster of binges. Many nights of drinking ended at his daddy's house. Most times Jamee would make it inside where Austen gathered him up and poured him into the spare bedroom, but there were times Jamee would pass out in his car at a bar, in his father's driveway, or somewhere in the landscape. A few times Lester had helped Austen carry Jamee into the house.

"Do you need help?"

Austen looked over at Jamee, then back at Lester without saying a word.

"Let's get him inside," Lester said.

Austen nodded, then the two men walked over to Jamee and began the task of pulling him to his feet.

WE NEED TO TALK

LESTER PULLED into the short driveway, parked beside Toots Richards's red Cadillac, then cut the engine. Helping Austen walk Jamee to his childhood bedroom had tempered Lester's anxiety. Jamee could not stand without each man wrapping an arm under a shoulder and holding him up. They didn't carry him, but he couldn't walk on his own, his steps heavy as stones. Austen thanked Lester after they eased Jamee onto the bed and removed his shoes. The old man remained calm and focused. He shook Lester's hand which quickly melded to a firm hug.

"I know I don't have to say this, you know it, but you need to keep reminding yourself that you're the best thing he's got right now."

Austen nodded while staring down at his son. "I know."

During the entire drive he thought of little else but Jamee and Austen, but when he pulled into the driveway his mind flipped to the present. The sudden realization that now he was about to face a patient on his own produced frayed nerves, instant sweat. Within seconds, he felt burdened with being by himself and on his own. He held his hands out, palms down, and watched the steady shake.

Just follow protocol and all will be fine. Stay in the moment. This is expected; embrace it.

Irene's car was not in the driveway, only Toots's red Cadillac, which disappointed him since he was hoping she had somehow arranged to be home for his virgin solo call to her father. *Irene.* He parked his truck next to the car, then turned to look out his back window, down the driveway, and across the street to a neighbor's home, another brick rancher. He had noticed the family before on previous visits to see Toots: African Americans, one ten-year-old son, a mom and dad. He remembered waving one day as he walked back to his supervisor's car in the driveway, the mom and dad both returning his wave. When he mentioned the family to Irene on his next visit she said they "are sweethearts. Richard works at the Chrysler factory and Belinda is a schoolteacher, teaches third grade at Davis Hills." The neighborhood, like many in Northwest Huntsville had been integrated over fifty years ago; back then, this section of town mushroomed due to its proximity to NASA and the Marshall Space Flight Center. Wernher von Braun's surrender to Americans had first landed him in Texas but they soon moved him to Huntsville to build the rocket, the Saturn V, which would take Americans to the Moon. When von Braun moved to Virginia in 1970, the Huntsville population stood at 140,000, an avalanche of growth from the 16,000 who lived there in 1950. The rocket economy enticed out-of-state college degrees bearing faith in integration, many tasting Southern culture for the first time. This cultural brew caused Huntsville to be the first integrated town in the state of Alabama, yet the integration was misleading. During the '60s and '70s North Huntsville's three high schools, Lee, Butler, and Johnson were fully integrated, but the two South Huntsville high schools wore their segregation as a badge of honor. Beginning in the '80s, whites began to abandon North Huntsville. Realtors promoted the move from integration to segregation with the Black population growing to over 70% in the Northwest. Toots decided not to abandon this side of town, even holding a grudge against realtors. "The racist realtors resegregated Huntsville. Hate springs eternal," he told Jenny Lynn and Lester one recent afternoon.

Lester turned his head and looked back to the house. Irene, who taught fifth grade at the James I. Dawson Elementary School a few blocks away, had promised she would be at the house for Lester's first independent visit, so her current absence surprised Lester. He stepped out of his truck and looked down the street in both directions. His anxiety and fear began to bubble. He decided to lie down in front of his truck between the front bumper and the house. He squatted down, fell back onto his rump, then reclined until he was completely horizontal and looking at the cloudless sky. He rubbed his face for a few seconds, keeping his eyes closed as he listened to a car pass by the driveway.

He thought of Irene, her walk, her smile, her lively flirtations. When he finally pushed Irene out of his mind, the thoughts of his children filled the void.

Lizzy's request to spend Friday night at her friend Jill's house danced across his mind, including how he didn't like Jill's money obsession. He'd only met the parents once, the meeting confirming the cause and effect he hypothesized: their daughter was a bad scout for the family.

From Lizzy, his mind turned to ten-year-old Chuck and his desire to create a sexually graphic comic strip. "Sexy, but very classy and age-appropriate," Chuck had told Lester a couple of days ago, three days after Jase gave Lester a head's up on what he heard Chuck tell his friends one Saturday night. "Porn, Dad. Chuck wants to be a porn king."

Lester laughed at the idea, "That's preposterous." But seeing a couple of initial drawings, one an illustration of a young woman disrobing, confirmed his belief that his son possessed artistic talent. He didn't see this endeavor turning out well. A neighborhood ostracizing was probable, the law stepping in quite possible.

Jase's anxiety of stepping up to the next-age level in basketball wove through Lizzy's and Chuck's endeavors. The anxieties stacked up like cords of wood. He thought of Toots, Irene, Lizzy, Chuck, and Jase, an armful of anxieties in his life, but none more than Toots, a seemingly honest and caring man confronting his death. Toots would probably be the first person to die under his care. And he speculated that how he handled the loss would be the first barometer for his hospice capability. He feared his compassion would spell doom for a hospice career. Would he truly be able to help the dying for the next twenty years? He had read the literature concerning hospice nurse burnout, the warning symptoms: chronic physical exhaustion, frequent illness, inability to emotionally disconnect from patients during time off, losing the joy of helping the dying leading to cynicism or indifference.

Jenny Lynn had talked to him on more than one occasion about being able to leave at work the deep emotions encountered in hospice situations. "Everyone has to learn to deal with the stress of a job. I bet you had your own stresses with that car-wash business."

"Right. Always something," Lester said.

"But hospice is a different bird altogether. You're working with and growing an emotional attachment to people who are dying and, many times, to their family, friends, and caretakers. Just human nature, Lester. You're gonna have the ideal, the good death, when all involved are on the same page and everything works the way you want it to. But let me tell you, there will be lots of experiences that are not even close to the ideal. One time I had an eighty-year-old client who had moved into her daughter's house for her remaining days. The woman was a nightmare, just mean as a hornet to everyone, family and friends, me included. I finally came to the conclusion that this woman had some mental illness that had never been addressed. I had a mental health professional come in to diagnose her, which provided some relief, but the tension in that house was atrocious. The daughter, her husband, even the grandchildren couldn't stand her because of her attitude. I'll never forget talking to a grandson at the funeral. He was the one person the old woman was halfway kind to, her favorite. I asked him if he was gonna miss his grandmother. He looked at me like I was crazy and said, 'No, I'm glad she's gone. She was a mean woman.'"

"That must have been fun."

"No siree, it was uglier than ugly. Lester, I'm telling you this for your own good. You gotta be able to leave your hospice world with the hospice world if you want to continue this job into the future. Keep a journal, take walks, garden, get a massage; do whatever it takes to help you separate your personal life from your hospice life. I had a nurse tell me he flipped on *The Three Stooges* as soon as he walked in his front door, claimed it helped him close the door on his hospice world for the day. I went through a period when I had to listen to Led Zeppelin on the drive home after a full day. With the sound cranked up, mind you. Can't tell you how many times I listened to 'Black Dog,' 'Immigrant Song,' and 'When the Levee Breaks' while I made my way to the house. I wore 'Stairway to Heaven' out. Bottom line: it helped me survive."

Lester smiled as he scanned the small brick rancher, needing something to focus on. A quick glance revealed the neat and tidy red brick house, the house's quality assessed from earlier visits; the black mortar outlining the dark red brick portrayed class for the small home in Northwest Huntsville, Alabama. Large hollies at each corner, the grass cut and edged. The black-wood trim freshly painted, even the metal roof just a few years in age. The surrounding houses not rundown but clearly a couple of steps below in appearance and upkeep. Toots's pensions provided the needed funds for such maintenance. Irene's living expenses decreased while living with her father; the single, young elementary school teacher with three small children would be struggling on her own.

Toots would probably be dead within a few months, yet the approaching end seemed just part of the show from Lester's perspective. Toots told a quick story of his life to Lester one morning during a visit with Jenny Lynn. Toots had joined the Army the summer after high school at eighteen and been sent to live in Böblingen, Germany at the Panzer Kaserne installation for his entire twenty-year career, a rare experience but such longevity at one base not impossible. At twenty, he married an eighteen-year-old German girl, Britta, and then became a father at twenty-one with Irene's birth. Britta died five years later from a freak hiking accident, leaving Toots to raise Irene alone. Retiring from the military at thirty-eight, he and Irene, seventeen at the time and an early high-school graduate, returned to the States, specifically Huntsville, Alabama, his hometown, where his mother still lived. Toots's father disappeared when Toots was a small boy, "Vanished without a trace except for his foul stink of being a lazy drunkard," his mother always said to whomever wanted to listen. She had raised Toots with the help of her mother and sisters. Three years ago Alzheimer's had taken Toots's mother from this Earth.

After earning a teaching degree from the University of Alabama in Huntsville, Toots became a history teacher at Ed White Middle School. Life felt smooth for a few years, until Irene gave birth to her three children from three different men, all rebels, all without a cause, and all completely devoid of responsibility. Her choices seemed to have derived from the men's sexual skills. Toots stepped in countless times to help her battle her poor choices in men. When the lung cancer diagnosis appeared like a violent stranger, the father and daughter walked as if in a thick fog, bumping into their day-to-day tasks and leaning into the world that was now turning upside down. They made plans for a losing battle, keeping the war in mind. Toots possessed a thirty-five-year smoking habit, which he balled-up and threw out the window as he said, "Fuck you!"

When he heard a car come down the street from the opposite direction and turn into the driveway, Lester raised his torso and watched Irene's car pull up behind her father's Cadillac. He quickly stood up and saw Irene looking at him as she stood by her car. She waved.

"What were you doing on the ground?" she asked.

"Oh, just checking to see if my truck is leaking oil."

"Is it?"

"Doesn't seem to be, but old trucks can spring a leak any time."

"The Green Machine," Irene said with a smile.

Lester remembered Jenny Lynn giving him some friendly advice when she noticed Lester grinning every time Irene was at home during their visits: "My advice: be professional."

"I get that," said Lester.

Irene was a born flirt, joking and teasing constantly. He remembered while on one of his training runs a few weeks ago her mock wolf-whistling at the mailman while unloading groceries.

Be professional, be ethical, he thought as he looked at Irene. And he liked Toots, admired a man who faced his end with blunt-axe humor. Toots's well-grounded view of his approaching death demanded respect, at least in Lester's eyes. Lester encouraged and mirrored the gallows humor he saw in Toots. He filed this behavior in his mind, thinking he could draw from it for other patients and even his own final reconciliation.

"I'm so glad I was able to be here with you on your first day to see Daddy by yourself," Irene said as she walked up to where Lester stood in front of his truck.

"Me, too. I'm just surprised you were able to leave your students."

"A good friend is covering my class for this period. I can only stay a minute. My principal is a doll."

"Your boss loves you; now that's a pretty picture. I guess coming home to check on your father isn't a big deal with him," said Lester.

"Well, my boss is a she, not a he."

"Well, well, well, you do have it going on."

"Hush you. She's a sweet woman who is actually married to a good-looking man. I think he's the better looking of the two."

"Maybe they're swingers."

"Swingers? Those two?" Irene squinted, looked at Lester and then panned down to the ground.

Lester broke the silence. "So you think—"

"Hold it, hold it," Irene cut in. "Give me a sec here."

"Just you pondering the possibility makes it seem possible."

"Anything is possible, but no. Those two? Just no."

Lester laughed.

"It's actually one of the vice principals I have to avoid. Every time he sees me he gives me a big old hug. A bear hug. One time he spotted me across a room full of people and bee-lined through the crowd so he could hug me. He makes sure he presses against my chest. Every. Time."

"You should rig a safety pin to stab him in the chest." Lester covered his mouth with his right hand and quickly dropped it a few inches. "Did I say that out loud?"

"That has crossed my mind. I don't want to cause a scene."

"His own fault. He's the one not playing nice."

"I think I'm in love with you."

Lester tipped an imaginary hat. "The Lone Ranger fights for truth and justice."

"The men around here must keep you busy."

"Men everywhere, ma'am. Men everywhere."

Lester looked at Irene with a crooked smile.

"Thank you, Lone Ranger."

Lester followed Irene down the sidewalk and up the steps to the front door. She was a rather tall woman, blonde, big-shouldered, a blend of her solid parents, the six-foot, five-inch Toots and her stout German mother whom Toots affectionately referred to as "a refrigerator with a head."

Irene unlocked the door and walked to the den at the rear of the home with Lester a couple of steps behind, passing through several rooms added on through the years, the house stretching deep into the backyard. When they reached the den and within eyesight of Toots who sat in a chair next to a walker wearing jean shorts and a green long-sleeve Henley, Toots called out to his daughter without turning toward her.

"You did manage to come home." He cut Lester a sliver of a smile. "But you left the door open; a big rat came in behind you."

"Hey, Mr. Toots. Are you excited? Just me today. Don't worry; I know what I'm doing. This catheter won't hurt a bit. The last one I inserted, the guy only cried a few minutes."

"You're gonna kill me, ain't ya?"

"I told him not to kill you yet," said Irene. "I think we can get some more goody out of you."

"I just watched *Little Miss Sunshine* again," said Toots.

"No, get that out of your head, Daddy."

"Irene's not gonna score you any heroin, Mr. Toots. We've been through this a few times."

"Okay, not the hard stuff. I knew that was a longshot. Your reluctance is duly noted. Don't agree with it, just not right for a dying man, but I can live with that. At least for a few months. Just get me some cocaine."

Irene and Lester stood facing Toots a few feet from the ottoman holding his legs.

"What do I say to this?" Irene asked Lester.

"You say yes," said Toots.

"Why do you keep bringing this up?" asked Irene.

"Because I'm dying. Let me make it clear. D. E. A. T. H. Everyone in this damn room knows the fact that I'll be worm food within a few months, maybe weeks. Sitting where I'm sitting I should be able to do just about anything. How can you deny a simple request from a dying man? Your dying father. Amiright?"

Irene stared hard into her father's eyes. She turned to give Lester a searching expression, her eyebrows arching to the heavens.

"Irene, he has a point there."

"What?"

"He's not asking for China White."

"Actually—" Toots began.

"Are you crazy? Do you hear what you're saying?" said Irene.

"Humor," said Toots. "Another benefit of sitting where I'm sitting is that I can joke about anything. Nothing is off limits. Like the adorable Mrs. Adams a few houses down; she's in play."

"What are you talking about?" asked Irene.

"You could set a glass on her ass," Toots said to Lester with a nod.

"That's supposed to be funny, Daddy? Sounds sexist to me."

"It's sexual and humorous, not sexist. And I did see you smile, Irene. You should record everything I say. After I'm gone you can listen to me and think this is what freedom sounds like. But I ain't kidding about that simple request from a dying man. Just want to be honest here."

"Ain't happening, Daddy. You need to face the fact that you can't live like you used to."

"'Used to' ain't worth a damn," Toots shouted. "One's limitations are always shifting, the decline of the physical and the growth of the spiritual keeping you in balance."

Irene looked down at her father's bare legs. "Your legs are full of age spots. Did this just happen? I don't remember your legs looking like this."

"I'm an old man, Irene. Few want to talk about it, but you just get old and rot. Like every other living thing in this world."

"I don't care what you say," Irene shook her finger at Toots like she was scolding a child, "you are not hiring a hooker and snorting cocaine."

"Let me be specific," said Toots.

Lester laughed.

"I want a premium hooker. A super deluxe special. Actually, an escort, that seems more classy, something top shelf. Not asking for a streetwalker. Nothing against streetwalkers; everybody's got to make a living. I did meet a sweet strumpet one time in Munich back in the day who looked just like Marilyn Monroe. Spent a weekend with her the first time. I was nineteen and she was twenty-five. Lena was her name. She was ... uh, very skilled in the oral arts."

"Sweet Jesus," said Irene.

Toots nodded his head at his daughter then turned to Lester. "I'll pay five thousand dollars. Whatcha think, Lester? That'll get me a show pony, huh?"

"Five thousand dollars? Maybe. I have no knowledge of such transactions. I'm guessing what that buys is blue-ribbon material," said Lester.

"Blue ribbon?" asked Irene.

"Five thousand dollars, Irene; that's got to be top of the line for North Alabama," said Toots.

"You really would pay that, wouldn't you?" asked Irene.

"Money is no object."

"No, no, money is an object. That's money out of my pocket, out of your grandkids' pockets."

"Ohhhhh, so we're already there. Okay, okay, let's just peel off all the veneer and get right to it; no more cotton candy sweet talk. I guess we're finally to the ugly truth, just Ramen Noodles from here on out. Maybe chicken broth with saltines. Weaken the old man in order to hasten his decline. Have you been test driving Mustangs? I'm sure you're gonna buy a new Mustang once I breathe my last?"

"I was wondering if you saw me the other day when I drove by and honked."

"Hey, I don't have a problem with that. My money is your money; get you one if you want it, just at least afford me a little pleasure here at the end. Right, Lester? I'm not talking nonsense, just asking for a smidgen of empathy for her dying daddy."

"I can't argue with that, Irene."

"No, Lester." She shook her head. "Not happening."

"How much is a top-shelf lady of the evening?" asked Lester. "Hypothetically, Irene."

"Lots cheaper around here than in New York City," said Toots. "Of course, I don't know about such things; that's just the internet talking there."

"Of course, hookers are cheaper here than in New York City," said Irene. "Everything is cheaper here."

"I don't know, Irene, I think marijuana is pretty damn cheap up there. Might be the same with hookers, supply not being an issue," said Lester.

"Junior T says hookers are thick as gnats up there," said Toots.

"I don't trust a word out of that man's mouth. He told you he had an affair with Linda Ronstadt," said Irene.

"He did."

"Linda Ronstadt?" asked Lester.

"Now Irene, you're always bad mouthin' that man. Junior T was a bass player in a band back during Ronstadt's early days before she became a big star. Their paths crossed and fornication took place."

Irene shook her head and rolled her eyes at Lester.

"Daddy, please. If Junior T had an affair with Linda Ronstadt, then we're all whistling Dixie."

"Whistling Dixie? Do people still say that?" asked Lester.

"You're joking, aren't you, Lester?" said Irene.

"Hell yeah, boy. Old times here are not forgotten," followed Toots.

"'Segregation now, segregation tomorrow, segregation forever.' Just makes you swell up, don't it?" said Lester.

"Little George, a man of the people. Nothing like hate and racism to bring people together," said Toots.

"A politician extraordinaire," said Lester.

Toots threw his hands out. "Stop right there. I've had enough nausea ever since that goddamn chemo."

"You must be one of them pointy-head academics" said Lester.

"I sound like one of them professor agitators, don't I? George would call those boys up there to the stage so he could autograph their sandals," said Toots.

"Sandals? That's where that came from," said Lester.

"What do you mean?" asked Irene.

"Never understood mocking the sandals things. Mostly old-timers now, but I always thought it was a gay thing, homophobia bobbing up its ugly head. Part of it must be a holdover from the Wallace years during the '60s, going after the hippies, the student activists."

"I think you're right about that," said Toots. "Don't you be trotting in here wearing leftist sandals. I tell you one thing, he was something to behold. In one speech he'd denounce Democrats, Republicans, the U.S. Supreme Court, war protestors, Communists, and any person who didn't fit his vision for the country."

"A con man. He'd say whatever would get him attention and votes," said Lester.

"That's what I'm saying," said Toots. "His campaign slogan was 'Stand Up for America.' Fascism at its finest."

"Well, they say most ideas are just retreads," said Lester.

"Takes your breath away, don't it?" said Toots.

"Anyway, enough of that. How you feeling today, Mr. Toots?" asked Lester.

"Beer, cocaine, and a hooker. Bring me those things and I'll be just dandy."

"I'll get you as much beer as you want, Daddy, but I will not buy you cocaine or a hooker."

Toots stretched his neck. "Okay, whatever you say, sweetheart."

Irene smirked at her father and shook her head.

"What? I said okay."

She walked off toward the kitchen. "Can I get you something to eat, Daddy?" she asked.

"No, I'm fine. I finished off that pizza from last night."

"All of it? There were three slices left."

"Big Ed's makes a mighty fine pie. You've had Big Ed's, Lester?"

"Yes, of course."

"The Promised Land serves Big Ed's, son. Now the original Big Ed's was down in a little plaza off Oakwood. Did you know that?" asked Toots.

"I think I've heard that."

"I ate there in the '60s with the original owner, THE Big Ed, Big Ed Neusel. That boy had moved down from Michigan, I believe, but his wife was from up around Oak Ridge, Tennessee, so eventually she got a hankering to move back home, wanted to be around her family, so he opened another Big Ed's up there. He sold out the restaurant here to Steve Denton who had started working there while he was in high school at Butler. Steve ran it until his death a few years ago and then his kids took over. Now, let's see, Ed Neusel ran the Oak Ridge Big Ed's until he died in the late '90s, then his son took over. I think the son died just a few years ago and his wife keeps it going. There's a little pizza history for you, Lester."

"I never heard you say any of that before, Daddy."

"Dying makes you want to talk about stuff. I guess I figure I better get it out now, let people know these things. I'm about to be permanently off the grid."

"Your appetite's back," said Irene.

"Now that I'm off the damn chemo I can eat."

"You shouldn't be eating three pieces."

"Are you telling me to watch my weight? Do you hear that abuse? We're in the *Mommie Dearest* zone."

"That explains why you are so terrified of clothes hangers," said Irene. "I need me a CoCola. You want anything, Lester?" asked Irene from the kitchen.

"I'm good, Irene, thanks though."

Toots whispered to Lester, "I'm not sure I can survive the coke, but I do want a hooker. A nice one. You gotta help me out, Lester."

Lester laughed and then he shook his head. "My career would be over if someone ratted me out."

"I know that. Just talk to someone who can talk to someone who can call me."

Lester felt the vibration of his phone in his pants pocket. He pulled the phone out as he talked to Toots. "I can ask around, Mr. Toots, but this is off my radar." He looked at his phone: a text from Jase.

Found a stash of porn in one of Chuck's drawers. We need to talk.

Irene walked back into the den drinking a can of Coke. "I'm happy to hear you being so feisty. The hooker and cocaine talk is exasperating, but honestly such talk is comforting."

"Yes, I agree, Irene. You've been fading on us, but hooker and cocaine talk means … well …"

"That I'm back in the ring. Damn straight. I'm still a player, by god."

"My daddy, the player."

"Besides, these requests are for medical purposes, mercy medication actually."

"Okay, just for the sake of argument," said Lester.

"Not an argument. This is a request." Toots paused. "From a dying man."

"Let's say this happens. An escort rings your doorbell."

"She better ring my bell for the kind of money I'm willing to pay."

"I'm just lobbing them to you. But let's say it really happens. Humor me. You open the door, let her in. Then what are you gonna do?"

"When I learn that the woman is on her way, I pop a nice fresh Niagra."

"Got it all planned out, huh, Daddy?"

"Retired military. Planning is what we do."

"Okay, you need to plan how you are going to survive without cocaine and a hooker. I mean it, Daddy."

"Okay, okay, no need to ruffle your feathers. Honey, would you go bring me my gray sweater from the bedroom. I believe it's on the chair by the bed. I feel a little bit of a chill."

"Okay, but I've got to get back in just a minute."

After Irene left the room Toots motioned for Lester to come close. Lester walked up to Toots's chair and squatted down, face-to-face, inches apart.

"I need to tell you something."

"'Plastics?'"

"There's a scene for you," said Toots.

"'Mrs. Robinson, you're trying to seduce me.' They got that on Netflix?" asked Lester.

"Hell yeah, watched it not long ago. Saw it in a little theatre in London the year it came out. Now that takes me back. Look, all I'm asking is to see what you can do for me. This is a very reasonable request from a man breathing his last," he whispered.

Lester looked into Toots's eyes, glassy but focused, an honest glistening.

"Now, Mr. Toots." He grabbed Toots's right forearm with his right hand. "I know that you probably will not believe me when I say this, but, god, what am I saying? I'll try to help you here. You gotta tell me though: do you really want me to look into this?"

Toots placed his left hand on Lester's hand. A holy gesture, Lester thought. A stranger walking into the room might have thought that he had stumbled upon one man comforting a dying man, a scene of solemnity, a portal of wants and needs leaking from the older man's eyes.

"I sure hope you mean that, Lester."

Lester nodded. "Maybe I'm too soft for this job."

"Daddy, I looked all over your bedroom and couldn't find your sweater anywhere," Irene called out as she walked down a hallway, making her way to where her father sat.

"Oh, maybe I hung it up in my closet."

"Well, I'm not going back there again. You can ask your pimp to retrieve your sweater."

"Pimp?" asked Lester. "That's got such a negative connotation, like I'm whipping my girls to keep them in line."

"Yeah, I don't like that either. Pimp doesn't fit you," Toots said with a smile. "How about fancy man. People don't say that anymore, but it leaves a better taste in your mouth."

"Okay, never heard that before but I like it. Lester Gordon, fancy man. Struggling for a little supplemental income, a father trying to raise three kids by himself, so he turns to being a fancy man. I'm a man of mercy, Irene, just helping people who need help."

"A selfless man. A giver, not a taker. And, lest you forget, your commission would be a very healthy compensation. Don't know what the percentage breakdown would be, but that's your business. No one would ever know. Tax-free. And cash, not traceable. You're helping the dying. Isn't that your job, the focus of your line of work here? Need I go on? You'd be a fool not to, Lester," said Toots.

"Those are all good points, Irene."

"And the future is what it is. You can't add days to my life, but you can add life to my days. I'm asking you to add life to my final days, young man."

"How can I refuse this man?" said Lester.

"Cash? You got a stack of cash hid around here I don't know about?" asked Irene.

"Maybe," said Toots as he looked straight ahead. "Maybe not," he said with a wink to Lester.

"I saw that wink. Is it safe for me to leave you two here by yourselves? I don't want to come home to a keg of beer on the patio and a room full of strippers dancing naked."

"Huh, well now," said Toots. "My sweet daughter has made a very good point. Maybe we'll start with the kegger and some strippers, then see what the gals are up for. Have an open mind, right, Lester? Junior T has said on more than one occasion that the Bugtussle has the best gals. I think he's a frequent patron of many of those fine gentlemen clubs."

"Junior T, Linda Ronstadt, strippers: that man is worthless. Men are hopeless," said Irene.

"I'm a dying man, Irene. Green bananas are worthless for someone like me," said Toots. "As for Lester, he ain't nothing but a man."

"You gonna own that, Lester?" asked Irene.

"Thanks, Mr. Toots."

"These words carry some weight, my hospice compadre," said Toots.

"Okay, I've gotta go; I don't have time to listen to you talk in some kind of pimp code."

"Pimp?" said Lester.

"Sorry, fancy-man code. I've got a room full of children to get back to."

"Just negotiating my last few experiences in this world, sweetheart. How about another pizza tonight?"

"No, I'll fix something when I get in."

"I might put you and the babies up at a nice motel tonight. Lester and I will be negotiating with the Bugtussle for an evening of adult entertainment."

"Don't worry, Irene, I'm an adult and a professional."

"That ain't never stopped a man before," said Irene as she walked to the front door. "Behave, Daddy."

Lester followed Irene outside. When they drew even with her driver-side door, she stopped and turned to face Lester.

"Hey," said Lester, "I just wanted to touch base with you. How's he doing? You know, really doing. Pain? Any problems with his lungs?"

"I think the right one is filling up with fluid again, but going in and having it drained is taking its toll."

"Ending the chemo and radiation is a brave choice, but remember that we need to be careful with taking him to the hospital. We'll do it if we need to, but I'd have to take him out of hospice so the government will pay. Then, when he comes back home, we'll reinstate him into hospice."

"Okay, I'll keep that in mind. Not my choice about the chemo; he's just worn out and sees the end very clearly. His life, his choice. I understand him, and this fits him; live it full until you can't, face it head-on. All this is him to a T, really."

"You never know about these things. Everyone is different," said Lester.

"The road is about to get rocky. I'm glad you're here helping him. And me. I've tried to prepare myself, but I'm thinking that's not really possible."

"Just try to help him be comfortable; be there for him. Let him know you love him, appreciate him."

Irene let out a big sigh. "Most of the punches I've taken in life have been self-inflicted, but this one is out of the blue. My kids and me, I don't know."

"Most people don't know their strength until they have to use it. Right?"

"Every day, it seems," said Irene.

"He's in good spirits. All that talk in there is from someone who feels good about the day. Let him say what he wants to say. He's earned it."

Irene looked at the roof of the house, then back to Lester. "I guess I'm still believing that he might not die. Just hoping."

"My advice is to let him play; have some fun."

"I know. You're right," she stepped into the car, cranked the engine, and rolled down her window.

"Make sure you let me know any news about what you see in the old coot's condition."

"From what I've seen so far today I think he's doing great; playful energy is a good sign. Your daddy should be a poster child for hospice. Make your last days as good as they can be."

"Take care of him, Lester."

"Don't have to worry about that," said Lester as Irene pulled out of the driveway. The car slowly drove away, Lester waved and gave Irene a thumbs-up.

Lester walked back into the house and checked Toots, his eyes, his mouth and throat, his pulse, his lungs, limbs, weighed him, made him cough, walked him around the backyard, and asked him questions about his breathing, his pain, his sleeping, and his appetite. When he finished, he left the house and drove to a local convenience store for some coffee. He turned the truck into the parking lot and then shifted into park. His phone buzzed.

"Hey, Jenny Lynn. Perfect timing, I just finished up with Toots."

"Hey, good, good. How's he doing?"

"You know Toots; that man is face first into the wind. He's still swinging for the fences, good humor. May we all have his attitude."

"Yeah, he's a fighter, for sure. I was calling you to not only see how your first call turned out but to give you a little pep talk for your next patient."

"Otis Johnson?"

"Yes, he's a mixed bag."

"Only details I know are what Phyllis told me. The worst of what she said is that he's an asshole. That assessment has me on my heels."

Jenny Lynn laughed. "He's prickly, like a cactus, but I think part of the issue is that he and Phyllis didn't see eye to eye."

"So why'd you give him to me on my first day? Throwing me in the deep end to see if I can swim?"

"I'll put it bluntly to you, Lester. Phyllis just couldn't take him anymore. And she had a problem with Otis being a transgender man."

"Yeah, I kinda figured that. I don't have a problem with it, if you're wondering."

"It put a bad taste in her mouth. She just doesn't understand it. Like most people around here. You know that. And Otis, well, I'm sure it's a reaction to the bigots around here, but he can be abusive."

"So you think I can do a better job of taking his abuse?"

Lester opened his door and stepped out of the truck. He walked over to the side of the store and looked into the woods the building nestled into.

"I don't think you'll give him reason to be ugly."

"No big deal for me. I came to terms a long time ago, high school actually, that, like everybody else, my sexuality is my business."

"Exactly, that's the main reason why I think you'll be a good fit for Otis. And I think you being a man will shore him up, not be so quick to pull the anger trigger."

"So what's his deal with anger? Is it all about being trans in Alabama? Or is he just a hothead?"

"I'm sure there's some bitterness about how some people treat him. He told me one time that this is his home and if people around here have a problem with him then they can just kiss his ass," Jenny Lynn said and then laughed.

"I like his attitude," said Lester.

"He's certainly none too happy that he's dying, of course. His pancreatic cancer was discovered too late. He'd been having problems breathing, which is due to the adenocarcinoma spreading into his lungs. According to his caregiver, he saw hospice as giving up, so he fought the idea for quite a while. He finally came to terms with what's been thrown in his lap. Phyllis says he's supplementing his pain meds with his own pain meds; marijuana is what she smelled. She thinks he also might be smoking crack. I don't know about that. No evidence, just her gut feeling."

Lester faced his truck and began tapping the bumper with the toe of each foot.

"What do I do about the weed? And crack?"

"See no evil, hear no evil," Jenny Lynn said.

"How about smelling evil?"

"It'd be a different issue if Alabama was a medical marijuana state. Looks like medical marijuana might happen fairly soon, but since it's still a no-go under the eyes of the law then no smoking, no eating, no growing. Personally, I'm for anything that will help the dying. Anything. I'm so pissed off that you can't hardly find morphine anymore. Dilaudid is okay, but morphine is so much better at relieving severe pain. Many of my nurses find it difficult not to relieve a patient's pain in any way, so they use what they can. As your supervisor, I'm telling you to be careful."

A small silver car pulled up to the gas pumps, stopped, and then a huge, young white man stepped out and walked across the parking lot to the entrance of the store. He had to be nearly seven feet tall, Lester thought, and he was built like a football player, thick-muscled.

"And relatives?"

"Had a sister. Can't remember her name. Lucy maybe? But she died a few years back. My understanding is that they were very close and her death was very hard on him. She had a daughter who is a bit of a wild child. Phyllis says she saw her around looking stoned all the time. That's the only two we know about. Don't know much beyond that; he's a very private person. There's a friend living with him, the caregiver. Her name is Lilly."

"What about Lilly? Is she the voice of reason?"

"Very kind. Phyllis loves her. Thinks she's a lesbian, kind of masculine. I can see that. Of course, that's just Phyllis creating more gossip."

"This should be a treat. Helping an angry, bitter trans man with pancreatic cancer who self-medicates with weed, maybe crack, whose niece is a stoner and who has a lesbian friend taking care of him. Maybe he needs better weed. Maybe Berry White would be good for him. Have you heard of Berry White?"

"Berry White is good indica, so that might do him right. From what I hear," said Jenny Lynn.

"Right, right, you are the real deal, Jenny Lynn," said Lester.

"I'm just trying to help people, Lester."

"Anything else I need to know concerning his transgender issues? Anything from a nursing standpoint?"

"He's had surgery up top, not down below."

"Good to know."

"Phyllis didn't mention this?"

"She talked all around it."

"Phyllis is good people, just a bit limited in her worldview."

"Hey, one more thing. Can you tell me something about his house? Phyllis brought it up, so it must be something. Mentioned it's like a resort, said it's down off Harvest."

"Nice doesn't touch that place. Otis's mother was the daughter of one of the Double Cola owners, before they sold out, back in the '60s, I think."

"Really?"

"Oh yeah, knee-deep in money. Not Coca Cola money, mind you, but the family did well when they sold their share of the company."

"All right, the more info the better."

"There are people who admire him. He's not a monster. Lester, I just know you and Otis are good for each other, that you're the tonic for this guy. Take a stab at it today and see how it goes. Okay? Call me after the visit."

"Sure, sure, I'll give him a try. Anything else? Hobbies? Just trying to arm myself."

"Well, there is one more thing that is very unusual about Otis Johnson. I'm surprised Phyllis didn't say anything about it."

"What?"

"He claims he was abducted by aliens."

"Oh come on."

"No, no, I'm serious. He claims he went to bed one night and the next thing he knew he was in some sort of spacecraft, strapped to a huge black metal table with a room full of eight-foot-tall creatures giving him the stink eye."

Lester laughed. "What?"

"This isn't a big secret and it's not recent. Something like thirty years ago it made the national news when he first reported it. You don't hear much about it these days, but he still stands by his story. If you bring it up, he'll fill your ears with all the details."

"Abducted by aliens."

"Oh, and he's a racist, according to Phyllis. He'll drop the N-word on you without batting an eye."

"A transgender racist who was abducted by aliens. I can't wait to meet this guy. Does he pack heat?" asked Lester.

"Wouldn't be surprised. Seems like everybody is packing heat these days."

"I'll see what I can do."

"You'll do fine. Y'all are gonna hit it off."

"Wish me luck."

"You got this, Lester."

Lester ended the call and began walking to the entrance of the store. When he grabbed the door handle, he noticed the tall young man standing by the entrance with a smile on his face.

"A good day so far?" Lester asked while holding the door open.

"My mama is getting out of the hospital today," said the young man as he walked by Lester.

"That is good news," said Lester. "Bless her heart."

"Thank you, sir."

Lester walked into the store and noticed another young man, this one a few inches under six foot, standing behind the counter and wearing a khaki ball cap with an orange A and a navy U. He watched the tall young man walk to his car and begin to pump gas.

"You know that fella?" asked Lester.

"That's Wayne, lives down the street," said the clerk. "A gentle giant, that man is."

"Hey, let me ask you something. If it makes you uncomfortable or you don't know anything about it, just let me know."

"Okay, shoot, boss," said the young man.

"Do you know anything about high-end escorts in Huntsville?"

The young man gave Lester a hard look and then he smiled. "What you looking for? I've heard a few things."

"No, not for me, for a friend."

"Oh, we all got friends, don't we?" said the young man with a wink.

"No, no, really, a friend of a friend."

"Whatever you say, boss. My advice would be to go down to Jimmy's, ask around, tell them what your friend is interested in." He gave Lester another wink. "I'm sure you could talk to some people in the know down there."

"Jimmy's? That makes perfect sense," said Lester.

"There's all kinds of people down there. You'll find what you need," said the man.

"Amen, brother," said Lester and then raised his right hand for a high five.

The clerk popped a high five to Lester's palm, then said, "You on the clock?"

Lester nodded. "Afraid so."

"I was gonna see if you wanted to head down to Jimmy's for some pool. I'm off around noon."

"Like a beer and pool brunch?"

"That's what I'm thinking."

"Wish I could. Rain check, partner."

Lester walked over to a coffeepot and made himself a cup of coffee, walked back to the register, and paid the young man. "You have a good day, man."

"Hope you find an escort," the young man said and pointed at Lester, "for your friend," and then laughed.

Lester walked out of the store. He sat in his truck and checked to see if there were any more texts from Jase. Nothing since the porn alert concerning Chuck. Lester contemplated how to respond. He couldn't blow it off. A ten-year-old boy stashing porn needed to be addressed. But he needed more information. What did Jase mean by porn? Were there nude photos of women he'd gotten off the Internet? Sex acts?

He texted Jase: *I need more details. We'll talk tonight.*

Lester took a couple of swallows of coffee and then smiled to himself. He was about to shift the truck into reverse when his phone vibrated on the bench seat. He read a text from Jase: *I heard him say this morning, "Look at them beautiful titties." Dad, Chuck is off the rails.*

Lester shook his head and whispered to himself, "'Look at them beautiful titties.'" He shifted the truck into reverse. "'Look at them beautiful titties,'" he said again as he pulled out of the parking space. He looked at the man behind the counter who gave him a smile and a wave. Lester waved back, then said, "'Look at them beautiful titties.'"

IT AIN'T OVER TILL IT'S OVER

LESTER STOOD in front of the largest front door he had ever seen on someone's house, like a small castle door, a door that made a statement. He studied the wood: thick planks of oak stained dark brown, nearly black. He pushed the doorbell and waited for the door to open.

"Hi. I'm Lester Gordon. I'm Otis's new hospice nurse. Did Phyllis tell you I was coming?"

"Hi. Yes, Phyllis did mention you. I'm Lilly, Otis's friend, and I suppose you can call me his caregiver."

Lester stood for a second with a smile on his face. Not only had he felt curiosity for working with a transgender man, but within the past five minutes he felt like he had made a turn into Southern California.

"Are those olive trees?" Lester asked as he pointed out to the landscape between the home and road.

"Yes, you're right. Those are Arbequina olive trees."

"I didn't know you could grow olives in Alabama."

"The Arbequina does well in this climate."

"And over there, are those figs?" He pointed to a cluster of trees to the left side of the house."

"Right again."

"Hmm."

"Otis lived in Carlsbad, California for a while, so his landscape is flavored with Southern California touches. He seemed to embrace the influence. Even the house here."

"Yeah, yeah, I see that."

"It's in the Southwest adobe style. Some people call it Baja Mission, I think. How do you know about olive trees?"

"I've spent a little time out in Southern California. Had a girlfriend there several years ago. I traveled all over the West Coast."

"A beautiful part of the country, especially, for me, the coast, the beaches."

"It's a different world out there."

"In many ways," Lilly said.

"They don't stick their noses in your business out there. Live and let live. Don't like it, then fuck you. What are we doing here, right?"

The woman looked at Lester, first, with a blank expression then with bewilderment. Lester knew he had said something out of place, maybe inappropriate, but he truly had no idea.

"Oops, sorry about the 'fuck.' The desert has its own beauty. Always loved the deserts. Some just see it as a hot wasteland."

The woman smiled. "No harm, Lester. All a matter of perspective. Everything is beautiful in its own way. Having to be told what's beautiful is a tragic way to live, don't you think?"

Lester nodded. "Oh yeah, one of the most beautiful girls I ever met was a buddy's ugly sister."

Lilly smiled. "Oh my, never heard it put that way before. Won't you come in, Lester? Otis has just finished breakfast and is reading the news here in the den."

"That's old school."

"Reading on his iPad, which means also watching clips. Otis keeps up with current events."

"Current events? That can be a fast track to rage or depression. Maybe both."

"Indeed," Lilly said. "There's a fine line between laughing in jest and laughing in rage, juggling engaged and disengaged."

Lester nodded. "A damn shame. As soon as you allow yourself to become involved you end up red with rage. I'm sorry; enough of all that."

"One step up, then one step back. Follow me," said Lilly.

Lester followed Lilly into a huge great room, which included a den area with a couple of leather couches, one white and one black, two zebra easy chairs, and an open kitchen with a white marble island. A man lying down on a very large black chaise longue, facing out at a wall of windows, two sets of French doors, and a screen-covered pool with the roof of the house jutting out to the near water's edge. A couple of round iron tables with chairs and three white rubber pool loungers filled the patio. And to the left of the pool stood a long counter facing the pool, the edge of an outdoor kitchen that included a gas grill and sink.

"Otis, this is Lester Gordon, your new hospice nurse," said Lilly as she stopped next to the chaise, then waved at Lester to stand next to her.

"That Phyllis, bless her heart, she was a chore. She couldn't take a joke," said Otis.

"Hi, Otis, nice to meet you," said Lester as the two men shook hands.

"Do you have a sense of humor?" asked Otis.

"I think I do."

"Black?" asked Otis.

"Black?" Lester responded.

"Yes, your humor. Is it dark? Better be black," said Otis. "Don't you think, Lilly? Otherwise, you'll just walk around here like a zombie, your face all scrunched up. Like Phyllis." He looked straight at Lester.

"She didn't get you, no doubt about that," said Lilly. "Especially your use of the N-word."

"And I don't understand that at all. Seems like the N-word," Otis made the quotation marks with both hands, "would have been nothing for her. Why would she even blink an eye at that?"

"You're generalizing. I think Phyllis was a soft racist," said Lilly.

"'Soft racist?' Isn't that like calling someone a kind murderer?" asked Otis.

Lester laughed, a little too loud.

"Her bite did not produce venom," said Lilly.

"We've talked about this before. Maybe you're right. I can be hard on people. Point taken, but I've seen a thing or two, actually too many things. It's a mean cold world out there."

"Context," said Lilly.

"What?" asked Lester.

"Oh, that's just Lilly. Yes, yes, you can say anything you want if you know the context, what you say and whom you say it to. Phyllis laughed a lot, which threw me off. Complete miscalculation."

"You know better than that," said Lilly.

"But that's what I'm saying. Do you ...?" Otis looked at Lester and raised both hands into the air.

"Lester."

"Would you, Lester, know that I'm—"

"Stop it, Otis. Don't dig yourself another hole."

"I believe in reason," said Lester.

"In this world, that ain't nothing but trouble," said Otis. "Logic, many people think that's a fool's world."

"If reason is useless then we're doomed," Lester said.

"That's not the issue, Lester." Otis gave Lester a huge smile. "We've always been doomed. There is reason, but you have to have people who want to reason. You've heard about Nietzsche's butterfly?"

"Are you talking about a butterfly flapping its wings in Argentina causing a tornado in Kansas?"

"Sure, the idea that everything is connected but out of our reach for understanding. Another way to look at it is that, and I'm paraphrasing Nietzsche, if people see you dancing but can't hear the music then they'll think you're insane."

"Exactly," said Lester, "That's why when we see someone dancing to no music we forget that they are dancing to music in their head. Is that a sign of crazy? Then I'm crazy."

"I like this fella," said Otis.

Lilly smiled and shook her head. "It's easy to say we live in an age of willful ignorance. I'm a feminist, been a feminist for over forty years. I was a soldier on the front lines back in the '70s when most of these 'take no prisoners' feminists were in diapers. A blanket conviction is for fools."

"Yeah, maybe you're right," said Lester.

"Where are you from, Lester?" asked Otis.

"I'm from Huntsville, but I lived on the West Coast for a while, a few places in Southern California."

"You grew up in Huntsville?"

Lester nodded.

"Where did you go to high school?"

"Johnson."

"A Johnson Jaguar. Local talent. Lots of Jags on this side of town."

Otis gave Lester the once over. He looked down at Lester's feet and then panned up to his face. He had his hands resting on a bedside table that included an iPad and a cup of coffee. He wore a black V-neck T-shirt with an antique quilt pulled over his legs, the patches mostly different shades of blue and red.

"So what have you heard about me? That I'm a son of a bitch? Be honest."

Lester grinned. "Not much really."

"Not much? I think Phyllis would have told you lots of much. Bad much. Right, Lilly? That woman surely had to say a few disconcerting words about me."

"You have to admit that you were not very civil to Phyllis," said Lilly.

"Civil? I claim self-defense, Your Honor. That woman drove me insane. Let's not sugarcoat it; she didn't like me one bit, Lilly."

"I think Phyllis is a nice person," said Lilly.

Otis looked at Lilly, then let his jaw drop open. He looked over at Lester. "I respectfully disagree with that opinion. Her loss. Speaking of honesty, I do have a big helping of honesty I'd like to drop on the both of you."

"Otis, I'm sure Mr. Gordon here—"

"Lester, please," Lester corrected her.

Lilly smiled then continued, "I'm sure Lester has a busy schedule and doesn't have time to listen to you ramble about—"

"No, no, I will not ramble. In fact, I've written something that Lester needs to hear. You are a hospice nurse, here to comfort me in my time of need. Right?"

"Yes, that's true," said Lester.

"Right, and what I have here is something that pertains to my death. I'm writing my obituary, Lester. It's an early draft, a bit raw, rough around the edges but a very honest early draft. I'd like to hear both of your responses." He looked back and forth between Lilly and Lester.

"That's fine," said Lester.

"See, Lilly? Lester understands the situation here. He's here to help a dying man, not pick at his wounds."

"Okay, Otis, read us what you have, but I will caution Lester to have a very open mind here," said Lilly.

"Overcautious, noted. Let's see, there's something here for everyone." Otis cleared his throat and began reading from his iPad. "'Otis leaves behind a relieved community and countless other victims of his kindness, including doctors, nurses, former lovers, and random strangers. At a young age, Otis quickly became a model example of not conforming to society's standards: a young girl who realized that she had been born in the wrong body. Many believed he possessed a mental illness. He pleaded guilty to living an honest life. Otis's hobbies included being abusive to the people who abused him in their ignorance and gardening, a passion which provided countless hours of pleasure.'" Otis looked up at Lilly. "How do you like that? A nod to the disrespected world of horticulture."

Lilly smiled. "I'm sure horticulturists everywhere will applaud that decision."

"Right," said Otis, "so let's see ... 'Otis also received unprecedented accolades for his courageous contact with alien life forms.'" Otis looked up and gave Lilly a wink.

"Alien life forms?" asked Lester.

"Let's save that little topic for a later day," said Lilly.

Otis glanced at Lester. "Oh, I have a story to tell you about that."

"Just not right now," said Lilly.

"Fine, my in-house censor has a hard edge, paranoia. Now let's see ... 'courageous contact with alien life forms. Many in the community believed Otis's life was devoid of obvious purpose, failed to contribute to society and serve his fellow citizens, and possessed no redeeming qualities besides quick sarcasm. The truth of Otis's passing is a shining beacon in confronting the darkness of the world, an icon of truth, and a loving friend. At Mr. Johnson's request, no services will be held since most community members would offer no prayers for eternal peace and no apologies for their own rotten behavior toward such a bulwark against hate and intolerance. His remains will be cremated and spread around the base of his beloved olive trees.'" Otis half-glanced at Lilly. "As per horticultural passion."

"You walk the walk," said Lilly. "Are you sure it's legal to scatter your ashes in the garden?"

"My land is private property, so why couldn't my ashes be spread on my property around my trees? And ashes are not a health hazard."

"Yes, you are right, Otis," said Lester. "Disposal of ashes is governed by state law and Alabama doesn't have any laws against spreading ashes on private property, as long as you have permission of the landowner."

"I give my permission," said Otis.

"Public land is another issue. If you wanted to have your ashes spread in a park, say the Smoky Mountains or Yosemite, then the ashes would need to be spread in a deserted area. Sort of a covert operation."

"You a cremation expert?" asked Otis.

"Did a little digging one time. A patient wanted to know about spreading his ashes, and I was curious myself. One's ashes are not, as you stated, harmful. It's just the ashes of the bones. Your organs and fluids are burned off. Spreading them on water is a different issue. You can spread them in the ocean as long as you are at least three nautical miles from land. Dumping them in rivers and lakes is even stricter; you have to follow the laws in the Clean Water Act."

"Problem solved," said Lilly. "And I will always think of you when I see those olive trees."

"I do like that idea. Now stand back; here's the grand finale, a beauty of a last line. Are you two ready?"

"Let the wisdom wash over us," said Lilly.

"It's a true closer. A doozy. 'Otis's passing proves that kindness and compassion do, in fact, die and that light does not always conquer darkness.'" Otis placed the iPad on the small table, then stretched his arms straight in front of himself and twisted both hands while rolling his ringers. "Well, whatcha think?"

Lilly smiled.

"I think people will appreciate the honesty," said Lester.

"I will say that I've never heard of an obituary that attacked a community," said Lilly.

Otis nodded. "Just raw honesty, Lilly. People don't know, they assume. Assume all kinds of lies that help them justify their hate-filled world." He looked back at Lester.

"Now tell us, Lester, what have you heard about me?" he said as he waved his right hand in a sweeping motion.

Lester looked at Otis, "Well," then he paused, turned, and looked at Lilly.

She nodded, then looked down at Otis. "We do not believe in killing the messenger. Right, Otis?"

"I am a soldier for honesty," said Otis.

"Well, okay. I, uh, was told that you are very angry about your diagnosis."

"There's some truth in that. Who wouldn't be, right?" said Otis. "There were a few days of tsunami rage, but that has subsided to gentle waves lapping the peaceful beach of acceptance."

"A few days?" asked Lilly.

"Yeah, well, maybe a few weeks. Anything else?"

"And that you are self-medicating by smoking weed."

Otis and Lilly nodded their heads.

"And maybe crack," added Lester.

"Crack? I don't smoke crack. Where did that come from? I betcha that's Phyllis. That damn woman thinks I smoke crack. I knew she was crazy," said Otis.

"Maybe she thought your pipe was a crack pipe," said Lilly.

"Possible. She had a contorted look on her face that day she saw it," said Otis.

"Like I said before, she didn't know what to make of you, Otis."

"Out of sight, out of mind. So, what else, Lester? Surely, crack is the worst you've heard."

"Your alien abduction was mentioned. About being strapped down in a spacecraft with twenty-foot creatures standing around examining you."

"Here we go," said Otis. "That's another lie. They were eight-foot creatures. Twenty-foot creatures, give me a fucking break."

"And that you are a racist, that you use the N-word all the time. I believe we've covered that issue," said Lester.

Otis pointed his right index finger at Lester, "Check that one off." He turned to Lilly, "Do you think that most people think I'm a racist?"

"That's just Phyllis," said Lilly.

"I forgive her. One must forgive the ignorant. 'Father, forgive them, for they know not what they do.' Misinterpretation, even in my own damn house."

"You threw caution to the wind around Phyllis."

"Actually, this proves my point. Lester, I am not a racist. I do not smoke crack. But, here's the kicker: I am a transgender man. And that's the root of all these lies, been dealing with it for most of my life. Did you hear that about me?"

"Transgender? Yes, there were discussions concerning that issue."

"Good to hear. I assume you're okay with it?"

"No issue. Just a part of who you are."

"Yes, my dear Lester. Of course, you need to know this, because ... because you need to know this information to help me emotionally and physically as my life comes to an end."

"Otis, that's so true. Very true. To hear that is music to my ears. I'm here to help you live your last days to their fullest. But," Lester shook his head, "but ... but—"

"Don't be afraid. Say what's on your mind. Believe me, Lilly and I encourage you to express what you feel."

"Okay. Well, you see, I've had a very interesting morning, crazy really. You wouldn't believe the things people have said to me, texted to me."

"What?" Otis asked. He gave Lilly a look of confusion.

"It's hard to explain," Lester said.

"Have you been drinking, Lester?" asked Otis.

"No, not at all."

"You sure you didn't take a couple of nips on the drive here?"

Lester laughed. "Do I sound drunk?"

"Are you married?" asked Otis. "Sometimes that makes people sound like they're drunk."

"I'm a widower."

"Do you have any children?" asked Otis.

"Three."

"Good lord almighty, you're a single father raising three kids."

"It's not easy, but we manage."

"Losing your wife and the mother of your children, I'm so sorry to hear that," said Lilly.

"There's a hole there, you know, but you move on. On the other hand, my wife used hospice, which is how I ended up here. I apologize, didn't mean to get into this."

"Nonsense, I'm the one who brought it up. That was a little nosy, and none of my business. Please accept my apology," said Otis.

"Apology accepted. In the context of this situation trust is paramount. I think we must be friends in order for me to help you."

Lilly smiled. "I'm glad you did. Otis and hospice have been locking horns. He's been avoiding the situation. And there was little trust between Phyllis and Otis."

"None," said Otis. "I'm just rolling the death thing around in my mouth, softening up the stone of all pills."

Lilly looked at Otis. "Let's step outside, Lester."

"While you're out there, why don't you step back to the greenhouse and bring me back a refill," said Otis.

"You're out? No wonder you've been in a good mood," said Lilly.

"Doctor's orders," said Otis.

"And you're the doctor?" asked Lilly.

"Dr. Otis. I have a very private practice."

Lester followed Lilly to the patio surrounding the pool where she gestured for him to sit down at a table with chairs. The sun's warmth had driven the early morning cold from the day. Looking past the roof, Lester noticed the sapphire sky, how it seemed bluer than the early morning baby blue sky.

"Nice pool."

"Otis loves to swim, though his days of swimming are coming to an end, I believe. He still wades into the water, but he must be accompanied since he is so weak."

The oval-shaped pool sat thirty feet from the house, and a concrete patio surrounded it. Beyond the pool was a yard that ran fifty yards to the beginning of a stand of pine trees. In the middle of the yard was a small vegetable garden, at least sixty-by-sixty. To the left of the garden sat a small greenhouse.

"Otis seems to be quite the gardener," said Lester.

"A green thumb for sure, though now he's just a crew chief. He misses working with his plants."

"My wife and I planted some plum trees a few years back. And I have a few tomato plants, but that's the extent of my gardening."

"Raising three kids by yourself doesn't give you much time for gardening."

"My days are full, no doubt."

"Listen, Lester, I want to be upfront with you concerning Otis. I think we made a mistake with Phyllis. Though she seemed like a nice person, I believe she was a little too ... uh ... white-bread for Otis and his situation. They just didn't click and I won't even get into all the little barbs they tossed at one another. On the other hand, I felt a connection with you as soon as we met. I hope I'm not wrong about you. Otis and I are old friends, so my focus is to make sure Otis's last days are good ones."

"Then he has two people in his corner," said Lester.

Lilly grinned and nodded. "Yes, that's our goal."

"And I meant what I said about Otis being a transgender man."

"Yes?"

"Absolutely not an issue. I decided when I was a teenager that a person's sexuality is just part of who they are."

"True, but transgender is about gender, not sexuality. Just wanted to be clear on that. People seem to be more accepting of a person's sexuality than a person's gender."

"Right, sure, one's gender. If you are born with a dick, then you are a dude. Period. If you think you are a woman, then you are mentally ill. I find suppressing another person's true self that does not infringe upon other people's rights rather repugnant. We are a beacon of liberty. 'The last best hope of Earth?' Only if freedom is open and accepting."

Lilly nodded. "Well, Lester, you have no problem speaking your mind."

"I'm sorry if I offended you."

"No offense taken. And I agree with you."

"People want it simple. They refuse to accept the complexities of being human. And really, it's nobody's business."

"I can't tell you how relieved I am to hear you say that."

"I am a little curious as to how people treat Otis. People in the area, I'm talking about. I've never really worked with a trans person before, so I'd like to know if he's had trouble with people not understanding him. From his creative obituary I'd guess he's confronted some ignorance."

"What I believe is that many people in the community around here know the truth about Otis being a transgender man. He's never tried to hide the truth about himself. Most leave him be, not exactly friendly but they cause no harm. A few treat Otis like a pedophile. There's been some vandalism through the years, to his car, to the house here. Standard bullshit. Several years ago, a bunch of ignoramuses jumped Otis outside a bar but didn't realize whom they were confronting. He's fought the good fight, but he's tired, and now he's dying."

"I read in his file that he's sixty-five," said Lester.

"That's right; he transitioned in his early twenties, back when such things were completely underground. I just want you to know that even though Otis can be abrasive, he's a good soul who's learned to always have his guns loaded. On top of all that is his anger of having to come to terms with his terminal cancer. He raged at first, like he mentioned earlier, a red-hot ball of anger, but I think he's beginning to turn the corner. I just hope you can help him make peace with his situation."

"I'm here to help."

"You grow up, live your life, then you die. He's three for three of having each one be a clusterfuck. Pardon, your openness has made me let go of the reins. I'm just relieved you are here for Otis. Bless your soul."

"I feel lucky to be here with you and Otis. Honestly," Lester said.

Lilly smiled. "Your lucky day," she said and then turned to look at Otis through a window. "I love Otis. He's been so courageous all his life, but now I think he's afraid. I don't want him to die full of fear and anger."

"That's why I'm here," said Lester.

"Lilly, come in here and look at this religious trash. Who's behind this con job? Is it Ernest Angley?" screamed Otis from inside.

"Oh dear, I think he found that religious flyer that was in the mail," said Lilly. "I meant to throw that out."

"There's a picture of a fire-breathing dragon on here. And holy moly, there's Jesus on a white stallion rearing up like the Lone Ranger and Silver."

"These religious charlatans drive him crazy. He'll be worked up all day if I don't throw water on this. Why don't you walk down to the garden while I calm him down, Lester. I'll make him a strawberry smoothie. Give me a few minutes before you come back up."

"Okay," said Lester.

Lester walked around the pool, then down a pebble path to the vegetable garden. He strolled through the rows of vegetables, taking note of how healthy the plants looked. He squatted down between rows of cabbages to have a better look at the size of the heads when he heard music. He turned to face the sounds and realized the music came from the greenhouse. Lester couldn't place the song, the music too faint. He stood, focused his eyes on the edges of the greenhouse, then saw a figure walking behind the smoky glass. On the walk down to the garden Lester had noticed the greenhouse door on the front of the structure facing the pool, so he walked down the vegetable rows and then over to the door, pulled on the handle, and entered. There was a center aisle that split several rows of tables full of plants. He spotted someone at the other end of the greenhouse, but he couldn't see the person because of a row of tall ferns near the back obscuring his line of sight. The music was clearer now, a woman was singing, but he still couldn't place the song. He also noticed something else, an aroma of marijuana.

"Hello," said Lester. "Anybody here?"

The movement behind the ferns stopped. He decided to walk down the aisle and introduce himself. As he walked he calmly said, "Just want to introduce myself. I'm the new hospice nurse for Otis." No reply. No movement. When he reached the row of ferns the figure seemed to crouch down in the right corner of the greenhouse. He stopped, looked at the ferns, debated his next move.

"Look, I don't care if you're smoking." He walked a few more steps to the last row of plants, turned right, and then down the short row to where the figure partially crouched under a table.

"Oh my god," said Lester.

The figure stood up. It was a young woman in tan shorts and a green T-shirt with "OREGON" written in yellow letters across her chest.

"Ardor?"

The young woman gave Lester a puzzled look. "Lester?"

A few years ago, Ardor and her boyfriend, Wade, lived down the street from Lester and his family. Lester hadn't seen Ardor since she and Wade moved out to Oregon.

"What are you doing here?" asked Lester.

"Back atcha, cowboy. I'm dumbfounded. As for me," the young woman pointed at herself as she stood up, "long story. Short version: a good friend is Otis's niece. And you?"

"I'm a hospice nurse. Otis is my patient."

"So you replaced Phyllis?"

"Yep. I can't believe you're standing right here. You know I always wondered what happened to you," said Lester.

"My life has taken a turn ... like always, right?

"I remember."

"Right, it's a twisted road."

"Whatever happened to Wade?"

"We're still together. Sort of."

"I remember that, too."

"Lots of complications. I'll tell you later. I'm really happy to see you again. Just can't believe you're right here, taking care of Otis," said the young woman.

Lester smiled, then walked up and gave the woman a hug. "I thought you were in California."

When Lester attempted to unhinge the hug he realized that Ardor was not letting go. At first he believed his timing was off, as was often the case when he felt called on to give a hug. That he had been too quick to release the hug, probably caused by his now practiced and well-executed ritual, a way to act within the bounds of normal behavior. Pull the trigger too early and you were an odd duck, but give a full and loving hug, especially with a woman, and you were a creeper. Lester squeezed Ardor again, even letting the moment of intimacy linger. When he attempted to release a second time, her hug held tight, in fact, increased in intensity before suddenly her arms dropped to her sides.

"Things happen. I'm back. For now," she said. "But you know me, that could change any minute. Right now, change is a-coming."

Lester smiled, "Yeah, a restless soul. A nomad. That's the Ardor I remember."

"I seem to have an aversion to a peaceful existence. Not sure why that is."

"I've got a few theories," said Lester.

"Ha."

"I remember you as an instigator."

"An instigator? Like instigating a fight?"

"Always pushing buttons. Does that make sense?" He turned to look back to the front of the greenhouse.

Ardor shrugged. "Youthful indiscretions. Most harmless."

Lester challenged her with his expression.

"Most," she said, "not all, most."

"Didn't say a word."

"So, you're Otis's new hospice nurse? How in the world did that happen?"

"Can you believe it? When Connie was dying, I went straight to hospice. I probably would have drowned in my depression without their help. There was a lot of sadness in our house. Each kid mourned differently. We all came through together, and hospice helped us face the issues of death and loss. Especially Connie, but all of us really. Then that led to, I know this sounds trite, but I felt a calling, a need to help others."

"Yeah, Lester, I can see that. Fits you. And even better from my side is that it means Otis is in good hands with you."

"First impression: he seems like a fighter."

"An extremely interesting and caring person. What happened to that Phyllis woman? Did she quit?"

"No, she's still a hospice nurse. My boss thought I'd be a better fit with Otis, which from what Otis and Lilly said is a good change."

"Yes, they did not line up at all. She was decent enough, just couldn't figure out Otis. There was such a chasm between them. You and Otis should be simpatico. I'm very happy to see you here. And I guess you smelled the weed?"

Lester pointed at the four marijuana plants sitting on the table in front of Ardor. "No big deal. Good for Otis. But to cover myself I don't need to be around it while I'm here. I never even walked into the greenhouse."

"Sure. Do you want a hit off this joint I just put out?"

Lester smiled.

"See what I'm saying? Instigator. So, you're friends with Otis's niece, Lee Ellen?"

"Yep, we go way back."

"Okay, how did your friendship with Lee Ellen turn you into Otis's marijuana grower?"

"First, I do have horticulture skills. Thank you very much. Wade and I ended up in Oregon, right outside of Eugene. I got pulled into the growing side of things in the pot industry."

"Of course."

Ardor grabbed a hose and began watering the five-gallon pots of marijuana snuggled between two rows of ferns.

"Just another day of attending to your marijuana crop?"

"Hey, I actually have some kind of green thumb for growing marijuana."

"But how did you end up here," Lester pointed to the ground, "tending the dope garden of a dying man?"

"Lee Ellen is actually his gardener. She's been helping for a few months, ever since the diagnosis, but she decided to pull an Ardor and left a few days ago with some dude on a motorcycle that she just met. I understand her motivation while you're young and all, but the dude's a dick."

"Then she'll be back rather quickly?"

"Maybe. She'll learn."

"Experience is a cruel master."

"I've learned my lessons."

"Okay," said Lester with a wink.

"No, really, I've turned over a new leaf."

"There's lots of leaves right here you can turn over."

"No, no, I'm here helping Lee Ellen. She's been gone about a week ... wait, more like two weeks when I think about it. Heard from her yesterday, only the second time since she left. Said they're up somewhere along the North Carolina coast. She asked if I'd look after things for a few more weeks. I'm doing a good deed."

"Now I run into you here in the greenhouse. Life's funny. Especially if you're smoking weed."

"I am a little stoned, I admit it, but I had just one hit, enough to knock the edge off."

"You're doing well, you and Wade?"

"I've learned through the years; you know, it's dog eat dog out there, eat or be eaten. Thick skin is a requirement. I mean no harm; we can be winners together, but if things turn ugly then I'll do anything and everything to make sure I win."

"That's winner gospel. Preach it, sister."

"And trust is a four-letter word."

"Five."

"Are you sure? That throws my whole worldview off," said Ardor.

"'Trust, but verify,'" said Lester.

"Reagan?"

"Right, right, I'm a little bit of a U.S. history buff. 'We are never defeated unless we give up on art.'"

"Don't you mean God?"

"Same thing. Reagan said it, but he was always confused. I need to get back to the house and check up on Otis. I'm down here so that Lilly could calm Otis after he read a religious pamphlet from the mail. Also, I'm about to give the signal for the SWAT team to pounce on this place. I'll see if I can talk them into sparing your life."

"I'd be careful with that signal. I've seen your closet and it's mighty deep."

"I've got a skeleton or two, but not a platoon like you."

"Youthful indiscretions, like I said, running to live and living to run."

Lester smiled. "Is that what you tell yourself?"

"It works. So far. No guarantees."

"So that time at the party—"

"Easy now. What happens at parties stays at parties."

Lester nodded. "It is certainly good to see you, Ardor."

"Hold on a minute. Let me water a few more plants, then I'll walk up to the house with you. I'll let them know that you and I are old friends and that you're a narc."

"Got to earn your keep. And show 'em you're honest."

"Just a person with lots of scars," said Ardor.

After Ardor finished watering that table's plants, they both walked out of the greenhouse, up the path, through the pool area, and into the house.

Lilly was handing Otis a glass of smoothie when the pair walked up to where he sat.

"You will not believe this," said Ardor.

"What is it, my beautiful Ardor?" asked Otis.

"'My beautiful Ardor?' She has you wrapped around her finger, doesn't she?" said Lester.

"In a good way," Otis said.

"Don't listen to him. He's a fool. And believe me, I know. Lester's an old friend. That's what I wanted to tell you. My boyfriend and I lived down the street from Lester and his family a few years ago. We hung out some."

"A little bit. Saw each other at parties. I think Connie and I came down for a couple of your parties," said Lester.

"But he had a crush on me way back then. I was flattered, of course, yet felt truly embarrassed by his latent lust."

"Of course he had a crush on you," said Lilly.

"That is not true. You do know her well enough to know her taste for theatrics," said Lester.

"Isn't that cute how he tries to hide his obsession with me," said Ardor. "Don't worry, I won't hurt him; I won't ghost him."

"All fantasy. Just play along, doesn't hurt anybody."

"I'm gonna be objective here. Since I haven't seen any signs of obsession, I'll just wait and see how Lester comports himself in your presence," said Otis.

"This won't take long," said Ardor.

Lester smiled at Ardor, his eyes rolling from her face down her body and back to her face.

"Like what you see, sailor?" Ardor asked.

"Okay, I think I've seen enough," said Otis.

"What?" asked Lester.

"Good lord, man, you looked at her like she was a platter of fresh-fried shrimp," said Otis. "We got any shrimp, Lilly?"

"No, but don't forget that Jeffery Lloyd said he was coming by today to drop off a few pounds of the shrimp he brought back from Destin."

"I'd like to have some fried shrimp," said Otis.

"Hey, hey, I'm not looking at Ardor like fried shrimp," said Lester.

"Not just any shrimp, fresh Gulf shrimp from Destin," said Ardor. "Some things you just can't help."

"I feel outnumbered," said Lester.

"Paranoia, that's not a good sign," said Lilly.

"Especially from your hospice nurse," said Ardor.

"Okay, I'll leave you with Otis," said Ardor. "Let's get together."

"I'll walk you out to the pool."

"Does Lilly need to come with you for safety concerns?" asked Otis.

"He's harmless," said Ardor.

"Wow, you are so easily fooled," said Lester.

They walked out to the patio.

"Hand me your phone, Mr. Bourne," said Ardor.

Lester handed his phone to Ardor who tapped it a couple of times then handed it back. "Open it." Lester opened the phone and then handed it back to Ardor who tapped it several times before handing it back once again. She pulled out her ringing phone from her back pocket. "Call me. We'll go have some beers."

"Okay, you can tell me about your marijuana-growing experiences," said Lester.

"Really good to see you, Lester Gordon."

She gave Lester a quick kiss on the cheek, a smile, and then a quick punch to his shoulder.

Lester raised both hands up in the air while flashing peace signs. He then turned and stepped back into the home.

REST IN PEACE

As Lester approached the home of his next patient, a few miles north of Otis's house, he saw cars parked bumper-to-bumper on both sides of the road and in the yard. He had driven north out on Ardmore Highway, past Harvest and between Toney and Ardmore, and turned west out in the country. People stood in small pockets all over the front yard and on the front steps where they peered in the front door. He remembered Emma Wickwire had a large family and a thirty-two-year teaching career. The mourners included all ages: small kids ran around the yard, around the house, a muted playfulness; teenagers in groups of threes and fours crammed hands in pockets, sad smiles creased their faces; young adults' wore sullen expressions, many covered with tracks of tears; middle-agers carried on conversations with bobbing bowed heads; and the elderly stood upright, stiff as tree trunks, facing every direction, rebuttals to the moment.

After passing a long line of cars parked just off the road, he eased the truck to the shoulder and parked. This was the moment he dreaded more than all others. He checked his phone once more. There was a message from Ardor.

So good to see you today. I'm in a dangerous situation. Will explain. How about that beer tonight?

A couple of slammed car doors echoed from the cars parked in the driveway. Lester shook his head, muted the phone, and stepped out of the truck. He girded himself with the stoicism he kept loaded for the emotions he sensed drifting through that yard like fog.

As he approached the crowd, he felt all eyes cut to meet him. He reasoned it was probably nothing more than curiosity since few people here knew him, but all those heads turning also brought a wave of silence as if he was somehow responsible for the recent death. The small group on the steps and porch parted as he walked up and through the doorway. Once inside, he searched the blank faces for the husband, the one person he had met besides the patient. He saw no one but strangers as he walked from den to kitchen. The forlorn faces he encountered since walking through the yard now seemed an acknowledgment of the somber tone that had seeped into the air, the inevitable greeted not with respect but with acquiescence.

A pudgy man who looked to be in his late twenties walked up to Lester and with red-rimmed eyes asked matter-of-factly, “Are you hospice?”

The man was strikingly attractive, like a chubby movie star, which for a moment drained all thought from Lester; the anxiety now replaced with the human trait of instant awareness of human beauty. Lester knew at that moment that he stood in the middle of an emotional volcano, people bubbling with the loss of a dear soul, yet all he processed at that specific moment was a chunky movie star doppelganger. A tubby Brad Pitt came to mind as he greeted the man in front of him. He then remembered that this man was Emma Wickwire’s only son.

“Yes,” Lester said, then suddenly thought of the man’s name, Buddy. Behind Buddy hung several pictures on a kitchen wall, most of them of Buddy and his two sisters.

"Mama," the man said, then stopped and looked up at the ceiling. Lester felt the man struggle with a moment of grief. A woman walked up and hugged the man from behind.

"It's okay, Buddy. It's okay," she said.

"My mama," the man started as he shook his head and then stopped again. He wept while the woman hugging him from behind rested her head on his shoulder, rubbing his back. After a moment, Buddy suddenly began nodding, slowly at first, like a bobblehead doll in honey.

Lester followed the man's eyes as they locked onto a spot high on the opposite wall.

"Ain't this something? Ain't this goddamn something?" Buddy said with a pain-ripened grin. The nodding now quickened in pace like he was on stage with his band segueing into the rhythm of the next song. "Daddy and the girls are in there with Mama now. Nobody's been called. I mean medical people. Hell, this whole damn house and yard is full of people, so I know for a fact some calls have been made. Nicky said you would be here sometime around noon, that you'd know what to do, who to call."

"Sure, Buddy, I understand. I'll take care of things. This is what I do, why I'm here." Lester rested his right hand on Buddy's left shoulder. "Let me tell you something, Buddy, your mama was a good woman. Just look at all these people around here who loved her. And she told me more than once that she was very proud of you. That a mother couldn't ask for a better son." He rubbed the shoulder for a few seconds. "Her passing hurts. I know that, but she deeply loved you and your sisters."

Lester patted the young man on the shoulder and then weaved his way through the kitchen and down the empty hallway to the closed master-bedroom door. He tapped the door a couple of times before he cracked it open a few inches to peer inside. The father, his two daughters, and a young woman Lester did not know stood around the bed looking at the middle-aged woman as she lay there in peace. Lester pushed open the door and walked up to the side of the bed. The oldest of the three women, the stranger, in her upper thirties Lester guessed, bent over and kissed Emma on the forehead. "I love you, Emma," she said. She covered her mouth with the fingers of both hands. "What will we do?" The woman gave a quick glance to the other women and then turned to the husband. She tightly hugged him for several seconds, at least a minute, Lester thought. After letting go she nodded her head to Lester and soft pedaled out of the bedroom, gently closing the door after her.

"I can't believe you let that woman in this house, Daddy," said one of the daughters.

"Nicky," the father began, "I don't want to hear it. She was your mama; that's what you know. She was also a wife and a friend. Do not," he said, pointing a finger at the daughter, "assume you know everything about your mama. Because you don't. She was a damn good mama to you and a damn good wife to me."

Silence filled the room for a couple of minutes as Nicky gave her father a bewildered look.

Charley looked to Lester. "I'm glad you're here."

Lester walked up to the bed, looked at Emma for a few moments, then to the girls and said, "I'm so sorry. This is never easy."

They each nodded and thanked him.

"I want you to know she enjoyed you being with her; she told me that many times. You really helped her. Hell, helped all of us," said Charley.

"I'm a better person for knowing her, and I know she loved her family," said Lester. He turned to face Charley. "As we discussed earlier, I'd like to give you as much time as y'all need before I begin bathing the body. I need to examine Emma first, then I'll go out and call the coroner. After the coroner comes, you can call the funeral home. Let me know when you are ready for me to begin her bath. Y'all and Buddy are welcome to participate. I'll leave that up to you."

The father and two daughters nodded. Charley turned to face Nicky, gave her a stone stare, then walked out of the bedroom. After Lester checked for a pulse and looked at Emma's eyes, he said to the two daughters, "Take as much time as you need." He walked out of the bedroom, down the hallway through the whispering crowd, and didn't stop until he stood in the front yard a good thirty feet from the various groups of people. He called the coroner, gave the details, and turned to face the people in the front yard and on the steps.

"Can I have your attention, please?" said Lester. He scanned the crowd, looking at the faces, but as he skimmed over the people on his left, the ones closest to the road and facing the house he saw what looked like a pack of dogs. White dogs, seven, maybe eight, standing in a wide circle in a wire-fenced field across the road. A huge oak sat twenty yards behind them, the branches weeping downward in huge arcs. And the dogs all seemed to be looking at him. He exchanged stares with the canines for a few seconds, three, maybe five, and then he quickly returned his gaze to the crowd, back to the people by the front door. Another slow pan until he was back to the people on his left. He looked to the field to see the dogs still standing there, still looking at him. He thought this was just a pack of country dogs roaming the area, maybe even from one residence, one farm. They just happened to be all white. And all staring at Lester.

"Hi, I'm Lester Gordon, Miss Emma's hospice nurse. I personally want to thank all of you for being here, for showing your love and support for her and her family." Everyone stopped talking and looked at Lester. Many people began filing out of the house. "Oh, hi. I'll give you a couple of minutes," he said to people walking down the steps. "We all know this is a very difficult time for the family, so your presence is deeply appreciated."

He looked at the cars parked in the driveway and yard. He looked up at the sky, noticing the white cumulus clouds drifting across the blue. He turned to see a mother tell the group of young children at the corner of the house to settle down. Finally, he slowly panned back to the field across the road. The dogs all seemed to be in the same position. And, to Lester's astonishment, all were still looking at Lester in what seemed to be the same position as before. He looked very closely at the dogs, thinking they were some crazy farmer's strategy to ward off predators by using life-size dog decoys, the opposite use of duck decoys used to attract other ducks. Suddenly, as if to answer his curiosity, they moved. One sat down; a few turned their heads; a couple scratched. Real dogs. And he noticed that they were different sizes; two looked to be short-haired small dogs, three average-sized, like labs, and a couple of large ones, a bit smaller than Great Danes.

"Okay, is that everyone?" A young woman standing at the door nodded her head. "I want to tell you that the funeral home van will be here shortly, so all these cars in the driveway and front yard will need to be moved." A couple of people began walking toward the cars. "Wait, before you begin moving your cars I want to say something to everyone." The two people stopped and looked at Lester. "When people die, there's lots of good that can be derived from the death. Lots of good stuff taken from the death environment. Showing love when someone is dead is a beautiful thing. Thank you for showing so much love in such a death situation." Lester looked at the faces in the crowd and noticed looks of surprise, of horror, with a few giggling.

A young man held up his phone, recording Lester's garbled speech.

"Did you record that?" asked Lester.

The guy nodded.

"Are you still recording?"

The guy nodded again. "That was priceless. I think this might go viral," said the young man.

"I'm new at this, so I ask for your understanding. Just getting my feet wet here."

Most gave Lester a smile, a few returned is-this-a-crazy-man stares.

Lester looked at the young man recording. "Always wanted to be famous," he said.

"Your wish is about to come true."

"To tell you the truth, this isn't the first time I've made a fool of myself."

"I bet," said the young man.

After Lester finished his announcement, he stepped back from the crowd and looked to the field again. The dogs were still there. He looked to see if anyone had noticed the pack of dogs. He studied the crowd as they began to mill about and restart conversations, most returning to groups. Not one person noticed the dogs. He decided to turn his back to the dogs and begin searching for the coroner's number in his contacts list. To his right he heard two car doors slam shut, and when he turned to see who was there he saw Charley standing behind a car parked next to the road. Charley was talking to the woman who had kissed Emma's forehead. They hugged, their bodies shook from a constant ripple of sobs. He watched this embrace knowing that he shouldn't, that he should give these two the privacy they deserved. But he couldn't take his eyes off these two people. He thought of what Charley had told his daughter in the bedroom. Did the old couple have an open relationship? Was Emma bisexual? Had he been given a peek into some sort of menage á trois? When the couple finally pulled apart, Charley whispered unheard words in her ear and then quickly made his way to within a few steps of Lester.

"Lester, I'm going to have a drink with Linda," he said and pointed at the woman. "Give me about an hour before you begin bathing Emma. Tell Buddy and the girls that we will both be back before too long."

"Sure, Charley, I can do that."

"I just need a drink right now. Might be some stormy weather this afternoon," Charley said.

"Thought I heard some thunder in the bedroom," said Lester.

Charley smiled. "They'll be fine," he said.

"I'm sure they will."

Lester made the call to the coroner as the pair drove off in what must have been the woman's old Honda Civic since she was behind the wheel. After explaining the situation, he ended the call and turned to face the house. He was startled to see Buddy, Nicky, and Cindy, the youngest daughter, standing a few feet from where he stood.

"Where in the hell is Daddy going with that woman?" asked Nicky.

"Charley said they were going for a drink and would be back in an hour or so. The coroner should be here before too long. We'll begin bathing your mama when your father returns," said Lester.

"Well, I'll be goddamn," said Buddy.

"That just ain't right," said Nicky.

"Right ain't got nothing to do with it, Nicky," said Cindy.

Lester turned and gave the field another look. The dogs were not in their spot. He scanned the field a couple of times, guessing they were on the move. The dogs were nowhere to be seen.

Later that afternoon, Lester found himself lying in dense woods a couple of miles from the home where he had spent the past several hours. Driving down the country road, he had spontaneously turned right onto a dirt road that led into this stand of oak, hickory, and ash trees.

He lay on the road, mostly a trail with its obvious lack of traffic, directly in front of his car, making sure to block the view of someone by chance, however slight, also driving through these woods from the main road.

Lester closed his eyes and placed both arms across his face. He took several deep breaths. A few moans led to silence for several minutes. Eventually, the silence gave way to the natural sounds in the few acres of thicket. Birdsong provided the melodies of this tiny forest. Suddenly, sounding within a few yards of his head, a large animal or two was heard galloping through the trees and brush. He raised himself on his right elbow and turned to find the source of these sounds. He saw nothing. Lester quickly jumped to his feet to have a better look at what he thought was at least one deer. He was able to see the movement of undergrowth deeper in the trees, but he did not see any animal. No deer, and certainly no white dogs. Lester pulled his phone out of a front pocket to check the time and noticed Jase had sent him another text.

Found one of Chuck's drawings. The girl is completely naked. Tits and ass. Chuck is off the chain. We need to reel him in, Dad.

Lester read the text three times. He shook his head. "'Tits and ass?'" he said to himself. "What the hell?" He walked around the truck and opened the driver-side door, then looked around the woods one more time before sitting in the cab. He cranked the truck and then turned on the radio. While finding a station, Lester kept whispering to himself, "Tits and ass. Tits and ass." He found an oldies station playing "Spirit in the Sky," closed the door, turned up the volume, then put the truck in reverse.

HELL HATH NO FURY

"JILL'S MOM and dad have lots of money," said Lizzy, then took another bite of her slice of cheese pizza.

"How do you know that?" asked Lester. He turned to Ardor who was waving at the waitress for another beer.

"You want another one?" she asked. "I think the waitress is avoiding me."

"Yes, I would. Why would she avoid you?"

"She looks like the younger sister of a guy I went to high school with. His name was Billy. Billy Lunchmeat, something like that."

"Are you drunk? Why would Billy Lunchmeat's little sister avoid you?"

"We were hot and heavy for a while, but he started to become attached, saying things like 'You're my girl; Hey, here's Ardor, my girl.' I needed to amputate that before the cancer spread."

Lester winced.

"Sorry, that was too close. I'm an idiot."

"Don't have to tiptoe around me. You know that."

"I know, but still." Ardor looked at the waitress again. "Yeah, that's his sister. I had to make a quick and clean break, which didn't go over too well with not only Billy but all his family and friends."

"You ghosted him?"

"It was for the best. Better a little pain now than lots of pain later. I did him a favor. A humanitarian act of mercy."

"I betcha the Lunchmeat clan begs to differ."

"I did receive a few rude looks and gestures from his kin. They found displeasure in my act of mercy." Ardor waved her right hand at the waitress. "Hey, hey, over here, please." The waitress did not look her way. "Did you see that? I mean really, it's been nearly ten years."

"How did he take it, the recipient of the ghosting?"

"Not well. Bad actually. He did himself a little harm. Not really a suicide attempt, though he wanted everyone to believe that I made him want to end his life. A big baby, so dramatic."

"What did he do?"

"Drove his car into a tree. He dented the front end but was traveling much too slow to really off himself. And we weren't in love. I never said anything like that. He acted like I broke off a ten-year engagement."

The waitress walked from the front counter to the table where Ardor, Lester, and his kids sat. She looked at Ardor, but neither said anything.

"We'd like two more beers, please," said Ardor.

"Two beers, coming up," said the young woman.

"Hey, I don't know if you remember me, but I believe I use to date your older brother, Billy."

"I remember you, Ardor," said the waitress wearing a handwritten "Julie" on her nametag.

"How is Billy these days?"

"Billy is living in Florida, down around St. Pete. He owns a bar not far from the beach. And he has a girlfriend who really loves him and appreciates him. I'll get your beers." Julie walked back to the counter.

"That young woman holds a grudge," said Lester.

"Whatever, ain't my problem."

Lizzy looked at Lester. "Dad."

"What is it, Lizzy?"

"You asked a question about Jill."

"Yeah, sorry. How do you know Jill is rich?"

"They're rich because that's what Jill said. And they have a big house and new cars and can I spend the night over at Jill's house Friday night? You said you would think about it."

"Okay, but I need to talk to the mom or dad before you go. You understand?"

"Yes, Dad. I'll tell Suz you want to talk to her."

"Suz? Honey, you shouldn't call an adult by their first name."

"Suz told me to call her Suz."

"Lizzy, it's about respect. You should respect people who are older than you. Like me," said Jase.

"You?" said Chuck.

"I'm older, thus I deserve respect."

"You're twelve, numbskull. Dad's talking about adults."

"No, he's not. He's talking about respecting your elders. Tell him, Dad," said Jase.

"There is respect for adults and then there's respect for kids older than you. Both deal with respect. Respecting adults is a little more important." Lester looked at Ardor.

"More important?" Ardor asked, then looked to the counter and Julie.

"Yeah, respect for adults is more important than respect for people who are just a few years older than you, carries more weight; there's reverence. Of course, both are connected to how the older person conducts himself."

"What's reverence?" asked Lizzy.

"Higher regard, an admiration."

"Hear that, Chuck? You should admire me," said Jase.

"Admire you?" asked Chuck, then began laughing.

Ardor laughed, too. "I like the part about 'how the older person conducts himself.' But there's more to it than that, don't you think?'" Ardor asked.

"What?" asked Lester.

"Just sayin'. How about a little admiration for the female."

"Conducts?" asked Lizzy.

"Yeah, what the person says, what the person does. Respect is also earned. If the older person doesn't deserve respect, then don't give it to ..." he looked at Ardor, "... her."

"And the one who doesn't deserve respect is a woman. That's very interesting," Ardor said.

"I can't win."

"Fair and just don't have a thing to do with winning."

"Are there hidden cameras around here? Because I'm being schooled everywhere I go. Coincidental? A dream? A new dimension I've suddenly stepped into?"

"If your new dimension is a dimension without male privilege, then yes," said Ardor.

"I need that beer," said Lester.

"They're coming, but I can't make any promises as to whether or not she spit in them."

"Dad, I think it's time to talk about the porn issue," said Jase.

"'The porn issue?' What porn issue?" said Ardor.

"Chuck seems to be very curious about sex. Which is fine. Nothing wrong with a little curiosity about sex for a ten-year-old," said Lester.

"It's more than curiosity, Dad. Chuck wants to make porn," said Jase.

"Porn? Look, I've seen porn and my book is not porn. Sexy, but not—"

"You've seen porn?" blurted Lester, and then he quickly looked at Ardor.

Ardor grinned and nodded her head.

"Of course you've seen porn," said Lester. "Porn is ubiquitous."

"What?" asked Lizzy.

"Ubiquitous means something is here right now and it is everywhere. Like air is ubiquitous," said Ardor.

"So God is ubiquitous," said Lizzy.

"Right," said Ardor.

"Then love is ubiquitous," said Chuck.

Ardor turned and looked at Chuck. "What did you say?"

"Love is ubiquitous," repeated Chuck.

"Whoa." Ardor grinned and turned to Lester as she placed her hand over her heart. "Be still my beating heart."

"Already a heartbreaker," said Lester.

"You might want to take him to a clinic so they can study him and save the human race. Where was I?"

"Ubiquitous," said Lizzy.

"Right. So, your dad said porn is ubiquitous which means porn is everywhere, but I can't go along with that," said Ardor.

"Really?" asked Lester.

"It's easily accessible on the internet, that's a given, very easy to find but not everywhere. Male privilege is ubiquitous."

Lester gave Ardor a flat, pained look. "Okay, sure; I get it. Point taken. And that's what I meant, easily accessible. Kids, like my kids, can look at porn with pushing a few buttons. Honestly, I've been waiting for when this would happen."

"Your kids looking at porn?" asked Ardor.

"Yes."

"Then I'm assuming you've had time to create a plan of action for this very moment. What's your plan?"

"I'm in a quandary. First, I've had to ask myself what I would have done at their ages with such easy access."

"And the answer?"

"I would have been all over it."

"Honesty, acknowledging your male lust is a breath of fresh air," said Ardor.

"Well, that's as far as I've gotten. What's your advice?"

"I'd say just be honest, explain how sex is healthy and fun."

"Like eating an apple?" asked Lester.

"Eve would agree with that. Of course, it has a dark side. Respect other human beings." Ardor raised her hands in a welcoming gesture. "Just one of the stones of our foundation." She smiled at Lester and looked around for the waitress. "Now Julie is gone. I guess she went to the back to fetch the poison. But you know, please don't teach 'em it's sacred and fuck 'em up for the rest of their lives." She looked at the kids. "Sorry for the salty language. My passion got away with me." She gave Lester a wink.

Lester laughed and patted his cheeks. "Whew. Yeah. Okay. Look, you're too young to look at porn," said Lester as he gave Chuck a serious smile. "You don't have the experiences to process those images. This can cause you harm. And that kind of harm could be deep harm." He turned to Ardor. "I'm not making any sense, am I?"

"Not really, but that's expected. Learn as you go; do your best," said Ardor.

"You think I'm too young to learn about the birds and the bees? Is that what you're telling me, Dad?" asked Chuck. "I respectfully disagree with you. Sex is part of who we are." Chuck smiled at Jase, who immediately rolled his eyes.

"No, no, not too young to learn about the birds and the bees. Younger the better." Lester nodded at Ardor. "Right?"

"I'm sex-positive here," said Ardor. The waitress walked up and placed two fresh mugs of beer on the table and took away the empty glasses. "Thank you very much, Julie." The waitress didn't say a word as she walked away. "I don't feel good about this mug of beer. Poisoning might be a reach, but spitting is certainly in play here. I don't think Julie appreciated the pain and humiliation I caused the home team. I see revenge in those beady eyes." She looked at her mug and then over to Lester's mug. "Would you mind switching?"

"Oh no, I didn't do anything to Mr. Lunchmeat. Billy is a good guy in my eyes. There are consequences when you almost kill someone."

Ardor raised her mug, sucked in her breath, and chimed, "To the birds and bees!" She swallowed two big gulps of her beer. "I think sex should be explained at a very early age. Maybe two or three."

"Two or three? What? A two-year-old has no concept about sex. None," said Lester.

"All the more reason," said Ardor. "Hasn't been corrupted by our sexualized society. Has seen very little of the capitalistic objectification of women. Clean slate. Be clear. Be objective. It's a natural part of life. Explain the natural beauty of it, no big deal."

"Yeah, sorta my point, Chuck," said Lester. "Your mind is so fresh that it's unable to understand the different ways to look at sex."

"'Look at sex?'" asked Ardor.

"No, I mean understand the different types of sex."

Ardor laughed. "'Different types of sex?'"

"Your first understandings of sex should not be those types of images. Porn's purpose is to arouse your sexual desire. That's closer to what I mean. I think."

"I don't know about that. My first observation of sex—" Ardor was cut off by Lester.

"No, no, don't go there."

Ardor raised her eyebrows at Lester, paused, and then said, "You're probably right."

"Look, Chuck, porn can corrupt your views of sex, especially if you are ten years old. Just please back off the sexuality in your book."

"Yes, listen to your dad, Chuck. You need to fully understand sex before you jump into porn. Let's start with orgasm." She pointed at Lester, "Men—"

"Wait, wait, wait. How many beers have you had?"

"Same as you. Are you keeping count?"

"Just no," said Lester.

"Okay, then Chuck can just find out about the big bad orgasm by watching porn."

"Let's just end this right now. We're not gonna talk about sex with my children at the local pizza joint. That's just too seedy."

"What's seedy?" asked Lizzy.

"I thought we were talking about Chuck and porn," said Jase.

"Yes, good point, Jase," said Lester.

"Let's cut to the chase. What are we talking about here? I'm just asking for clarification." Ardor raised both hands, palms out. "How does Chuck want to make porn?"

"Chuck wants to write a fantasy book with illustrations. I guess like a graphic novel," said Lester.

"That's cool, little man," said Ardor and then gave a high five to Chuck.

"Yeah, good, good, but he's made some preliminary drawings that are a little questionable, a little sexual," said Lester.

"'A little sexual?' I think naked women are more than a little sexual," said Jase.

"You drew pictures of naked women?" asked Lizzy.

"The women are not naked," said Chuck.

"You show their breasts," said Jase.

"I do not show the nipples."

"Dad?" said Jase.

"Do you have to show their breasts?" asked Lester. "Can't you draw the females without the breasts?"

"Then they wouldn't be females," said Chuck.

"Perhaps," Lester waved his right hand in a circle, "just imply there are breasts."

"Chuck wants to make money from porn," said Jase.

"Sex sells. That's what Terrance said," said Chuck.

"Terrance?" asked Lester. "Who is Terrance? How old is Terrance?"

"He's Jase's friend," said Chuck.

"Can I borrow your phone, Dad? I need to remind Jill to make sure Suz gives you a call," said Lizzy.

"Lizzy, please call Jill's mom Mrs. Moore, not Suz," said Lester. He pulled out his cell phone and handed it to Lizzy.

"Terrance is your friend?" Lester asked Jase.

Lizzy punched in a few numbers on Lester's phone.

"Yes, he's been to the house a couple of times."

"How old is he?"

"Thirteen, maybe fourteen."

"Hi, Suz; this is Lizzy."

"Lizzy, what did I just say?" said Lester.

Lizzy nodded her head. "I'm sorry, Dad wants me to call you *Mrs. Moore*," said Lizzy with her eyes bulging toward

Lester. "He needs to talk to you about me spending Friday night with Jill. Okay, he's right here. Okay." Lizzy handed the phone to Lester.

"Yes, hi, Suz. How are you?" said Lester.

"So, how do you and Dad know each other again?" Jase asked Ardor.

"Like your dad said earlier, my boyfriend and I used to live down the street from y'all. Just a few blocks from where you live now. Do you remember me?"

"Not really. How long ago was that?"

"About five years, I think."

"Where do you live now?" asked Chuck.

"I live with one of your dad's patients actually. He's the uncle of one of my best friends. I help take care of him and his place."

"Are you a hospice nurse, too? asked Lizzy.

"No, I mostly just help take care of his yard and garden. His niece and I are kind of like his gardeners."

"Where does this man live?" asked Chuck.

"Out in Harvest. You know where that is?" asked Ardor.

"That's fine, Suz; I'll drop her off Friday evening. I'll have Lizzy give me a call on Saturday when she's ready to come home. No, on second thought, I'll come pick her up around ten since she's coming to her brother's basketball game. Sure, right; thanks again," Lester ended the call. "There you go, Lizzy. Friday night with Jill."

"Thanks, Dad. So you get to call her Suz because you're an adult?"

"Yep, that's the way it works; adult friends don't have to be formal with each other, though some people believe very old people should be called by their last name. You give them respect because they've lived a long time."

"How old is very old?" asked Lizzy. "Like one-hundred years old?"

"Certainly one-hundred, but not very many people live to one-hundred. Eighties for sure. Seventies. I'd say sixties, too. But we're talking about young adults. A person in his forties probably doesn't give a person in their sixties or seventies that type of respect."

"In the South, maybe so," said Ardor. "Southern culture is still kind of *Gone-with-the-Wind*ish."

"Maybe so, but that seems to be dying off," said Lester.

"I try every day to help kill it," said Ardor.

Lester shook his head.

"Now Chuck, I have no problem with you writing a story, drawing pictures. In fact, that's wonderful. Go for it, man. Can't encourage you enough to create art. However," Lester paused to look at Jase, "let's not draw any pictures that are sexual in any way, especially pictures with females."

"How about female aliens?" asked Chuck.

"No, absolutely not. You'll go to jail," said Jase.

Chuck looked at his dad. "He's crazy."

"Well, if anybody is going to jail it would be me for allowing a ten-year-old boy to draw sexual pictures of females, even female aliens, for people to look at."

"Really?" asked Chuck.

"I'm afraid so, sport," said Lester.

"So how old do I have to be?"

"For what? To legally make porn? See, this is what I've been talking about, Dad," said Jase.

"Chuck, you have to be legally an adult for anything like that, which is eighteen in this country. How about you just not use anything sexual in the book. A bit too young for that right now. Okay?" asked Lester.

"Okay," said Chuck.

"Good. If you have any questions just come to me and we'll talk about it."

"I will say, and I'm saying this with all honesty, that discussing porn with your family is very impressive. Kudos to you, my friend," said Ardor. She raised her mug toward Lester, which Lester tapped with his mug. She took another gulp. "Very good beer. I especially enjoy that saliva aftertaste."

"Funny, mine doesn't have that. I guess you aren't around too many families these days," said Lester.

"Happy families are all alike, but unhappy ones are different. Something along those lines," said Ardor.

"Tolstoy, and that's very much a paraphrase," said Lester.

"I'd also add that no family is completely happy," said Ardor.

"Yada, yada, yada. Don't teach my kids to be nihilists."

"What's a nihilist?" asked Jase.

"A puddle of a human," said Ardor.

"So you gonna tell me about this dangerous situation?" asked Lester.

"Not in front of your kids," said Ardor.

"Really? This is coming from a woman who wanted to describe orgasms to my kids here."

"Orgasms are healthy. And fun. What I'm about to tell you is not healthy. And not fun."

Lester nodded his head. "I'm intrigued and terrified."

"It's not a happy tale, but it is entertaining," said Ardor.

"To a nihilist maybe," said Lester.

"So that's what you think of me?" asked Ardor.

"Nope, not at all." He looked at his children. "I'll give y'all five dollars to play the video games back there," said Lester.

"Five dollars? Dad, please," said Chuck.

Lester laughed. "Right. Gotcha. I'll give you five dollars each," said Lester as he looked at Chuck. Chuck gave his dad a thumbs up.

"Now you're cooking with gas, Dad," said Chuck.

"Where'd you hear that?" asked Lester.

"Terrance," said Chuck.

"Terrance. I need to meet this Terrance," said Lester.

"You'd like him. He smokes," said Chuck.

"He smokes?" asked Lester.

"No, he doesn't," said Jase.

"I was there when he smoked at his house," said Chuck.

"He was showing us how his older brother's vape pen works," said Jase.

"That's called smoking," said Chuck.

"It was a demonstration," said Jase.

"And he also showed us some pretty cool websites," said Chuck.

"What?" asked Lester.

"Nothing. Do we have to go play video games?" asked Jase.

"Yes. Ardor and I need to talk alone for a few minutes. Here," Lester pulled several folded bills from his pocket and then proceeded to give each child five dollars. He gave Lizzy five one-dollar bills and a five-dollar bill each to Jase and Chuck.

After the kids left for the game room, Lester took a bite of pizza and said, "Well?"

"I've got some people after me," said Ardor.

"After you? You mean like the mafia?" he said with a chuckle.

"Kinda."

"Dear god," said Lester.

"Wade and I found ourselves in the weed-growing business in Oregon. He met a guy who worked as a master grower. We needed money since both of us were between jobs. With Wade's knowledge of growing stuff—"

"Wait. Growing stuff? You mean growing weed here in Alabama?"

"Yes, small stuff, a couple dozen plants out in the woods. And he's worked at a few nurseries. Garden nurseries. Anyway, he quickly landed a job as a master grower at this cannabis farm. A few weeks after Wade started, they hired me, too. I did some trimming for a while, but that's a grueling job, man, trimming off the leaves from the buds. You're paid by weight, so people put on headphones and try to find a groove. Assembly-line grunt work. I eventually became Wade's assistant. He convinced them I knew almost as much as he did about growing weed."

"Did you?"

"No, not even close. I didn't make near what he did, but it was better than trimming. Then, well, Wade being Wade, he thought we weren't being fairly compensated for our skills, especially since he has a degree in horticulture."

"A degree in horticulture? I didn't know that. Where from?"

"Faulkner State, down in Bay Minette. I think they changed the name not too long ago, something like Coastal Alabama Community College. Just north of Mobile and Pensacola. His mother loves gardening, that's where his interest came from. I love her, but she's kinda crazy. Hippie crazy."

"Like you?" said Lester.

"Groovy, man. Make love, not war."

"My point."

"Wade loves the Redneck Riviera. Had lots of fun down there; it's the place he calls home. That's where he and some other hort students grew weed in the woods on somebody's farm."

"Oregon would be a good place to use his skills then."

"It was, except his knowledge of growing weed far exceeded the people who owned the operation, though they didn't think that. Because of Wade their plants really improved, grew bigger, bushier, better buds. He knows his hort shit. More importantly, their profit margin greatly improved thanks to Wade. So, he thought he deserved more money. I was there when he explained his reasoning to them, but they didn't give a damn. Just greedy assholes. They paid him as little as they could without him quitting, so he began to skim a few buds. We sold it on the side to a few dealers he knew. Made more money than I thought we would with the stuff."

"How much?"

"A couple of backpacks full of cash. That's not really all of it. Wade said he bought some land in South Alabama with some of it. Somewhere along the Florida line. Not sure exactly where it is. Anyway, the last time I added it all up the total was $100,000 plus. And that was a year ago."

"That's after he bought the land?"

"Yeah."

"There's people who will hunt you down for that kind of money," said Lester.

"Obviously. We did it so long I suppose we pushed our luck. A few months ago, Wade told me on the way home from work that they were on to us. I laughed at him, but he was serious. He said he overheard the owners talking about us stealing weed. We went straight home, packed up some clothes and the money, then left. After a few days in the Seattle area, we split up. I came here, and Wade said he was going to the northeast to stay with an old friend. Said we should meet up at that land after the New Year."

"Are you feeling a little paranoid?" asked Lester.

"Hell yeah. I've tried to be very careful about not seeing too many people in town," said Ardor.

"And here I was thinking you'd gotten yourself in trouble with some dude's wife," said Lester.

"Hell hath no fury like people who think you've cheated them out of thousands of dollars," said Ardor.

"This is a very ugly situation," said Lester.

"Hideous," said Ardor.

"Why don't you just give them the money?"

"That's what I said, but Wade sees it differently, believes they owe him this money."

"Does he have all the money with him?"

"Most of it. And no, he's not going to fuck me over."

"Okay, now you want me to help you out of this incredibly dangerous situation?"

"How about letting me move in with your family?"

Lester chuckled. He turned around and looked at his kids playing in the game room. "I can't endanger my kids, darlin'."

"I certainly understand that. I wouldn't think of putting your great kids in any danger. Lee Ellen said she would be back in a few weeks. That's when I'd move in with you for just a couple of months, until after the New Year. I'll leave for the land in south Alabama on January 1."

"How wouldn't that be putting my kids in danger?"

"Wade and I told them we were from North Alabama, but I don't think we said anything about Huntsville. They have no way of tracing me."

"The name Ardor shouldn't be that hard to trace," said Lester.

Ardor paused. "That's probably true, but I've told no one in town that I'm here. Except for Lee Ellen. And I will not tell Lee Ellen where I'm going when I move in with you. I'll just say I'm heading back to Oregon."

"So, she doesn't know what you just told me?"

"No, you're the only one. Aren't you lucky?"

"Oh yeah, lucky me. How much of the money do you have?"

"Enough to pay you for your trouble."

"Huh. Well, now, that puts a different spin on things. You can move in today."

"Money is magic."

"Like rubbing the lantern. How much are you willing to pay?"

"For two months?"

"Yep, room and board for two months."

Ardor mouthed, "Ten."

Lester sat back in his seat, looked straight ahead at Ardor, and then he scratched the top of his scalp with fingers from both hands. "Good lord, Ardor." He gave the restaurant a slow pan then whispered, "Do you mean thousand?"

Ardor nodded.

"Welcome, roommate. Please stay as long as you like."

"Are you sure? Maybe you need to talk to your kids about it."

Lester took a long swallow of beer from his mug, placed the glass on the table, and then slapped it with both hands, "You're probably right." Lester turned and looked toward the game room. "Done!"

Ardor raised her right fist to Lester for a bump. After a couple of seconds Lester fist-bumped Ardor and said, "Honestly, let me think about it. Okay?"

"No problem. Lee Ellen probably won't show up for another week or two," said Ardor.

Lizzy walked up to the table. "Can we go now?"

"Blew through that $5, eh?" said Lester.

Lizzy nodded her head.

"Okay, go tell the boys we're leaving in a few minutes." Lizzy walked back toward the game room. Lester leaned forward and whispered, "I was wondering if you could do me a favor?"

Ardor leaned into the table. "Already asking for a favor. You get to it, don't cha?"

Lester smiled, "Can you acquire some nose candy?"

"Yeah? Well look at you, Mister Hospice Nurse."

"No, no, not for me."

"Sure. A friend, right?"

"That's the truth. A terminally-ill patient."

"Really?"

"And maybe a hooker?"

Ardor sat back. "And a hooker? For a friend?"

"Helping the needy."

"Whatever you say."

"This guy is breaking my heart. Stupid. I'm stupid."

"Don't let your heart make you do stupid things."

"Yeah. I know it sounds crazy. Completely foolish."

"Hey, who am I to judge. I'm the queen of bad decisions."

"Yeah, you're right; let's just forget it."

"Tell you what, let me look into it. Wouldn't hurt to find out some numbers, availability. Just to satisfy your curiosity. And mine. I have a little knowledge with the white lady, but hookers are a vice I've never had the pleasure to dance with. I'll ask Lee Ellen, see if she knows anyone who can help. She's got lots of friends in the area. Don't worry; your name will not be mentioned."

"I'm pretty sure I won't go through with it. I just feel for this guy. Like you said, won't hurt to see what she can find out. And one thing for sure: the fewer people who know you're in town the better. Right?"

"You got a heart as big as a melon, man. I'm pretty sure I wouldn't be able to help the dying."

"Just remember to stay low."

"I'm a ghost."

FOR A FEW DOLLARS MORE

THURSDAY AND FRIDAY brought Lester patients who struggled with the symptoms of old age, which now included the unavoidable, the rank march of darkness. He knew hospice meant young people slapped across their faces by the sudden appearance of approaching death, those were tough; the old, the grannies and grandpas seemed resigned to their fate rather than angry. They knew their days were coming to an end, so the days bulged with thoughts of their end times. "Later" suddenly was no longer an option. A seventy-one-year-old wife, mother, and grandmother given a terminal diagnosis was a different creature from a seventeen-year-old girl dying of a brain tumor.

He found each client a separate world. Most navigated the final trip as clean as possible, sometimes confronting, sometimes avoiding. Pleasure, pain, loneliness, love, bitterness, regrets, and despair. An eighty-five-year-old man suffering from the latter stages of Alzheimer's, lost in an ever-changing world, including his wife's death two months earlier, was no less sad than the sudden snuff of a life just beginning. With each new patient Lester felt punch-drunk. His maiden visit, the duo of Irene and Toots, full of humor and Toots's heartfelt plea for drugs and sex seemed a perfect launching pad for his new altruistic career, but the accumulation of dread, the dread of the patient, family, and friends, and even Lester himself always colored the moment. Some bathed in relief, a struggle coming to an end. Some believed the end was the end, kaput, finis, that their final days were their final days. Most of these people seemed content with their circumstances. Others were unsure what lay ahead; thus their faces revealed a confused expression, an ever-growing apprehension, and still others took solace in their faith and their god. Most of these took Southern refuge with the Father, the Son, and the Holy Spirit, hoping and believing the next journey brought the promised land of mourned loved ones. One thirty-nine-year-old possessed a Buddhist's calm and kindness, the journey for the Four Nobel Truths never-ending. And then a twenty-six-year-old man recently informed of his Stage IV pancreatic cancer decided to wear his anger like steel armor, embracing his fury for having his life cut short.

Lester felt dizzy with his proximity to death's unceasing deep hum, that low menacing tone heard in movies when evil was close. He now understood what experienced nurses emphasized again and again: how one must learn to weigh detachment in relation to compassion. Go cold, hard professional and you commit to being a machine, focusing on doing your job well, and allowing no room for heartbreak. "Some will think you have no emotions, that you just don't care, but the truth is that you are trying to survive so that you can help others," a nursing professor told one of Lester's classes one evening. Even his first steps into the hospice world brought Lester to the understanding that the skill one most needed involved calibrating the scale to prevent an emotional beating.

The first day Lester met Jenny Lynn she told him, "You should do everything you can to help the patients, physically and emotionally, come to terms with what we all will face: our deaths." Lester nodded his head. "But more than anything else, Lester," she had said as they sat in her car in front of a country home north of Huntsville, one of Phyllis's patients, waiting for her to arrive, "and you'll think I'm crazy for saying this, but more than anything is survival, your survival. If you care too much, then you'll just burn yourself out and what's left after that is, plain and simple, we've lost a good nurse. Which means one less caring soul who helps the dying. Now that's the truth."

He had given that idea little thought until Friday morning, when he allowed the seventeen-year-old too close, moved by the young woman's plight. Her sadness was deep and cold. Within the first minute Lester had walked into her bedroom, she lashed out at him with her hopelessness.

"Is it really just bad fucking luck? I'm going to die because of bad fucking luck? 'Sorry Cathy, just bad fucking luck that your DNA grew a tumor in your fucking brain that will take your fucking life.' This ain't right. This is not fucking right. Everyone keeps telling me that I've got to accept it, 'Just accept it, Cathy, find the joy in your last few days.' That's easy to say when you are not the one about to die. Tell me how to find fucking joy with death bearing down on me like a runaway fucking train."

"Cathy, we're not capable of understanding all of life's pains. God has plans we just don't understand," said the girl's mother who stood at the foot of the bed.

Lester looked around the dying girl's bedroom. Finding a desk chair behind him, he rolled the chair beside the bed and sat down.

"Mom, I'm tired of you and everyone else saying that shit. I'm about to die. Do you understand that? Jesus-fucking-Christ."

Lester looked at the mother; tears ran down her face.

"Oh baby, I know. I'm so sorry," she said.

"Cathy," Lester began, "I'm not going to pretend to have any answers. Because you're right; there are no answers. You've been given a bad hand to play. The worst. It's not right. It's not fair. You have a right to be very angry. But you need to realize that you get to choose how to live your last days. You can be angry until the very end, just go down spewing your rage at the unfairness of what's happened to you. Another choice is that you make peace with your circumstances and find joy in your remaining days. Honestly, I can see the benefits of both for you. Letting out that bitterness has to feel good; relieving that rage certainly calms you, like you're hitting back, punching cancer and death right in the face."

"I'd trade places with you if I could, sweetheart," said the mother.

Cathy looked at her mother. "I believe that and I love you for it. But, honestly, where you're standing right now saying something like that seems very easy. Where I am right now lying down in this bed waiting to die, it don't really do me much good. Fuck dying," she said with venom. She turned to Lester and spewed another, "Fuck dying."

Lester nodded. "Indeed, Cathy, 'Fuck dying.' But you need to understand that you control this situation for the people who love you. You're gonna lose the game no matter what you say, but you still have a little time to be with the people who love you. And remember that everyone's journey ends the same. Your call, Cathy. But remember your decision is about your final days and the final days the people you love have with you. I guarantee you that if you go out raging, the people you love will forgive you because they love you, but destroying these last memories of you shouldn't be how you want them to remember you. They didn't do this to you. No one did; it's just bad luck. I'm not telling you what to do, I'm just trying to be honest about your situation. One option is to love with all your heart the people who love you. This isn't easy, we all know that. Just think it through; think how you want to spend these last days with the people who love you."

Lester looked at the young girl's face. She was thin and pale; the radiation had removed most of her hair. A long Frankenstein-looking scar on the right side of her skull was several inches in length.

"What does it matter? You know? What does it fucking matter?" the young girl said.

Her mother walked to the other side of the bed and then kissed her daughter's cheek. "I love you so much," she said.

"I love you, too, Mama. I just don't want to fucking die."

The one patient who shook Lester more than all the rest that Friday was his last call that afternoon. Her name was Wendy White. She was eighty-three and living with her nephew and his family just outside the northwest city limits off Blake Bottom Road. She had lived with Lisa Haynes, her partner, for forty years, but when Lisa died four years ago Wendy was forced to enter a nursing home. The home she had shared with Lisa for nearly thirty years was suddenly taken away from her. Lisa's grandmother had left the home to Lisa, but upon Lisa's death the grandmother's will stated the house would be bequeathed to the grandmother's church if Lisa had not married nor produced children. The small Baptist church did not bend in the presence of a lesbian relationship.

At the nursing home Wendy endured bullying for nearly two years, verbal and physical abuse, all connected to her being a lesbian. Wendy's nephew, Wayne Holman, had taken Wendy into his home when he heard of the abuse at the nursing home. He told Lester at the front door that his family had very little to do with "Aunt Wendy" because of her homosexuality.

"I just couldn't allow Aunt Wendy to suffer like that. Those people at the nursing home were cruel. One old man bashed his walker into Aunt Wendy's scooter on several occasions, screaming his disgust at her 'perversion.' They ostracized her, forcing her to eat alone in the cafeteria. One day a lady rammed her wheelchair into Aunt Wendy's table, knocking it over and screaming 'y'all will burn in hell.' And in the mailroom someone slapped the back of Aunt Wendy's head while she was checking her mail slot. Several spit at her and on her. When I finally heard what was going on out there, I just told my wife that we couldn't let her live like that. She certainly doesn't deserve the cruelty. I saw how mean people can be, even from her own family, my family." He shook his head. "I love Aunt Wendy; she was always kind to me. I was the only person from our family who attended Lisa's funeral. My wife loves Wendy. So do our son and daughter."

Lester shook his head. "I'm so sorry to hear that, Mr. Holman. People who call themselves Christian. I don't get it."

"One more thing, Mr. Gordon. Wendy is a retired schoolteacher, so she can be ... how should I say this?"

"Opinionated?"

"Yes, that's true, but even oafs can be opinionated. She is very adamant with her opinions and her knowledge about things. She doesn't suffer fools very well. Just wanted to warn you. She can put people off."

"Ignorance carries no weight with me. It's like trying to play a two of clubs on an ace of spades. An old friend of mine use to say that teachers got on his nerves because they are so self-righteous, always walking around with a smug look on their face. Honestly, I've never met a really smart person who wasn't a little bit smug and self-satisfied. The people who I have trouble tolerating are the idiots who are smug."

Wayne laughed. "I know what you mean. The ones who are all puffed up in their ignorance."

"Sorry, Mr. Holman, I have a tendency to run my mouth, to say things I shouldn't."

"No, no, you're fine. Aunt Wendy is right back here." Lester followed Wayne to the back bedroom of the home where Wendy was lying in bed.

"Aunt Wendy, this is Mr. Lester Gordon. He will be your new hospice nurse."

The old woman was sitting up in bed with a book opened in her hands. She possessed a full head of short white hair and wore a bright green pair of glasses.

"Hello, Ms. White. Very nice to meet you. What are you reading if I may ask?" asked Lester.

The old woman looked up from her book. "Hello, Lester Gordon. I am happy to meet you. I'm reading Maya Angelou's *I Know Why the Caged Bird Sings*. Are you a literary man, Mr. Gordon?"

"I read some, though I would never refer to myself as a literary man. I don't believe I've heard of that novel."

"It's not a novel. It's part of Ms. Angelou's autobiography, the first of seven volumes. She's a famous black poet. Did you know that, Mr. Gordon?"

"I do know that. I believe she read a poem at Bill Clinton's first inauguration."

"Yes, that poem made her famous outside the literary world. This first volume is quite astounding. It was nominated for a National Book Award when it was first published back in ... let me see," Wendy flipped to the copyright page, "back in 1970. I've read it several times. I find it very inspirational. Do you know why I find it inspirational, Mr. Gordon?"

"Please call me Lester."

"Fair enough. You may call me Wendy. Do you know why I find it inspirational, Lester?"

"I have no idea."

"As a toddler, Maya and her brother were sent by their mother to live in Arkansas with their grandmother. Arkansas is where she first encountered the cruelty of racism. She also describes being raped at the age of eight years old. The book is stunning in its revelation that through strength of character one can overcome such trials and tribulations. I can tell by your expression that you are mystified. Am I right, Lester?"

"I'm a Southerner, so I'm fully versed in the South's velvet glove of cruelty. However, raping an eight-year-old is a level of cruelty that is beyond my understanding."

"Well, well, Lester, curiosity is a trait of an active mind. I'm no different than anyone else. I've been tested, had my share of bullies and bigots, but what I've learned is that one must be true to oneself, must believe in one's true self in order to make it in this world."

"That's very true, Aunt Wendy."

"Now my nephew Wayne is a curious soul, mind as sharp as a tack."

Wayne smiled.

"A bright boy," she said as she pointed at Wayne. "This book certainly teaches such ideas, though not pedantic, which of course makes the argument for labeling this autobiography as a beautiful piece of literature." She placed a blank index card in the book, closed the cover, removed her glasses, and then studied Lester's face. "You are a very handsome man, Mr. Lester Gordon. I hope I'm not being too forward. As my nephew will attest, I'm a lesbian, so my appraisal is only mildly sexual."

Lester smiled and looked at the nephew.

The nephew grinned. "'Only mildly.' Aunt Wendy is very honest. She won't tell you something unless she means it." He looked at his aunt.

Wendy quickly said, "My dear sweet Wayne, one may tell those so-called white lies in order to avoid being rude, hurting someone's feelings. But I feel I'm on solid ground by stating that for most all other occasions honesty carries the day."

"I suppose now you know where Aunt Wendy stands on honesty."

"Well, you certainly are charming," said Lester.

"Be careful, dear boy; I did have a few boyfriends in my day."

"I'm not surprised to hear that," said Lester.

"I never knew you had boyfriends," said Wayne.

"There're lots of things you don't know about me, Wayne. I almost married a man once. I broke it off after we had sex. It became clear that he thought of me as something to give him pleasure. That would not do. I saw my road ahead as a road full of sexual frustration."

"So, you gave up men after that experience?" asked Wayne.

"No, that's not true. I gave up men after I had sex with women. I'm being a bit unfair toward your sex, but the anecdote does possess some truth."

"Some of us know what we're doing," Lester said with a smile.

"People surprise me all the time, but I don't think I would be surprised by you, Mr. Lester Gordon."

"Aunt Wendy, you behave yourself," said Wayne.

"If we would have met when I was a younger woman, I'm pretty sure we would have been very good friends. Wayne, go pour Lester and me a taste of bourbon. I'm a Dickel woman, myself. About a finger's worth, neat. You are welcome to join us, Wayne. And please don't deny a dying woman's wish."

"Aunt Wendy is in a drinking mood."

Lester knew at that very moment he would deeply mourn the death of Wendy White.

Lester pulled into the parking lot of the YMCA, gliding the car to a space a few rows from the front door. He and his kids were in a black Mercedes, a sedan he inherited from his mom. Lester's wife drove the car after his mother's death, the kids associating the car with their mother, even calling it "Mom's car." Lester thought the car ostentatious, even if just for the car being a late-model Mercedes, but everyone in the family, including Lester, enjoyed the car's luxury. He felt more confidence in the car's dependability over the truck, which was mostly due to the multi-green truck being several years older.

"Can you play that song again, Dad?" asked Jase. "Just one more time to make me feel good about the beating today."

"'Us Vs Them?' Excellent choice," said Lester.

"You really think those guys are going to pound you?" asked Chuck. "Grow a pair, bro."

"I'm positive. I'd like to see you play them," said Jase.

"I'd love to. Do you think your coach would let me. I've been working on my jump shot. Ask him, Jase. Tell him your little brother is a wizard on the court. You've seen me, it's true."

"I hate to admit it, but you've gotten better, Chuck."

"Thank you very much. I'll help the team."

"What do you think, Dad?" asked Jase. "Chuck is good. We could use his shot."

"No, you can't play unless you're on the roster. Didn't Jase ask you to play at the beginning of the season?"

"Yeah, but that was before I developed this jump shot. I got it working, Dad."

"It's true; he's got him a shot now."

"You can't just walk out and begin playing on the team. You both know that."

"Anyway, you should pull for us, not against us," said Jase.

"I'm just saying that you shouldn't be thinking you're going to lose before you play the game. You gotta think you have a chance. Right, Dad? What's the point of playing?"

"The team we're about to play beats everybody. Beats them badly. By forty, fifty points. They're so tall. And good."

"Jase and them can win, right Dad?"

"Just please play the song, Dad."

Lester pushed a few buttons on his smartphone and the song began to play. He turned to Jase. "Chuck has a point. Yes, these guys have hit puberty; they're big dudes for their age, and their skills are good. Doesn't mean they can't be beat. Everybody loses at some point. I know losing is no fun, but all you can do is give your best."

"They're huge. You remember watching them a couple of weeks ago. We won't hardly get a rebound."

"Big boys for sure—" Lester's phone rang, the opening notes of "Blue Rondo a La Turk."

"I haven't heard that ring before, Dad," said Chuck. "That's jazz music?"

"You're correct, Chuck. I just downloaded it yesterday," said Lester. "One of my patients was listening to this when I visited him." Lester looked at the phone. "Hey, this is Ardor. Why don't y'all go on in? I'll be there in just a couple of minutes." All three nodded their heads.

"Hey," Lester said right after the last car door slammed.

"Hey," replied Ardor.

"What's the scoop on my man's request?"

"Huh?"

"The nose candy and the hooker?"

"Actually, I forgot about that. Lee Ellen came in yesterday completely unannounced. We ended up going to some crazy party last night. This guy she took off with is really shady. He's got lowlife written all over him. I tend to give people a wide berth, but this guy is stupid and a thug. A hide-your-wallet type of guy. He kept trying to fuck me last night, wanted to fuck both of us last night. I'm sex-positive, right, willing to try most things and all that, but I'm not fucking a drunk dickhead."

"What does Otis say about him?"

"Otis banned him from the property."

"Good for him."

"Anyway, what about my room-and-board request?"

"Sounds like you need to get out of there. Not a good situation for you."

"Yes, I need a decision about me living with you, ASAP. I need to get out of here, get far away from this creep."

"Didn't Otis solve your problem with this guy?"

"If I'm around Lee Ellen, then I'll be around him. I've got to cut her off, too."

"Right."

"If you're not up for it, then I'll need to find someone yesterday."

"What's Lee Ellen doing with him?"

"I don't know; maybe he's a good lay. She does have a thing for bad boys. But he ain't no cool bad boy, some hip rebel. His neck is as red as a stop sign. If you aren't comfortable with me moving in, which I fully understand, then I'll find somewhere else to go. I just need to know so I can find an escape."

Lester watched the steady stream of parents and kids leaving and entering the YMCA.

"Okay, well, let me think about it a little while longer."

"Nope, can't do, cowboy. I need an answer now. This jerk is walking trouble. I need to start looking for another place if you say no."

"Sure." Lester scanned the front of the YMCA. About ten yards to the right of the building where the mown grass met the property line of several acres of undeveloped land stood a white dog. The dog looked like a white German shepherd. And it seemed to be looking straight at Lester. A family walked in front of the car, blocking the view of the dog for a few seconds. When the family passed, the dog still stood at the edge of the woods and still seemed to be looking straight at Lester. A few yards behind this dog were three other white dogs standing in the underbrush. Lester leaned forward to look closer at the dogs, but his left arm bumped the steering wheel which caused him to drop the phone, sending it ricocheting against the dash and seat until it hit the floorboard. Lester bent down to pick up his phone, grabbed it, and then raised back up and looked at the dogs. All four dogs looked at him, turned, and ran into the woods.

"Hey, you still there?" asked Ardor.

"Yeah, sorry about that. I dropped the phone. Now, you said you would leave at the beginning of the year. Are we on the same page here?"

"If not sooner," said Ardor.

"We're looking at about two and a half months."

"And don't forget the money."

"I haven't forgotten the money. God, I'm such a whore. You're going to pay me to help you hide from these folks."

"This is America, dude. You pay someone to do everything."

"Still doesn't make me feel good about it."

"A simple transaction, a business deal. And you're no more a whore than the rest of us. I'm not sure how long they'll chase us, but I'll do everything I can to avoid them. I'm thinking I'll be safe with you."

"I would hope so, but you never know."

"Not one-hundred percent foolproof. There is risk. Everything involves risk."

"I know that too well. I just don't understand why you don't take off down south, hide out in some motel by the beach."

"I should tell you the truth: I sorta already told Wade that I'm staying low by living with you. He's going to pick me up right before Christmas. He thought it was a great idea."

"Presumptuous?"

"Sorry, just had a feeling. The land he bought in South Alabama has a trailer for us to live in. He has this plan for us to live off the grid. I suggested, again, we give the money back."

"Might be your best choice."

"He said I was crazy."

"He thinks he deserves that money, doesn't he?"

"Yes."

"Why doesn't he come now?"

"It's all rather complicated, a complete shit show. Better that I not tell you any more. The less you know the better."

"Agreed. You've already told me more than I want to know." Lester looked back to where the white dogs had stood. Nothing. "Okay, I'll agree to this conditionally, which places me right in the middle of Crazy Town. I need to talk to my kids before a final decision."

"Of course, of course."

"And if they give it a green light, then you must promise that when Wade comes down to pick you up you'll meet him somewhere other than my house. I'll drive you anywhere you need to go."

"That's not an issue."

"Are you wanting to move in this weekend?"

"The sooner the better. This dude is insufferable, like being around a spoiled chimp. I got to go now."

"Right. I'm with you on that. Let me talk to the kids today. Maybe you could move in tomorrow afternoon. Can you escape his grasp until then?"

"He left about fifteen minutes ago, but he's an idiot, could show back up at any moment. Lee Ellen can't get enough of him. I keep telling her, 'Are you kidding me?' but all she does is give me a blank stare. This is her train wreck, not mine."

"She's blinded, sounds like."

"Dick drunk. I mean that literally and metaphorically."

"Not the first time I've heard of that. I'm pretty sure the kids will have no problem with you moving in. I'll probably put you in Chuck's room."

"I'm not tossing your son out of his room. I'll just sleep on the couch."

"For that kind of money, you get to have your own room. Besides, Chuck's room is tiny; we used it as a storage room before he made it his bedroom. And you need your own space."

"That will make things much more comfortable, for everyone really. I appreciate you thinking of me."

"And Jase has two beds in his room. They argue all the time, like most siblings, but they'll be fine together."

"If your kids are fine with it, then I'm fine with it. And I'll ask Lee Ellen to make a few calls to see what she can find out about your patient's request."

"Just don't tell her it's for me."

"Right, right, of course."

"I have to admit, I'm having second thoughts about the request," said Lester.

"I can see that."

"See what you can find out first. Maybe asking around will cure my need to do this. The guy just makes a good case for himself."

"Okay."

"And promise me this also. If you have one tiny suspicion that they have found you—"

"Who?"

"The Oregon thugs. Whatever they are. If someone seems to be following you, watching, then you let me know."

"Yes, of course, I'll tell you immediately. And I'll hightail it."

"Okay then, I'll let you know something by tonight," said Lester.

"That sounds wonderful. And thank you again."

"And you're sure that no one knows you're in town besides me and Lee Ellen?"

"You, Lee Ellen, Otis, and Lilly. And Wade."

"And the monkey boy," said Lester.

"He's just a fool trying to get in my pants. He has no idea about me. Hell, he has very little idea about anything."

"Do Otis and Lilly know your family?"

"No. Wade does, of course. And Lee Ellen, but she is under strict orders. She's as wild as a June bug, but I can trust her. No doubt about it. I'd bet my life on it."

"I think you are."

"Maybe I should get a gun."

"No, I don't want a gun in my house."

"You don't have a gun?"

"A couple of shotguns."

Ardor let out a sigh.

"And you're not telling Lee Ellen that you'll be living with me, right?"

"Nope. In fact, I'll have a taxi drop me off at a gas station out in the country and you can come pick me up there."

"We have Uber and Lyft now, darlin'. Maybe to be on the safe side you can have one of them take you to a station. Then have the other company pick you up there and take you to another station, and from there you can walk to another location which will be where I'll pick you up."

"Goddamn, should I cut and dye my hair?"

"I was gonna ask that. Maybe starting to walk with a limp wouldn't be a bad idea."

"Maybe cut off one of my ears?"

"Cutting and dying your hair will probably suffice."

"You like that with your women, don't you? Mix it up a bit."

"Could you wear some knee socks?"

"How about a little short plaid skirt?"

"You got one?"

"I'm beginning to think this request for coke and a hooker is for you."

"Just trying to be on the safe side; cover your tracks. Y'all stole lots of money."

"Not according to Wade."

"I don't think his argument will carry much weight with these people. They are hunting you two because you stole from them. It's not a labor dispute."

"I know. You're right."

"And if you do stay here, then I think you should pretty much stay in the house, like you're under house arrest. All it would take would be for someone who knows you to see you and that person tells other people, and those people tell other people. A private investigator comes into town snooping around, and suddenly he has an idea where you might be. Then more people come into town to look around where you have been seen. This is an ugly picture I'm painting."

"I'm in an ugly place."

"Prepare for the worst."

"Living in the moment is my best option."

"I'll contact you tonight," said Lester, and he ended the call.

Lester walked into the Y slightly dazed from just the idea of what he was bringing into his house, his family. He found Chuck and Lizzy in the ping-pong room where kids played games on the four tables. He walked to where they stood along one of the walls.

"Hey, where's Jase?"

"He's in the boys locker room with his team getting ready for the game," said Chuck.

Lester looked at his phone. "They're supposed to play in fifteen minutes. Make sure you come see your brother play."

"To see him get whooped?" said Lizzy.

"No, not to see him get whooped. We don't know what's going to happen. Regardless, we need to support Jase, okay?"

"Gotcha, Dad," said Chuck. He gave a thumbs up which was followed by a thumbs up from Lizzy.

Lester buckled his seatbelt. "You played well. Ten points is a good game."

"They killed us," said Jase who sat in the front passenger seat.

"They only beat you by sixteen. Haven't they been beating teams by thirty and forty points?"

"Yep."

"I thought you were great, Jase," said Chuck.

"Thanks, Chuck."

"I'm proud you're my brother," said Lizzy. "You're a star, Jase."

"Thanks, Lizzy."

"You play them one more time before the end of the season. You now know what you need to do in order to beat them. You'll be ready for them," said Lester. "That fear you had of them is not justified. They are good, but not gods."

"Thanks, Dad."

"Okay, before we take off there's something I want to ask y'all." He made eye contact with each of his children. "You all know Ardor." Each child nodded. "Ardor needs a place to stay for a while, so I'm thinking about asking her to live with us."

"Why?" asked Jase.

"She's found herself in a situation where she needs a place to live."

"Where does she live now?" asked Jase.

"She's staying somewhere that she can no longer stay. Let's leave it at that. So I'm asking you if there are any problems with her living with us for a few weeks."

"A few weeks?" asked Chuck.

"Until around Christmas."

"Where will she sleep?" asked Lizzy.

"In Chuck's bedroom," said Lester.

"Where will I sleep?" asked Chuck.

"You would sleep in Jase's room."

The slamming of car doors in the Y's parking lot filled the silence of the car. Lester started the Mercedes. He looked at Jase and then turned to look at Chuck and Lizzy in the backseat.

"Well, any more questions? Any comments?"

"Count me in, Dad. I like Ardor," said Chuck.

"She seems like a nice person," said Lizzy.

"She is a nice person, Lizzy," said Lester.

"I think this conversation is for show," said Jase.

"For show?" asked Lester.

"Sounds like you've made up your mind. Not that I'm against it. That girl is cool," said Jase.

"What?" asked Lester. "I haven't made up my mind; that's why I asked you guys. We can say no."

"She likes us, right?" asked Jase.

"Yes, Jase, she does like our family."

"Do you think she would model for me?" asked Chuck.

Jase rolled his eyes. "This can't be healthy for a ten-year-old."

"See Dad, he acts like he's a preacher or something. Our family is a loving family. That's what you said, Dad. Those are your words."

"No, what I'm saying is that my brother is porn crazy. We love everyone, Chuck, but you're the one who is porn crazy."

"I'm making a book about aliens, not about sex."

"That is so ridiculous. Right, Dad? Chuck is wanting to live in the gutter."

"No modeling," Lester said to Chuck.

"Okay, but I can use her shape without her actually modeling for me."

"No, Ardor will not be used in any of your art. Do I make myself clear on that?"

"Okay, okay. I'm just so surprised that art has no respect in our house."

"She'll be our guest, so give her respect. That goes for everyone. I'll let her know she can move in tomorrow," said Lester.

"Tomorrow?" questioned Jase.

"Problem?" asked Lester.

"No, no problem. She's a grown woman, right?"

"Sort of," said Lester.

"What?" asked Jase.

"Nothing. We're all good here, right?" asked Lester.

Chuck gave a thumbs-up.

"Lizzy?"

"I like the idea of another girl in the house," said Lizzy. "I love you guys, but I'd like another girl in the house."

"Right, sisterhood, a little solidarity."

"What does that mean?" asked Lizzy.

"Solidarity is when people feel unified over a common interest. Like you and Ardor both being female gives you two a feeling of being together, solidarity, over issues that females have. Like lots of women agree and feel unity over issues that women have together."

"Ardor and me have girl power."

"You got it, Lizzy. Okay, then. I'll let her know. One more question, though. What did you mean Jase when you said, 'That girl is cool?'"

"I don't know, Dad. I can't describe it."

"Do you mean charm, Jase?" asked Chuck.

"Maybe," said Jase.

"Maybe she's got some kind of girl voodoo," said Lester.

"Voodoo solidarity," said Lizzy.

Lester pulled his phone from his jeans' front pocket. He texted Ardor, *It was unanimous. Welcome aboard.*

"You been here long?" asked Lester after he stepped out of his truck and walked up to where Ardor stood next to her two duffel bags, one blue jean and the other an Army green. They stood next to a convenience store.

"Hey, what's wrong?" asked Ardor. She crossed her arms.

"What do you mean?"

"Are you having second thoughts? You look like you got the world on your shoulders."

"No, no, just a little upset about one of my patients. Got a call about an hour ago telling me that he had a heart attack this morning."

"But you just started, right?"

"Last Wednesday."

"Your first day was that day with Otis?"

"Yep , first day seeing patients by myself. The first patient I saw that morning was a middle-aged man dying from lung cancer. He had a heart attack this morning. He survived, but he's not doing well."

Lester picked up one of the duffel bags and placed it in the back of the truck. Ardor tossed in the other one right behind it.

"Is he the guy who wanted a date and some coke?" asked Ardor as Lester walked around the rear of the truck on his way to the driver-side door. He stopped and faced Ardor when he grabbed the door handle.

"Honestly, I wasn't going to find those for him. I was just looking into it so that he could dream. I don't think he really wanted all that, he just wanted to feel like he was still swinging for the fences. His eyes sparkled with energy when he talked to me about his wish list. Maybe I'm wrong; maybe he was serious. I just think you should let people have their dreams, especially at the end."

Lester opened the door and stepped into the cab of the truck. Ardor opened the passenger door and then placed her elbows on the seat.

"I need a beer," she said.

"You serious?" Lester shook his head.

"You want one?" she asked.

"It's Sunday morning," said Lester.

"Look," she pointed in the direction of the cash register inside the store, "That's nothing but a kid in there. I know I can get a couple of beers from that dude."

"Oh, that's right, I'm now living in Ardorland."

Ardor smiled. "I have my ways."

"Okay, do your magic and get me a tallboy."

"Any flavor?"

"I prefer cold."

Lester sat in the truck with the engine running as he waited for Ardor to return with the beers. The convenience store sat alone in a field. He was hesitant to look around, fearful he would see another white dog, certain he didn't want to add more evidence to that weirdness. He looked at Ardor as she talked to the young clerk with one hand on the counter while she pointed with the other one to the beer coolers on the back wall. The guy had the silliest grin on his face. Lester knew Ardor would be coming out with those beers. After a few moments, Lester could no longer fight the urge to scan the field on both sides of the store. He felt a relief when he didn't see any white dogs.

"Thank god," he whispered to himself.

Ardor walked out with two cans of beer in brown paper bags. She climbed in the truck and shut her door. She held up the beers.

"Magic," she said.

"You're a witch."

"I'm a good witch, like Glinda."

"All witches say that."

"They do?"

"All the ones I know."

"I gave him my number."

"You did?"

"Well, not *my* number. Somebody's number."

"You're definitely not a good witch. I'd be careful about a house falling on your head."

"I flirted with him; he gave me two beers."

"You didn't pay for them?"

"He said they were his treat."

"I like treats."

"I did see something really strange in there."

"What?"

"There was a dog in there."

"A dog ain't strange."

"This one was. He looked like a golden retriever, but he wasn't golden. He was white as snow."

"Okay, a white dog."

"That's not the strange part."

Lester opened his beer. He took a swallow, shook his head. "A white dog. A white golden retriever. So did he dance on his hind legs?"

"Did the Tango, brother. No, what he did do was walk up to the door when I came in. He seemed to be looking out at everything that was out there, like he was looking for something specific. But then he seemed to see you in the truck and just locked a stare, stiff as a board. Freaky. Isn't that how dogs react to vampires?"

"Look, you have nothing to worry about. It's daylight." He raised both hands, palms up. "Besides, you ain't no virgin, I don't want your blood."

Ardor popped the top off her beer and took a swallow. "That's a relief," she said.

He tapped the edge of the can to Ardor's can. "I suppose you haven't had to worry about vampires since you were thirteen-years-old."

"I know what I'm doing," she said as Lester drank a couple of swallows.

"That dog does seem odd though," said Lester.

"Right, that was freaky, man."

As they began the drive back into town, to the Five Points area of Huntsville, Lester decided to take a left turn where he should have turned right. They listened to music off Lester's phone, The Dead South's "That Bastard Son," when Lester rolled down his window.

"The Lord's day," Lester said and let out a deep burp.

"So, you worrying on this Lord's day had nothing to do with me moving in with you and your kids for a few weeks?"

"Our hearts are a pitter-patter with the thought of you moving into our family extravaganza."

"Are you high?" asked Ardor.

"I beg your pardon."

"Well, I just want to be honest here, but I got a little high this morning in the greenhouse. I brought some with me, if that's okay? I don't want to cause any problems here."

"You're good."

"You want a hit off a joint?"

"I'm fine. Thanks for the offer."

"Where you from, Lester? I don't think you ever told me. Are you a Southerner?"

"Yes, ma'am, southern Alabama. How about you?"

"Dothan," said Ardor.

"Get the fuck out of here. That's my hometown. What are your roots?"

"Now I remember, I think we've talked about this before, when Wade and I lived down the street. I think it was a Friday night; we came down to your and Connie's house for a beer. You told us you were from Dothan."

"Yeah? Huh. Don't remember that. Not surprising though; my life's been a bit hairy the last few years, so my memory is a shambles. I remember you and Wade living down the street, and I remember how you embarrassed yourself a few times in your obvious lust for me. That sticks with me."

"I lusted for you?"

"Yeah, yeah, Connie had to put a collar on you. You acted the fool; textbook lust."

"Acting the fool about you?"

"You were wanting in my britches mighty bad. It's okay, really; everyone knew you couldn't help yourself."

"Whatever you tell yourself. Anyway, my momma and daddy grew up down there. Still have some relatives in the area. I was four when we moved up to Huntsville. My daddy and my grandfather had a falling out. Actually, they just kept fallin'."

"I think I do remember now. I had forgotten you're from down there," said Lester. He looked over at Ardor. "You're probably wondering where we're headin'."

"I thought you still lived in Five Points," said Ardor.

"Look, I just wanted to get to the ass end of this shitstorm I seem to be grabbing by the horns and dragging into my house. You know what I mean?"

"Sure. Sure. You should dig up all the bones. What do you want to know? What can I do to dampen your anxiety?"

"Let's pull in here." Lester softly braked and then drove the truck into a closed gas station. He parked under the canopy of a large tree growing next to the parking area on the left side of the station.

"Black oak," said Ardor.

"The tree?"

"Yeah, my momma is a tree freak."

"Black Oak Arkansas," said Lester.

"'Jim Dandy to the Rescue'?"

"Uh huh, that's them. '70s band. You know your Southern rock. Here's the deal, Lucille. The more I think about it the more I'm convinced that I'm making a huge mistake for allowing your shitstorm into my family's life."

"Honestly, they might can track me down to Huntsville. Wade and I did tell them we were from here. But there's really very little chance for them to trace me to you."

"Very little? I got a feeling your 'very little' is different from my 'very little.'"

"What else can I tell you? They'd have to talk to somebody who has seen me. I've been a recluse, so I don't think that's gonna happen. Or they'd have to actually see me around town. It'll be like in witness protection, no one knows where I am, and I will make no contact with friends or family. Lock down, brother. Not one-hundred percent safe, but it's close."

"I should not help you. Really, I shouldn't. I got kids. You know? But I keep thinking I need to help you. Why? I don't know. I like you. Maybe it's your sexuality, which just drips off you. I'm a man; I'm not immune to your witch's brew of sexuality."

Ardor laughed.

"No, no, I'm not kidding. You reek of sensuality. Some women are cute, are beautiful, but there are others who have that look like they've been dipped in sex. Have them roll out of bed, slide on a T-shirt and jeans, and they still look sexy."

"And you think that's me. That I'm mega sexy?"

"It's true."

Ardor looked out the windshield, took a sip of beer, looked over at Lester, smiled and then laughed. "Obviously, I don't feel that way. I'm not trying to manipulate you with some sort of sexy vibe."

"Maybe, maybe not. I do know better than this, really, I do. So please, please, please, Ms. Ardor Hardwick, please let this not be a mistake."

"I don't think you're making a mistake," said Ardor. She turned up her can of beer, drained the rest, and let out a growl of a burp. "How's that for my sexual allure? I bet you got a hard-on now."

Lester laughed. He swigged some of his beer, looked at Ardor. "Boner City, don't you know it. Look, I still think there's a chance of bad things happening. I don't want to be a downer, but a slight chance of danger is still a chance of danger. Me, by myself, I'd help you in a heartbeat. But with my kids, I don't know. Just why am I doing this?"

"You're helping a friend in need."

"That's true, that's very true. But helping a friend has its limits."

"Maybe it's for the money, too. Most people need more money, especially a dad with three kids."

"Yeah, that's what I'm afraid of. I'm doing this for a few dollars more."

"Well, maybe you *are* feeling a little tug of lust."

"Damn my lust."

"We did kiss that time."

"We were drunk," Lester said. "We never kissed again, though we did have opportunities. We're adults."

"You know you've always had a thing for me."

Lester's eyes widened. "Now you're cocky."

"I've felt some things. A girl knows, right?"

"Guys aren't very good with concealing our attraction."

"It's not complex. I figured that out in junior high."

"We're pitiful. But it's more than that with you. Lots of guys have this thing for you."

"I know, I know, some guys even get obsessive. That gets old quick. It's very strange."

"I remember a friend of Wade's just couldn't get enough of you."

"I did not encourage that."

"To your credit, you didn't seem to play with him too much; you seemed to keep him at arm's length."

"That's boring to talk about. I just want you to know I wouldn't put your kids in danger."

Lester grabbed Ardor by the shoulders, locked eyes, and let out a big sigh.

"Are you really that worried?" she asked.

"I look forward to you living with us. And I also feel lots of fear. That can't be a good thing."

"Believe me when I say I'll do everything I can to make sure this works, that nothing will happen to your family."

"I know that, and I guess that's the main reason I'm doing this."

"Lester, you're helping a friend, making a little money, getting off by being close to me, and you know I will be extremely careful."

"Getting off?"

"Well—"

"Oh, I get it; like you get off by being close to me?"

"Whatever," said Ardor.

"Whatever," said Lester.

A MEAN BUNCH

When the truck rolled up the driveway the back door of the house opened and out poured Jase, Chuck, Lizzy, and Austen. The kids ran through the gate to greet their father and Ardor.

Lester turned to Ardor, "So, here we go. You know my kids. The old man there, that's Austen, my uncle; you'll be sleeping on the couch with him."

"I love old men," said Ardor.

"Good for Austen."

Ardor jumped out of the truck and hugged each child.

"Ardor, you're gonna live with us!" said Lizzy.

"Yes, I want to thank all three of you for allowing me to stay in your home for a few weeks. You are very kind."

She shook Austen's hand. "You must be Austen; I'm Ardor. Lester told me you're his uncle and not to be trusted."

"Good to meet you, Ardor. His life is nothing more than a tapestry of imagined worlds. But, as I'm sure you know, his fantasies are mostly harmless."

"Uncle Austen used to watch Babe Ruth play baseball. Even remembers when the Titanic went down. Don't you, Uncle Austen?" Lester winked at Austen.

"I do not run from my years. One should have pride in the wisdom gleaned from experience."

"He can teach you how to send a telegraph message. Isn't that right, Austen? He used to be a rider for the Pony Express."

"Lester did tell me that you are a beautiful woman, however, which is obviously true."

"You better be careful, Austen; she'll put a spell on you," said Lester. "She's a witch."

"You're a witch?" asked Lizzy.

"Your dad is just trying to be funny," said Ardor.

"He tries to be funny to hide his fear of women," said Austen.

"I do not fear women."

"Those are foolish words," said Ardor.

"So, you'll be staying here with Lester and his kids. Such a wonderful family, good people, the kids especially. Lester's just their keeper; most people learn to not pay much attention to him. To be honest, there's darkness in that man. I feel it in my bones."

"You can just feel the bleakness radiating off of him." Ardor raised her hands to within inches of Lester as if she was warming her hands by a fire.

"And another female in the house has to be a good thing, right Lizzy?" said Austen.

"Girls rule," said Lizzy.

"There you have it. Too much testosterone hanging in the air over here," said Austen.

"The boys and I are true believers in equality. We're part of the solution, not the problem. Right fellas?" said Lester.

"I love girls," said Chuck.

"Don't you start," said Jase.

"Am I missing something?" asked Ardor.

"You know, from the other night. Chuck likes to draw girls," said Lester.

"Oh sure, Chuck likes to draw girls who are—"

"No, nope, not now," said Lester.

"One must respect the female soul," said Austen.

"Have you heard of the great Cherokee Chief Ostenaco? Austen fantasizes he was named after him. That's just a ploy to put you at ease so he can con you outta money. He's a con man extraordinaire. His real name is probably John Smith," said Lester.

Ardor stared at Lester for a moment and then turned her attention to Austen. "What's the truth, Austen? Are you Cherokee or just trying to score with the chicks? Of course, I don't believe anything Lester says."

"Let's ask the little ones. Am I a Cherokee or just an old man who says he's a Cherokee?"

The three children smiled at Austen.

Jase stood closest to Austen and spoke first. "Austen is Cherokee. Not my opinion. I know that for a fact. I've seen pictures of his family. Some are old Cherokee people living on a reservation."

"Austen is Cherokee," said Lizzy as she gave Austen a big smile. "He makes Indian sausage."

"Dad just likes to pretend; he's pulling on Austen's chain," said Chuck. "We all know Austen is Cherokee. And he's a warrior."

"Then that's settled," said Ardor.

"Yeah, well, Austen has them fooled. Kids love fairytales," said Lester.

"It's not a fairytale, Dad," said Lizzy.

"What are we having for dinner?" asked Jase.

"Grilling some burgers," said Lester.

"Yes," said Chuck as he gave a fist pump.

"You want to eat with us, Austen?" asked Lester.

"I would like that. I will bring over some sausage."

"Austen makes sausage from venison," said Lester.

"That's deer meat," said Jase.

"Austen says he uses an old Cherokee recipe," said Lester. "However, I don't think Native Americans made sausage."

"You are right. We didn't make sausage at first. We dried meat and added types of seasoning. Sort of like jerky, a perfect food for those times, full of protein and fat. We called it pemmican. The meat used was from whatever lived around them, such as buffalo and deer, also elk and moose up north. The recipes for sausage arrived with our invaders. My recipe is derived from Europeans, I'm sure."

"What do you say to that, Mr. White Man?" asked Ardor.

"I love playing the fool with Austen. He puts me in my place every single time. He makes me a better person. And showing me the pleasures of a sweat lodge makes him a king in my world. Why don't you kids go in and clean up the kitchen."

Lizzy quickly ran into the house with Chuck right behind her. Jase turned back to Lester as he stopped on the back steps.

"I'll make sure they do a good job," said Jase.

"Okay, just don't be too harsh. No fighting."

Jase hollered over his shoulder, "No fighting," as he walked into the house.

"Hey, Mr. Wonderful Friend, when you go over to get your sausage why don't you bring over your peace pipe—" Lester said to Austen who returned the nod as Lester's cell phone rang from his truck. Lester walked over and grabbed his phone off of the front seat on the fourth ring.

"Hello. Hi, Kathy. Oh, really, ok ... right ... I see. Yes. Yes. I agree. No, don't do that, let her talk, doesn't matter to whom. Hallucinations are normal." Lester sat down in the truck. "What's the tone of the conversation? Talking to an old friend is very common. Let her go there. If you try to convince her that the friend is not there, then you risk making her angry and confrontational. No need for that. Talk to her as she talks to you ... Music is fine ... Sure, Elvis works. She loves Elvis, right? Then Elvis is fine, helps comfort her, and that's what we should strive to do. Give her peace and comfort; tell her you love her and that you're there for her ... Yeah, that's fine, too. Sleeping all the time is just part of the process at this stage ... Well, from what you've told me, I'd say fairly soon. Contacting friends and family would be appropriate. Keep them apprised of the situation. Sure, I can come over. I'll try to come by within the hour ... I'll let you know when I'm on my way."

While speaking on the phone, Lester had watched Ardor enter the backyard and begin playing with Georgia. When he ended the call, he stepped out of the truck and walked over to Austen who was leaning against the fence watching Ardor toss a tennis ball to Georgia.

"She has a good arm," said Austen.

"You ever play ball, Ardor?" asked Lester.

"A couple years of softball during middle school."

"You gave it up for boys?" asked Lester.

"I gave it up because I got tired of it. And for boys. And I got tired of the coaches. And I started playing tennis. And I was freshman class president. And I had a little issue that year with marijuana, suspended a couple of days for having half a joint on me," Ardor said as she waited for Georgia to trot back with the ball.

"At least you weren't selling it," said Lester.

"That was eleventh grade. Man, I had fun that year."

"Ardor and her boyfriend worked on a marijuana farm out in Oregon," said Lester.

Austen nodded.

"Was that a good experience?" Austen asked.

"Mostly good, until the end when things turned rather ugly."

"Lots of jobs turn ugly," Lester said.

"They tend to turn ugly when you are grossly underpaid," said Ardor.

Lester laughed. "Right. Hey, Austen, I need to visit a patient right now who, from what I was told, seems to be dying. Can you stay here with the kids and Ardor while I'm gone? I think that would be fair to Ardor, let her ease into the situation."

Ardor walked over to the two men leaning on the fence.

"Of course, I can stay with them," said Austen.

"I shouldn't be that long."

"Wow, going to help someone who's dying. How you hanging with that? Doesn't sound easy to me," said Ardor.

"I've got mixed feelings. I will say my understanding of living is changing."

"For the better?" asked Ardor.

"Of course. Lots of people are terrified of death."

"I'd guess most," said Ardor.

"But that's a waste of energy. Dying is part of living, you know."

"All journeys come to an end," said Austen.

"It's the unknown, that's what scares most. 'Is this it, lights out and you're done?' Not processing it until the very end doesn't help matters," said Lester.

"One isn't losing control; dying is having control. You decide to just let go. Nothing to fear," said Austen.

"Can't be that hard; everybody does it. No matter the road, we're all going to end up at the same place. Pretty simple to me," said Ardor.

"Ain't that the truth," said Lester.

Kathy Renfro led Lester to her mother's bedroom. The room was dark, drapes pulled, lights out but for a low lamp on the bedside table.

"She drifted off about twenty minutes ago. I thought she was sleeping, but I tried to wake her when I heard your knock and couldn't. Is she in a coma?"

"Not sure. Let's see here." Lester gently grabbed the woman's wrist and then called her name. "Lucy. Lucy. It's Lester. Can you hear me?"

There was no response, no movement. He turned to look at a small CD player playing on the dresser.

"The King," he said.

"She's told me a million times that she wants Elvis songs playing at the end."

"Nothing wrong with the boy from Tupelo." Lester turned back and gently shook the elderly woman's shoulder. "Lucy. Lucy." Still nothing.

"Is there something wrong?" Kathy asked Lester.

"I don't think there's anything wrong."

"Is she dying?"

Lester pressed the fingertips of his right hand to the side of the woman's thin neck.

"Her pulse is weak."

"She's dying, isn't she?"

"I'm not sure." He pressed his hand to her forehead. "She's a little cool to the touch."

He pulled back the blanket and sheet to check her knees and feet.

"See how her coloring is slightly purplish, a little pale. Has she been eating and drinking?"

"She's barely had a bite the past couple of days."

"Any liquids?"

"A few swallows of water, sucked on a few ice cubes, a little cranberry juice yesterday."

Lester stood up and looked Kathy right in the eye. She stood on the other side of the bed with a face of alarm.

"Kathy, I'm going to be honest. Okay?"

"By all means."

"The signs I'm seeing here, the weak pulse, a drop in temperature, the purplish color of her hands, knees, feet, the loss of appetite and thirst, and, of course, what seems to be a coma, these all point to imminent death."

Kathy simultaneously sucked in a breath and closed her eyes. "I was afraid of that."

"I'm sorry," said Lester.

Kathy opened her eyes. "I thought I was ready for this. But, obviously, I'm not."

"I understand. Everyone processes death in their own way. No right or wrong here. Are you okay?" asked Lester.

"I just need to focus on her. Help her in any way I can."

"That's exactly right," Lester said.

"How long will she live?"

"That's hard to say. Maybe a day, two days, could be a week or two. The body shuts down on its own."

"When will we know that she is truly dying? What will be the signs?"

"Do you want the graphic details?"

"Yes. I need to know this."

"There's usually irregular breathing, quick breaths followed by a pause. There can be what people call the death rattle, which is when the secretions pool in the mouth and throat due to a loss of the swallowing reflex. We can vacuum that out if need be. At the very end there can be a fever, which is usually from dehydration. Mottled skin will increase. The marbling becomes more apparent. The heart weakens and is no longer able to pump blood effectively."

"Will she be in pain?"

"Has she been in any pain the past few days?"

"No."

"Then no, she shouldn't be in any pain. If she shows signs of physical pain then we can medicate the symptoms. Morphine, OxyContin, and Dilaudid all do well for pain. Morphine is actually the best, but sometimes it's hard to get. For dying patients, there shouldn't be a problem in getting it, but they've overreacted to the addiction issue."

"A friend told me that morphine can kill a patient at the end, that you shouldn't give it to someone near death."

"That's not true. Morphine provides comfort to the dying. It doesn't kill them unless you give them an overdose. In fact, it relieves the stress of the body fighting to live, which helps people to live a little longer, at least a few more hours."

"You recommend giving morphine to my mom?"

"Absolutely. What happens at the end is that the control center for breathing begins to fail. The breathing muscles become weak, just like the other muscles in the body, so muscles other than the breathing muscles begin to help out. The body is shutting down but also trying to live. A dying body. There can be irregular breaths, pauses, faster and shallower breaths. Your body doesn't just flip a switch, even during the process of dying it is still trying to live. The morphine provides comfort. Some people use it, some don't. The ones who use morphine typically are much more at peace."

"This coma, is this it? Her death coma?"

"Probably. I do have one question for you. I should have asked you before now, but do you want to be present during her death?"

Kathy looked at her mother without speaking.

"That's your decision. Don't feel an obligation. Were you ever able to discuss what she wanted? Did she *want* you to be with her? For many, dying is a private affair. You always hear about people dying surrounded by family. Some yes, some no."

"She was very upfront with me. She wants me to be here but wants me to take long breaks so she can come to terms with letting go. I thought that was crazy, but I guess she knows how she wants to let go. Maybe I'm the crazy one."

"No, not at all. You learn by experience, and most people don't want that experience. Don't want to even think about it. I think you're lucky that she was able to talk to you about her death. I've heard of many people waiting to pass, not being able to let go until family members have left the room. And something else. There's lots of evidence that points to her being able to hear you right now, so please talk to her. Let her know you love her, that you'll be fine. I'd also recommend informing close family and friends that she has reached this stage. Just give them the information, and let them decide if they want to see her during these last moments. Again, they must come to their own understanding."

"I guess since the music is her idea I should keep it playing?"

"Of course, but give Elvis a rest every now and then. Even Elvis gets old nonstop."

Lucy suddenly opened her eyes, looked at her daughter, and then turned to stare at Lester. "He doesn't know? Why doesn't he know? He has to know. He's always known," she said, not really a scream, more of a shout, a passionate shout.

"What?" asked Kathy.

Lucy turned back to Kathy. "Does he know I'm in love with him?"

"Who are you in love with?" asked Kathy.

"Are you telling me you don't know either?" asked Lucy. She then closed her eyes.

Lester and Kathy looked at one another and then back to Lucy.

"Well, she seems to have something on her mind. Know what she's talking about?"

"Not really," said Kathy.

"This is common; you see it in patients at the end. Sometimes the patient will just blurt out little snippets of thoughts. Perfectly natural."

"So, I should just sit here with her, talk to her?"

"Right."

"Like you suggested, maybe take a break every now and then?"

"I think that's a good plan."

They both stood in silence looking at Lucy. Her eyebrows dramatically shot up and down for nearly a minute.

"Wow," said her daughter.

"She's working through something," said Lester with a grin.

"Bless her heart," Kathy said.

"Bless her heart, indeed," Lester agreed.

"Thanks for your help, Lester, especially coming out here on a Sunday on such a short notice. I can't imagine not having your help. You've been a blessing, for me and Mom."

"When my wife died, I felt the same way about the hospice nurse who helped us. She was so good, so compassionate during such a tumultuous time that I changed my career to hospice care."

"I remember you saying that."

"What I didn't know at the time and what I've come to realize since I've been working with hospice is that the relationship between the hospice nurse and the patient, especially the patient's family, is reciprocal. Human beings, we're so interesting, very caring and also so screwed up." Lester laughed.

Kathy began to weep, tears streaming down her face. "I'm going to miss her so much."

"I can tell you this. This is something I have realized and truly believe. I think about my wife and mother every single day. Your mother is leaving, but she'll always be here. My wife and my mom are always with me. I talk to both of them all the time. Right here," said Lester as he patted his chest.

"She's been a wonderful mother. I couldn't ask for a better one."

"That's what you need to tell her."

Kathy nodded.

"I need to go to the bathroom. I'll go out to my car for a few minutes. Just come get me when you're ready for me to come back in."

When Lester made it out to the driveway and leaned against his car, he checked his phone. There was a voicemail from Ardor:

Just wanted to tell you again how much I appreciate you letting me stay here. Thank you, thank you, thank you. You're a lifesaver, literally. Oh, and can you pick up some beer and vodka on the way home? I've got some friends coming over for a little party. Ha! Thanks; you're the best.

SOMETHING AIN'T RIGHT

MONDAY AND most of Tuesday involved a tug-of-war for Lester. He enjoyed Ardor's presence. She was a natural with children, having grown up with lots of cousins on her mother's side, including one who had nine siblings. She explained she was closest to the cousins whose fathers were "hell raisers." One uncle had eight kids with three different mothers and another one had four kids with four mothers.

"People think I was a wild child back in my late teens, but Uncle Dean and Uncle Alfred lived like pirates. When I graduated high school, I decided to distance myself from those worlds, hit the brakes, tossed an anchor over the side. Most of the girls were getting pregnant and the boys were in and out of trouble on a daily basis."

"You mean when I met you your wild days were behind you?" They sat on the couch in the den that first Monday evening, drinking a beer after the kids had been tucked in.

"I was living full throttle, not givin' a damn about what I did, who I hurt, who I lied to. I did some things I probably shouldn't have done."

"Like what?"

"You want the dirt, don't you?"

"Don't tell me anything you don't want me to know."

"You can be sure of that. Well, without naming names I did get to know a mayor rather intimately. Not saying it was the mayor of Huntsville."

"Get the fuck out of here."

"And his wife."

"Get the fuck out of here."

"And her best friend."

"Where was I? I met you too late."

"Not saying it wasn't fun." Ardor sipped her beer. "The wife's friend ..." Ardor stared blankly over Lester's head. "She was a very interesting person. I need to look her up one day."

"Now you're a retired pot trimmer who's kicking back with a family. Everybody calms down eventually, huh?"

"Turned over a new leaf."

"Ha. On the lam with a duffel bag full of money. Waiting to meet up with your boyfriend so you can enjoy the spoils of your endeavors."

"I know I keep saying this, but I really do appreciate you letting me stay here with you and your kids. From my heart, thank you." Ardor leaned over and planted a kiss on Lester's cheek. A smile formed on Lester's face as Ardor sat back on the couch.

"You are more than welcome. All of us love you living here. It's a shame you have a boyfriend."

"Isn't it, though?" she said with a grin.

Ardor liked having fun with the kids, playing Monopoly, Hearts, Yahtzee, teasing the boys about girls, laughter ringing throughout the house. She helped with breakfasts and dinners, the kids' homework, even reading to Lizzy at bedtime. And Lester had not been this happy for at least a couple of years. But late Tuesday night produced the truth, at least *a* truth. Lester decided that Ardor could not stay. While lying in bed he knew his decision was rock solid, beyond reproach.

He fretted all day Monday and Tuesday that Ardor's visit was a tragic mistake, at the very least a foolish endeavor to offer help to a friend in a dangerous situation. Ardor and her boyfriend had skimmed thousands of dollars from marijuana growers in Oregon, and these people wanted their money back. He felt for their situation, but it was self-inflicted, even if they were not being fairly compensated. You don't want to do this job for that amount of money, then go find a job that is better to your liking. They should have stayed until they found fairer jobs, he reasoned. He understood "fight the power," empathized with "fuck The Man," but most choices involved risks, and their risk was now his and his kids' risk.

The money provided a big incentive, had been the deciding factor in Lester's mind, of course, but the risk was too great. Men were probably hunting Ardor, and now Ardor was living in his home with his kids. In his mind, he repeated the mantra that his kids' safety trumped the money and his helping hand to Ardor. He would inform her tomorrow that she had to go. He would try to help her in any other way; she just had to find another location to hide. Living in his home could not continue. He regretted leading her on like this. She was happy, they were happy; these few days had created a sense of safety and security for Ardor, which she pointed out every day. But his family was the most important part of his life. Before he fell asleep that night, he made up his mind.

When he awoke Wednesday morning there was suddenly a sense of deep relief, the apprehension seemingly evaporated during the night. The decision was clear; family first was an easy call. Silly to think otherwise. What was he thinking? Yet this would also calm an anxiety that wormed its way into his daily thoughts. The chemistry between

Ardor and the kids seemed magical, as if the perfect au pair had suddenly dropped from the sky to help this family, his family minus a wife and mother. The sudden pleasure he derived from her presence surprised him, not that he didn't hope for her living there to be an enjoyable experience for him and the kids. Why wouldn't a smart young woman who helped with the kids and the household chores fill a void? Of course. But he thought himself an idiot for not foreseeing the obvious. She seemed to have as much fun with them, the kids and Lester, as they did with her. A deeper apprehension had now bloomed. Despair. His three children, and himself he admitted, would become deeply attached to Ardor; thus, her eventual departure would be another loss. All of that worry had now evaporated like steam off hot pavement. The decision to tell Ardor she had to leave had been emotionally difficult for Lester, even weighted with the knowledge that her departure would protect his family. Now he understood the decision provided more benefits. While looking at the sunrise from a den window, he drank his first cup of coffee with a pensive smile stretched across his face. He would tell her that evening after the kids went to bed. He would wait a few days before telling the kids so that she had time to look around for another place to hide.

But this smug disposition ended on Wednesday afternoon. While driving to his last call of the day he received a text from Ardor:

Lester, I walked to the store this morning and saw two guys sitting in a car staring at me. They didn't follow me home. I don't think. We'll talk about it when you get home.

Lester pulled off the road and reread the text. "Son of a bitch," he said to his phone as he read the text a third time.

Lester drove to his last call, an orientation call for a forty-five-year-old woman with Stage IV colon cancer. He explained hospice care to the patient, her son, and daughter-in-law. The initial call was one of Lester's most enjoyable parts of hospice care. His faith in the benefits of helping others during a time of death made the discussion effortless. He methodically explained the different phases, the different possibilities, and answered all of their questions. The patient and family members' intense focus and gratitude created the reciprocal altruism that motivated Lester and many other hospice nurses. The visit also momentarily pulled Lester from the horror of Ardor's text. By the time Lester was driving home, his initial fear had returned and now had added the terror of paranoia. He resolved to hear the details before surrendering to panic.

He walked into the home bugged-eyed and nearly hyperventilating. Ardor sat at the dining room table with Lizzy, a textbook opened and a worksheet in front of his daughter.

"Hey," said Ardor.

"Hey," said Lester. "Whatcha workin' on?"

"Lizzy has finished her homework, so we were just discussing some female issues."

"Female issues?" asked Lester.

"Dad, it's just girl talk and you're not a girl."

"This is true, I am not female. I fully acknowledge that. I hang my head in shame."

"Dad, don't be ashamed."

"Thanks, Lizzy. Can I borrow Ardor for a few minutes? She needs to tell me about her walk to the store today."

"Sure. Can I watch some TV?"

"For just an hour. Why don't you use the TV in my bedroom."

"Okay," said Lizzy and then quickly stood up from the dining room table and trotted into the bedroom.

"Grab a couple of beers, Lester. I'll meet you in the backyard."

"Yes, ma'am."

When Lester walked up to the picnic table with two opened beers, Ardor was throwing the rubber ball for Georgia.

"Okay, I'm ready for the details of the armed and angry men who are closing in on you. And us, I might add," said Lester as he placed the beers on the table.

Ardor grabbed a beer and sat down across from Lester who was now sitting while looking out across his backyard.

"I walked down to the store—"

"And why did you do that? I thought we agreed you wouldn't do that," said Lester, already exasperated.

"I needed some tampons, Mr. Stay-At-The-House," said Ardor and took a long swig off her beer.

Lester dropped his head. Rubbed his temples and then shook his head. He took a long swallow of beer.

"Okay. I see that." He bobbed his head a few times. "Why didn't you say something last night? We could have gone to the store last night."

"Lester, please. I needed tampons, all right?"

Lester looked at Ardor and nervously dragged his tongue across his upper lip. "Soooo, you walked to the store. I'm assuming Papa Jack's?"

"Yes."

Lester bumped his fists together. "Okay. Okay. Help me out here. As you walked into the parking lot, you saw two men sitting in a car staring at you?"

"I think this will work better if I, the one who experienced it, explains what I saw and not you evaluating what you think might have happened. You are not a lawyer, and I'm not on the witness stand."

"Sure. Right. Talk away. Paint your canvas, my dear."

Ardor shook her head. "Just hold on. Let's be patient here."

"Be patient? For all I know they're looking at us right now. Maybe they have a rifle aimed at my skull as I speak."

"I believe the rifle would be aimed at my skull," Ardor said as she reached down for the ball that had been dropped next to her on the bench seat.

"I'm sorry. I'm sorry. Just very concerned. This is just exactly what I was afraid of."

"I know."

"This could go very, very bad, very, very quickly."

Ardor threw the ball to the back of the house. "As I was saying, I walked to the store, not thinking anything about it. Keeping a low profile, wearing my hoodie." Ardor pulled her black hoodie over her head to demonstrate. "See? Being discreet. However, when I was about to enter the store, I noticed a car— "

"What type of car?"

"What?"

"What color was it?"

"Color?"

"Did you see the tag?"

"Fuck, Lester. Really?"

"I know. I'll shut up."

"Okay," Ardor pulled the hoodie off of her head, "as I pulled the door open, I turned and saw a car pull into the parking lot with these two dudes. How old? I don't know, maybe late thirties/early forties. Not young guys. They parked in the front, a few spaces from the door. I tried not to be obvious as I stared at them, but that was nearly impossible since they both gave me the stink eye. I went ahead into the store and searched for the tampons. I found them but kept walking around looking at things on the shelves so I could take peeks at these men in the car."

"What did you see?"

"They were looking at me."

"Fuck me," said Lester.

"Anyway, I walked around the store for a few minutes to see if they would come in. They didn't. But every time I looked at their car, I noticed they seemed to be looking right at me. I'll be honest, I felt some fear. I was shaking a little. Know what I mean?"

"Yes, I do, I do know what you mean."

"I'm thinking, is this it? Is the gig up? Are they gonna grab me, drive me out to the country, and torture me until I cough up the money?"

"Maybe," said Lester.

"Thank you; thank you for soothing my fear. That really puts my mind at ease. Glad to have you in my corner."

"Too honest?" Lester asked.

"Whatev, I know you're freaking out because of your kids. So, anyway," Ardor took a swallow of beer, "I'm thinking just what the fuck am I gonna do? Then something very good happened."

"They came in and gave you a hug."

"Yes, that's right. Said they were happy to see me, took me out to lunch. Great couple of guys. Said they came down here to tell me that all was forgiven and good luck."

"See, you were worried about nothing. A worrywart."

"I wish. Nope, a cop car pulled up next to them. Serendipity, my friend."

"Then what happened?"

"I made my purchase—"

"Of your tampons."

"Yes, of my tampons. I then walked out the door and greeted the cop who was just stepping out of his driver-side door. I said that those two men in that car had been following me. They seemed to be stalking me. I pointed right at those motherfuckers. The cop's partner stepped out of the patrol car and looked right at those two dudes. He then turned to me and said, 'Do we have a problem here?'"

"What did the two dudes do at this point?

"The dude driving cranked their car, pulled out of the parking space, and then drove away without looking at us one time. The cop I was talking to said, 'We need to talk to these fellas.' And oh, I did notice their tag. Oregon."

"Fuuuuuuuuuuck," said Lester with his hands covering his face.

"And the car was an Infinity SUV, one of those big tank-looking things."

"And the color?"

"An off-white, like a bone white, pearl white."

"And the dudes, anything stand out?"

"One seemed to be thin and the other rather stout, but they were in a car, man. I don't know. The thin one had a goatee. And he had a golf shirt on. I think, red, and the other one had on a green Oxford long-sleeve with the sleeves rolled up."

Lester lowered his head until his forehead rested on the table.

Ardor drank a few more swallows of beer. "The cops didn't go after them, of course. They couldn't do anything for them just staring at me. Told me they'd keep an eye out for them. And told me to contact the police if I had any more problems with them."

"This is not good, not close to good. Good has left the building," said Lester with his head still on the table.

"Here comes Austen," said Ardor.

"What?" Lester raised his head and turned to look at the gate in front of the driveway where Georgia stood with her tail wagging.

"May I join you or are you having a private conversation?"

"Yes, please join us," said Lester as he waved Austen into the backyard. He turned to Ardor and said, "I'd like Austen to hear all this, so he can give us his opinion. You don't mind, do you?"

"By all means. Austen is the wisest person here. No offense," said Ardor.

"None taken. Can I get you a beer?" asked Lester as Austen walked up to the table.

"Maybe later," said Austen as he sat down next to Ardor. "Or perhaps sooner if I consider the looks on your faces."

"He could sit here," Lester pointed to the bench next to himself, "or he could sit there," he pointed to where Austen sat, "and he decided to sit there. Isn't that strange?"

Ardor took a swallow of beer. She shook her head. "I'm a young woman; nothing strange about that."

"You seem to take pleasure in confrontation," Austen said.

"There is consternation, but its cause is not my doing," said Lester.

"I need to call Wade," said Ardor.

"Yes, very good idea. See if he's seen anything. You're in this together. Or we're all in this together."

"Okay. While I call Wade, you can bring Austen up to speed on those dudes. Have you even told Austen why I'm here?"

"Nope, but now is the time. One of my best friends and a next-door neighbor means he's in the inner circle, I'm afraid," Lester said and pointed at Austen, "We need your opinion here, and you need to know for your own sake."

"Good, yes, god yes. I really want your opinion on all this, Austen."

"Giving my opinion is certainly a task I enjoy."

Ardor pulled out her phone from her front pocket. "Here goes nothing," she said as she stepped away from the picnic table and walked to the two plum trees.

"Okay, my friend, time for me to tell you stuff you'd probably not want to hear. But you need to hear it."

"Let me guess. You two are having an affair but the boyfriend doesn't know about it."

Lester squinted as he looked Austen dead in the eyes. He turned to look at Ardor before turning back to Austen. "You caught us. And she's pregnant, already knocked her up. Couldn't help myself." He turned to look at Ardor one more time. "Sad to say, but the details are much more ridiculous than that. Much more. Lots more."

Ardor reached up to a branch and pulled off a couple of leaves. She rolled the leaves into a small ball and looked over to where Lester and Austen sat as she listened to the phone ring.

The phone clicked and Wade answered, "Ardor?"

"Wade, I need to talk to you," said Ardor as she sat on the ground under one of the plum trees and threw the ball of leaves to the ground.

"I'm glad you called. I need to talk to you, too. Is everything okay?"

"Yes. Everything is fine. No, that's a damn lie. Something happened today."

"Listen, first let me say something. I've got some news also, health issues. Bad shit, baby."

"Bad shit?"

"Yeah, dark bad. A few weeks ago I started smelling these strange odors, weird stuff. Thought I was going crazy at first."

"What strange odors?"

"It smelled like something rotten, like maybe rotten fish or maybe even rotten meat. Horrible smells, and no one else could smell what I was smelling. It would last about fifteen-twenty minutes, then suddenly go away. I saw a doctor who ran an MRI on me. That's when they found the tumor."

"Tumor? What are you talking about?"

"I've got cancer. And it's a rare form of cancer. I'm special."

"What the fuck?"

"It's called Neuroblastoma, and it originates in the olfactory nerve, which is why I smelled these odors that were not really there. They're called phantom smells. And as a bonus, it's a malignant form of cancer. The MRI revealed that it's spread into my sinuses and brain."

"You've got to be kidding me."

"Not fucking kidding. Right now they are deciding if it's possible to surgically remove it or use radiation or maybe chemotherapy."

"Are you gonna fucking die?"

"Maybe. Probably. Hopefully not. It don't look good, baby. You need to come up here. For one, you need to grab this money in case I die."

"I am living one hell of a bad day. I thought my news was bad. And it is, it's a nightmare come true, but it ain't cancer bad. I don't know what to say. I'm numb right now."

"What's your news? How bad is it?"

"Yeah, well ... it's like we're running in the Bad News Race and you beat me in a photo-finish. I'm sorry if I sound a little stunned, but I'm a little stunned."

"What is it? What's happened?"

"I don't know if I can talk after listening to you. My head's spinning right now. Okay, a couple of dudes at the convenience store down the street were staring at me today. Just staring a hole through me. It freaked me out. They were driving a car with an Oregon tag. Could they have found me here?"

"I don't think so, such a long shot, but yeah, anything's possible. You gotta get out of there. Don't take the chance."

"Lester and I were talking about me going somewhere, getting out of town. I guess I should come up there."

"On second thought, after what you told me, maybe that's not a good idea."

"You think they're up there, too?"

"Haven't noticed anything. I've been focused on my nose cancer. I'm gonna sneak out of here one night, just to be safe. I'm waiting on the doctors to tell me I'm not about to die. I'll come down there like we planned."

"Where? Florida?"

"No, go to South Alabama, the eastern corner. Get a room in Dothan. It's not far from the cabin. I'll call you when I'm on my way. Shouldn't be more than a few days."

"Do you have all the money?"

"We've talked about this."

"I know. I've forgotten. My mind is doing somersaults right now."

"I've got around a hundred."

"Oh my god. I thought you had about seventy-five. Do you think they have any idea that's how much you skimmed? How could they?"

"They couldn't know, just guess. I still think Crazy Davey is the one who tipped them. He saw us skimming some buds a few times. Said it was cool, said he did it, too. Never trusted that guy."

"Fuck Crazy Davey. Always coming on to me."

"You think he did this because you wouldn't fuck him?"

"I don't know. Maybe. He wouldn't let it go. No matter. I'll get down to Dothan soon as I can. And you let me know when the doctor says you're not dying. Okay?"

"Yeah, yeah, soon as I hear. Don't worry. We'll figure something out."

"Just get down here. Call me." Ardor ended the call, looked over to the table where she saw Lester waving her over.

"Come on, we've got a plan," called Lester.

Ardor walked back to the table and returned to her seat.

"Hey, Mr. G."

Lester looked over and saw Kwame waving him over to the fence like he was directing traffic.

"Oh god," said Lester.

"Who's that?" asked Ardor.

"That's Kwame, the neighbor's kid. Harmless really, but he's something else."

"Over here, Mr. G."

"Whatcha need, Kwame?"

"Come over here, I need to tell you something."

"Hold on a second." Lester turned to Ardor. "You haven't met him, have you?"

"No, haven't even seen him before."

"You should meet him. It can be an experience. Never know what's comin' out of that kid's mouth."

"He flies solo," said Austen.

"Come on," said Lester.

"Sure."

Lester and Ardor walked over to the fence where Kwame was standing. "Ardor, I want you to meet Kwame. He lives next door and is a good friend."

"Nice to meet you, Kwame." She reached out her right hand that he quickly grabbed and shook.

"Ardor is an old friend who is living with us for a while, Kwame."

"Nice to meet you, Ardor. You're spending the night like a spend-the-night party?"

"That's a good way to put it," said Ardor.

"Where's your Ali robe? You don't look the same without it," said Lester.

"My mom is washing it. She said it smelled. You are a very pretty woman. Are you two lovers?"

"What'd I tell you?" said Lester.

"What?"

"Never mind. No, we are not lovers. Ardor has a boyfriend. And that's really not any of your business."

"Whatever you say, Mr. G. I just wanted to warn you that my bike was stolen last night. Make sure you tell Jase, Chuck, and Lizzy to be careful and not leave anything out that could be stolen. I'm sure it was Blacks who did it. They're all thieves."

Ardor's face went blank, first blinking at Kwame and then over to Lester. He looked at Kwame and shook his head. "That's racist. You know that."

"No, it's not racist because it's true."

"Kwame, you can't call all Black people thieves because it is not true. And anyway, you are calling yourself a thief because you're Black."

"I'm not Black."

"You're not Black? What are you?"

"I ain't Black."

Lester smiled at Kwame. "You're playing with me."

"I'm not playing, Mr. G. My bike was stolen. And I'm sure Blacks did it; they're all thieves."

"Are you saying that if your skin is Black and you're not a thief then you're not Black."

"I'm saying all Blacks are thieves." Kwame looked over to Ardor. "I bet you must love sex."

Ardor laughed. "Why do you think that?"

"Because you are pretty and pretty girls love to have sex. Ugly girls don't because nobody wants to have sex with them."

Lester shook his head. "You are something else, Kwame."

"Well, I ain't a thief and I ain't Black."

"Whatever you say. Tell your mom and dad hello for me. We need to get back and talk to Austen about a few things. I'll tell the kids to be careful about leaving stuff in the yard."

"Tell 'em to be careful about leaving things outside when they see Blacks around here."

"Sure, I'll do that. You take care."

"Be careful, Ardor, I'm sure Mr. G will protect you," said Kwame.

"I sure will. Nice to meet you."

Lester and Ardor waved at Kwame and then turned and began walking back to the table where Austen sat.

As they sat down Ardor said, "That kid, I don't know what to say to that. I'm dumbfounded."

"There's something going on there. Autism, maybe? Hell, I'm a bit autistic, but I ain't that. He goes to the regular high school, tenth grade I believe. I've never really talked to his parents about him. They're nice people, though. Sweethearts. Were really sweet when Connie passed away, brought food over, were there trying to help. Willard even cut my grass a few times, came over and did it without me saying a word."

"You did tell him that you thought he was playing you," said Ardor.

"I really don't know. You almost have to think that, don't you?"

"I'm not sure if Kwame is kidding around with you, but I do think he believes whatever he says. He's worked it out in his head somehow," said Austen.

Lester nodded. "Could be. He told me the other day that he was going to run for sheriff."

"Run for sheriff? Don't you have to be like twenty-five or something?" asked Ardor.

"That's what I asked him. He said the minimum age was eighteen and that he just turned sixteen. That he has two years to plan his campaign."

"Why does he want to be sheriff?" asked Ardor.

"I avoided asking him, but he mentioned something about keeping greedy white people in line. If you give him lots of slack, he'll go off on all kinds of tangents."

"I smell weed. Must be your neighbor back there," said Ardor.

"I'm sure that's Marlin. He's part of your weed brotherhood."

"When is Alabama gonna legalize the cannabis?"

"Hell, Madison County is still one of the few wet counties in North Alabama, but there's a big push to legalize medical marijuana."

"Marlin knows the power of the smoke," said Austen.

"A wise man," said Ardor.

"One thing for sure, Marlin doesn't have a couple of jackasses from Oregon hunting him down. Look, Austen and I were talking it over, and we think you should just stay low. Don't leave the house for a while. Like even now you should go inside. If those guys are really looking for you then they could just drive around the neighborhood, seeing if they run across you."

"You're probably right. That's a good idea."

The three of them walked into the house and sat at the kitchen table. Ardor finished her beer in three gulps and then said to the two men, "But I can't stay here. I'd like to leave tonight, drive down to Dothan, and wait for Wade. He and I will figure something out down there."

"Okay, but at least wait a few days, let things cool a bit and then leave," said Lester.

"I'll drive you where you need to go," said Austen.

Ardor looked at Austen and smiled.

She placed both hands over Austen's right hand. "You'd do that for me?" she asked.

"We've already talked about it. An old Indian wouldn't catch their eye," said Austen. "Tell her, Lester."

"But we were thinking about you driving her to somewhere around town, in the county, not several hundred miles south. That's a couple of days on the road. Maybe it would be better that I drive you that far south," said Lester.

"I think he's right, Austen. Why don't you stay with the kids? I'm honored you would do that for me, that's so damn kind, but who knows what's down the road," said Ardor.

"People chasing money they think you stole from them is a great motivator," said Lester. "No worries, I'd give you up before things got really bad."

"Austen, maybe you should drive me."

"I do think you need to self-quarantine here at the house for a few days. Don't step outside the house, avoid windows, don't answer the front door. We'll leave Friday night or Saturday morning for Dothan. I'll be back as soon as I can. Might drop you off, then head home," said Lester.

"I think the sooner the better. Let's leave tonight, like now. Use the traffic as cover. I'll lie down in the backseat," said Ardor. She stood up and then walked over to the fridge, placed her empty bottle on the counter and grabbed another after opening the door. She then walked over to Lester and tapped the top of the bottle on Lester's chest. "The sooner I'm out of here the better: for me, for you, and for your family."

Lester smiled and grabbed Ardor by the shoulders. "Okay, I get what you're saying. But let's at least wait until tomorrow night. I think they are wild-eyed focused right now since they saw you at the store. If that was them. No guarantee, right? But let's play it as if they are driving down this street right now. After the kids go to sleep tomorrow night we'll leave. I'll tell them tomorrow night that you must leave, that you are going back to Oregon. You tell them you've decided to move back and I'm driving you to where your boyfriend is picking you up, which is the truth. Boom, bullet down there and then boom, bullet back. Easy-peasy."

"What do you think, Austen?" asked Ardor as she turned to face him.

"I think he's right. If those guys are looking for you then they are probably driving all over these streets in this neighborhood, especially around that store. Let them wear out a bit and then leave tomorrow in the early evening." Austen glanced from Lester then to Ardor. "I think you can slip them right now, but they'll not stop looking for you. Avoid using credit cards, only use cash. If you're careful, then once you're out of town it'll be near impossible to find you."

Ardor kept Austen's gaze for a moment. She stepped back from Lester's grasp, pulled the opener from the counter, popped the top of the local ale, and read the label. "Eight percent. Normally, that's a little strong for a Wednesday, but I think you're right, I'm sorta fucked right now." She shuffled by Lester and walked from the kitchen, by the table and chairs, to the open den, and sat on the sofa. She turned up the bottle for another long swallow and sat back with a smile on her face. "Wade and I are fucked," she said in a voice barely above a whisper, "but we'll figure out something. The point, right now, here, as I sit in this house, is that I slip from their fingers and make sure you and your family are no longer involved. I am so sorry this happened."

Lester and Austen walked into the den and sat next to Ardor.

"Nobody's fault. If those two guys are looking for you, then that was nothing but bad luck. I want to thank you for thinking of my kids. Once you and Wade are down south away from everything, you'll figure something out," said Lester.

"I suggest giving the money back. Perhaps shipping it to them from some obscure town. Like in Mississippi. Or maybe Louisiana. Might be your best chance," said Austen.

"Maybe so, but I just don't know if Wade will agree to that. He looks at that money like it's our fair share. And there's one more thing. Wade gave me some really bad news."

"More bad news? At least it can't be any worse than this shit show," said Lester.

"Actually, it can," said Ardor.

She explained to Lester and Austen about Wade's medical situation, the cancer, the possibility of terminal cancer. The two men listened in silence until she finished filling in all of the details.

"What the hell!" said Lester. "This is some damn Greek tragedy."

"Look, things are bleak. But Wade and I will deal with it. What else can we do? We have some money and that does help things. Anyway, Wade's cancer is not your concern. Right here, right now, get me out of your hair and you'll be done with me."

"Can I express my thoughts here?"

"Of, course," said Lester.

"Focus on getting Ardor to South Alabama right now. Once that is done, then you can help Ardor deal with Wade's health issues. Just focus, Lester."

Lester took a deep breath and then let out a sigh. "You're right. Of course, you're right." He pointed at Ardor. "Let's get you to South Alabama."

Lester awoke in his bed; his eyes darted to the strip of light at the bottom of his bedroom door. He thought he heard Ardor talking to someone. He heard her speak and then waited for a response and heard nothing. She was talking on her phone. He looked at his phone, 3:09 a.m., took a deep breath, and shook his head. "Great, the witching hours," he whispered to himself. He heard an "I love you, baby" and then swung his legs over the edge of the bed. Slowly standing, he stretched his arms straight out from his body, forming a cross, and then he slipped on a pair of sweatpants and stumbled his way out the door, down the hall, and into the den.

"Have you slept any?" asked Lester.

"A little. I've been up for a while," said Ardor.

"Were you talking to Wade?"

"Yeah, he's convinced he's got terminal cancer."

"What did the doctor say?"

"Nothing yet. Today's the day he finds out about the test results. Wade expects the worst, which is understandable for him. He's a pessimist, if nothing else. But he's also in the grips of a head-on paranoid downpour, on the edge times a thousand. He's just got it in his head that those Oregon folks are closing in on us."

"I guess today's a big day all around. Money, cancer, marijuana, being chased by thugs, very nice. 'A day which will live in infamy.'"

"Just a clusterfuck," said Ardor.

"I sure don't feel like making my rounds today," said Lester.

"Hey, I need to tell you something," she said.

"Yeah? I'm hoping you're going to tell me this is all a dream. That you're going to wave your magic wand while I click my ruby slippers together and repeat 'There's no place like home.'"

"Where are those fucking flying monkeys when you need them?" asked Ardor. "Really, I just want to say I'm sorry."

"No sorry's needed."

"I did drag you into this bullshit."

Lester sat down in the chair next to the sofa.

"Don't blame yourself. You didn't make me take you in."

"Who am I kidding, right? I didn't promise you sex, but I certainly flirted with you, used everything I could to persuade you to take me in."

"Not an issue."

"Not a good side of me."

"I was aware, at least of what it seemed on the surface. I'm not naïve, no innocent lamb here. Maybe a little bit. Here's something you don't know, so normal assumptions are meaningless for me. I'm serious. I'm a little heavy in the literal world. I saw how I was being lured into asking you to live here. I said it to you, remember? I'm also a guy; we think with our dicks quite a bit, which you are very familiar with."

"Huh."

"Huh?"

"Yeah, huh."

Ardor looked at Lester for several seconds without speaking. She could see his eyes, but the light from the stove in the kitchen wasn't strong enough to see where he looked.

"Okay," she said finally.

"Yeah, don't. I shouldn't have mentioned that."

"Anyway, I was close to being a wild child when Wade and I lived down the street from you."

"Close?"

"Yeah, ten miles a minute, collateral damage be damned. A walking and talking cliché, my friend."

"I seem to remember that most guys who met you were taken in by your ... I don't know what to call it. Charm. Charisma. Sexual allure. You had an effect on dudes."

"I know, it's freaky. We talked about this earlier. Never understood it. Can't really control it. It's like some sort of voodoo."

"Yeah, maybe voodoo."

"I was aggressive, I admit. Sexually aggressive."

"Men and sex. It's not a complicated formula."

"I've evolved from that."

"Evolved?"

"Rather than grown. I don't think people grow like a piece of grass. We change, like a chemical reaction, like adding water to bourbon."

"Okay."

"We're songs with lots of ups and downs. That was one note I played back then. It was a note I played for lots of guys."

"Whatever you say."

"Okay, honestly, I still like playing that note now and then."

"If you're good at it, why not?" asked Lester.

Ardor looked up and laughed. Rubbed the back of her neck.

"Okay, here it is, here's the deal, the truth of me, at least right now, from where I see it. Yeah, when I was in my teens, my late teens especially, I was one big ball of rebellion. Whatever was expected of me I did the opposite. I wasn't nice a lot of the time. Told lots of people to fuck off, kiss my ass, fuck you. I was in your face, confrontation was my modus operandi. I screamed at teachers, at cops, store clerks, co-workers, lots of people who just happened to cross my path. Why? Because I was young and didn't take too kindly to being told what to do. Youthful rebellion. Anti-authority. Lots of kids go through that. But what really pissed me off was the sexism I saw everyfuckingwhere I went. I get men's lust, that's why I learned to use it against them. It's an ugly trait for lots of guys. Most dudes can throttle it down, control it to a tolerable level. But what I do not understand is the misogyny, the fucking contempt for women. The discrimination against women, the belittling of women, the condescension. I stopped tolerating men treating me like I was dumb, that they were smarter all because they had dicks and I had a vagina. The mansplaining shit had to stop. Thus, I got a reputation for being a bitch. Who cares?"

Lester looked at Ardor for a couple of beats and then nodded his head.

"Well now," he said. "I get that. And I agree with what you said. How much shit can women take from men, right?"

Ardor grinned. Lester grinned back.

"I just need to get away from these guys."

"I know. And I've got to make sure those dudes stay away from my kids," said Lester.

"I'm terrified. Just want to put that out there," said Ardor.

"Your fear is real. It's as real as suddenly finding yourself alone with three small children to raise," said Lester

Ardor stood and walked over to Lester. She bent down and kissed Lester on his forehead. A couple of short kisses of kindness. She nodded. "Yeah," she said. "You're a good man, Lester."

100 MPH

LESTER STOOD at the foot of Toots's bed. He looked at Irene who sat in a chair on the left side of the bed with both hands holding Toots's left arm.

"They said it was a coronary artery spasm," said Irene. "That he's had a heart attack."

"Yes, I've talked to a nurse and doctor at the hospital. It's a minor heart attack, typically no major damage to the heart, but it can be a precursor to a major heart attack. He hits most of the risk factors," said Lester.

"Like his drinking," said Irene.

"He should no longer drink," said Lester.

Toots opened his eyes, blinked a few times, and looked from Irene to Lester, back and forth, back and forth.

"Hey, Dad. How do you feel?"

Toots smiled. "Can I have some water?"

Lester walked over to the other side of the bed, grabbed a plastic cup, and then poured water into it from a small pitcher sitting on a tray. He brought the cup over to the bed, placing the straw where Toots could reach it.

Toots took several quick swallows and then leaned his head back from the straw.

"Do you remember anything?" asked Irene.

"I remember chest pain, that's as much as I can tell you."

"That's what we were just talking about. You had a coronary artery spasm. The arteries in your heart tightened up. Yours was long enough to be a minor heart attack," Lester said.

"Prognosis?"

"You should be with us for a while longer," Irene said.

"But you need to get a handle on your party lifestyle, Mr. Richards. No more drinking, smoking, cocaine, and the orgies must stop. Mr. Toots, your party days are over."

"Just as well. I'm tired of drinking and snorting it up. The women have finally worn me out. Like most things, it's a sport for the young."

"And you should have a healthy diet, a very healthy diet," said Lester.

"No drinking and no more steaks. Bacon, too, I'm sure. Is now the time I start watching *SpongeBob SquarePants* while wearing an extra-large adult diaper?"

"I watch it all the time," said Lester.

Toots looked at Lester. "Oh, that's right, you have kids."

"My kids provided the gateway, but I'm a fan."

"I'm flummoxed by your taste," said Toots.

"I'm not ashamed of it. You got a problem with *SpongeBob*?"

Toots shook his head. "No, no qualms with the *SpongeBob* man. Do you bear good news for me, Lester?"

Lester set the cup back on the tray, took a deep breath, and continued to look at the cup.

"That is priceless," said Lester.

Lester grinned and then looked at Irene who held a look of puzzlement.

"I don't even want to know," Irene said.

"That's for the best, Irene. Trust me," Lester said.

Toots shifted his body and sat up most of the way. "While you're both here, I've got something I want to tell you two."

Irene and Lester looked at Toots. "No, I can tell you that, whatever you are talking about, no," said Irene.

"No matter what I say, just keep in mind that I'm king for the day since I'm wearing this crown of death. In other words, I don't have to worry about the repercussions of being completely honest. This just comes with the situation."

"Now Daddy, stop that kind of talk. You are not about to die."

"No, Irene, you're wrong. I'm about to die. Probably not today, fingers crossed, but sometime in the near future. Here me out now. That said, I want to air a few thoughts."

"I don't think Lester wants to hear you spewing your guts about the regrets in your life."

"I'm not gonna be talking about regrets. Regrets are for children and idiots. And if Lester don't want to hear this, then he's welcome to leave the room."

"I'm honored, Mr. Toots, that you want me to hear, as you said, your 'honest' thoughts concerning your life."

"Is that fine with you, Irene?" asked Toots.

"You're a grown man. You can make up your own mind," said Irene as she shook her head.

Toots gazed at his daughter, a couple beats passed before he began to speak again.

"And don't you fret any, Irene. I ain't gonna divulge any family secrets; those skeletons will not be dragged out from the closet by me. What you do with those bones is your business. And, of course, I'm sure you know I don't give a damn. I just got to say some things I want to get off my chest. The heart attack has pushed the schedule up a few notches. Okay?"

"Okay, Daddy."

"Lester?"

"I'm all ears, Mr. Toots."

"I've had an incredible life. Been blessed, as some say. Irene, your mother was the love of my life and I miss her every single goddamn day. Which is all fine, yada yada yada. Not mocking it, I know all that 'Love is the answer' shit is some kind of powerful force for us humans. Agreed? You don't have to answer that. It's a rhetorical question."

"Are you really gonna say this stuff, now, right now?"

"Irene. Please."

"Okay, okay, whatever."

"Okay, let's see, I was saying that I loved Britta for her honesty. The type of honesty that shapes how you lived, how you are true to yourself. That was the core of Britta's beauty. And it's the type of honesty that will piss some people off."

"Okay, that's enough," said Irene.

"Irene, the crown of death, okay?"

"Right, okay, the crown of death."

"Britta said if you want to truly understand honesty, then talk to some old Germans."

Toots looked at his daughter and then looked over to Lester.

"Do you need some more water, Mr. Toots?" Lester asked. He grabbed the cup with the straw and offered it to the old man.

"Thank you, Lester," he said and then sucked a few swallows of the water from the straw.

"Old Germans, Daddy?" asked Irene.

"Needed to be said," Toots confessed.

"Nothing but admiration here, Mr. Toots," Lester said.

"Of course, I'm not that old, so the relevance to me is that I'm at the end of my life, just like an elderly person who has ridden the train until the end of the tracks. The old Germans lived through the Nazis. They've seen us, all of us, is what I'm referencing here, at our worst. Now when you pull back the veneer of the pretty picture we like to draw of ourselves you find some ugliness. We can humiliate each other, kill each other at an astounding rate. Mass shootings in the good ol' U.S.A. are as common as crabs on a Bourbon Street whore."

"What?" asked Irene.

"I agree," said Lester.

"But what I'm driving at is the goodness that runs deep within most of us. That's what this honesty hayride we're on right now is all about. Where I'm pissing in the wind from right now is a perspective most don't face until much later in life. That's the clarity that has been dumped in my lap. I know I seem to be twisting in the wind right now, but I've suddenly realized that most of life is static, white noise, just stuff. You know what I mean?"

"I follow you," said Lester.

"It's something a little more than the 'live life like every day is your last' postcard philosophy. I don't know about you two, but if I knew today was my last day then I'd already be knee deep in my little request to you, Lester."

"Are you telling me that—"

"Here me out, Irene. What I'm saying is that I've come to see one should live his, or her, life as one sees fit. Don't live life like you're about to die, live life without the fear of asking for what you want. Most of the shit we worry about is ephemeral. Love the people you love with all your heart. That's easy, right?"

"Yes," said Lester.

"I'm saying this as someone who is on the edge looking into that vast pool of blackness." Toots popped his right fist into the palm of his left hand. "Don't worry about shit; just love the people you love and ask for the things you want."

Toots looked at Lester and nodded his head a few times. Lester nodded back. Then Toots looked at Irene and smiled. "I know you think these are the mutterings of a dying man who is slowly slipping into near-death delirium. I'll be blunt, baby. I should have asked for a harlot and some nose candy long before now."

"You sound drunk," said Irene.

"I'm drunk with the truth of honesty."

"I understand you perfectly," said Lester.

Irene and Lester stood in the driveway next to Lester's truck. The autumn sun warmed the cool morning breeze, dulling the cold bite of wind. Lester had stood for a few minutes in the bedroom after Toots had finished his declaration before he decided to leave, making sure he was stable and free of pain.

"We were here not long ago worrying about the old coot demanding hookers and coke; now he's had a heart attack and wishes he had asked for that stuff much earlier."

"You gotta learn to pivot in this world," said Lester.

"He seemed to be happy that we were both there."

"I think he's in a very good place right now. He's content, has wrestled with his situation and come out to tell us about it."

"I just want to thank you for being here."

"I need to tell you something, Irene."

"What?"

"I have to leave town for a few days. I'm sorry for the timing, but there is nothing I can do about that."

"When will you be back?"

"Hope to be back Sunday at the latest. I'll leave you with Ann's number. Do you know her?"

"I've heard her name mentioned a few times."

"She's a good nurse. She's been a hospice nurse off and on for many years. She has the most experience of any hospice nurse in this area. She's a damn good nurse. More importantly, she's one of the best human beings I've ever known. Hopefully, you won't need her during the few days I'm gone, but if you do, you'll be in good hands. Don't hesitate to call her for anything."

Lester pulled out his phone from his pocket, punched a few numbers.

"There, I just texted you Ann's number. She knows about your dad, I called her this morning to fill her in on the situation, bringing her up to speed. Leaving right now is not something I want to do; it's just a situation I can't ignore. I am really, really sorry, Irene."

"I understand. You have to do what you have to do. I hope it's not too serious and that we see you in a few days."

"You can count on that. And, Irene?"

"Yeah?"

"Your dad is in a very good place. He's rock steady."

"Very much so."

"I don't know if you can do it; you know, talk about it. But if you can, then I highly recommend that you reassure him; tell him you're gonna be fine, that you and your kids will be fine. That means a lot to people in his situation. That's their biggest worry."

"I'll try. That won't be easy to do, but I'll try with all my heart no matter how difficult because I love him."

"Tell him you love him. You can't tell him too many times."

Irene hugged Lester. "Hookers and cocaine. My daddy."

"May we all want hookers and cocaine."

"Are you ready?" asked Lester.

Ardor drew a deep breath as she lay face-up on the back-seat. She looked at her phone, 9:12. She closed her eyes.

"'There's no place like home. There's no place like home,'" she said to the headliner.

After a pause she exhaled and opened her eyes, staring straight into the darkness of the car. They had decided to take Lester's other vehicle, the Mercedes.

"So, you're ready to go home, Dorothy?"

"Yes, just get me away from these marijuana thugs."

"Easy as pie."

"What kind of pie?"

"I'm thinking chocolate pie. Easy as chocolate pie."

Lester backed the car out of the driveway and into the street, turning right. He drove to a stop sign that was ten houses down from his house.

"So far, so good," said Lester. "I feel better already."

"No signs of the sheriff and the town folk?"

"They're probably hanging back, waiting for the right opportunity."

"Ha, ha. Nothing like joking about someone trying to kill me."

"They want the money, not your life."

"Said the person they're not after."

"Focus on the mission, soldier. Okay, once I hit the highway I'll open her up to a hundred. We'll be in South Alabama before the bars close."

"Dynamite. We'll celebrate my safety with a few shots at a local dive."

"Bourbon or tequila?"

"High-grade tequila, you bitch."

"Patron?"

"Silver."

After a few blocks Lester turned onto a main road.

"Can we have some music?" asked Ardor.

Lester turned on the stereo. They listened to the end of a song.

"Pop country? Uh, no," said Ardor.

"Hey, if you don't like my music then you can get out of my fucking car." Lester turned off the radio.

"'The Dude abides,' man," said Ardor.

"Defy expectations. The Black cabbie wearing the leather hat loves the Eagles."

"Right! The Black dude loves the Eagles. That's at the heart of their art."

"Marge," said Lester.

"A pregnant police chief," said Ardor. "They pop lots of hipster balloons."

"I think they're setting fire to the smugness," Lester said. "Hell, everything is a style."

Ardor giggled. "Yeah, yeah, yeah, wearing jeans and a white T-shirt and drinking PBR is a style. Tattoos are now hipster cool."

"Anchor tattoos especially."

"Fixed-gear bikes."

"A gin cocktail served in a cucumber."

Lester noticed a white car not far behind that seemed to be following them. He didn't say anything to Ardor but decided to catch a red light to see if he could get a look at the occupants. He slowed the car to make sure he hit the red light a couple of blocks ahead. The white car pulled up behind them. There were two people in the front, white males. The thinner one, the driver, had a goatee. He examined the car, the hood, and the grill. He read the word Infinity on the front.

"Where are we?" asked Ardor.

"At a red light."

"Yeah? Which one?"

Ardor began to rise up and look around.

"What are you doing? Stay down."

"That's the Infinity!"

"Oh, fuck me," said Lester.

He quickly took a right turn and drove a few blocks before pulling into a baseball park parking lot. The white car drove by the entrance; both men turned and stared at him.

"Did they see me?" asked Ardor.

"How could they not?" He looked back at Ardor. "Please stay down."

When he turned to see if the car had driven off, he noticed the Infinity drive by again.

"We're in trouble. Only a few blocks from my house, and we're already in trouble."

"What?"

"I need to call someone."

"Who? The police?"

"I don't think so."

"Batman?"

"Let me know if you have his number." Lester reached for his cell, found a number, and punched dial.

"Did you bring that gun?" asked Ardor.

"No, I didn't bring that damn gun."

"Why the fuck not? We're defenseless."

"Just hold on. I've got a friend who can help us."

"A friend?"

"Sup, Ced. This is Lester. Can you talk?"

"Lester, how's the car wash business?"

"I'm out of the suds."

"Yeah, whatcha doing now?"

"Believe it or not, I'm a hospice nurse. Helping people with death, my friend."

"No shit. My mama used hospice."

"Mine, too. And my wife."

"Excuse me, we're about to be murdered," said Ardor.

"Yeah, I heard about that, man. So sorry. Your kids are still young. That shit had to be tough."

"Dark days, for sure. We're good now. Hey, I'm in a bind right this second and could use a little help."

"What you need, Les?"

"I've got a friend who's got some people after her."

"Is that right?"

"Afraid so. She and her boyfriend were growing marijuana for a company out in Oregon—"

"Legal weed. I should move to Oregon."

"Hear that."

"Legal weed, like peanut butter and jelly."

"I thought the shit would be legal twenty years ago. Anyways, she and her boyfriend got into a dispute over their pay. Long story short: they skimmed a little bit and owners got wind of it, so my friend and her boyfriend split. Now she thinks some of those Oregon people have found her here in Huntsville."

"Shiiiit," said Ced.

"I got her in the car with me right now, and it looks like there's a couple of fellas from Oregon sniffing all around us."

"Following you?"

"Sorta looks like it. I think they want to see what she's got."

"If she's got some of that money. How much they get?"

"Enough for a couple of men to hunt her down in Alabama. She's a local gal."

"Really? Who she be?"

"Ardor, Ardor Hardwick."

"Huh, I think I know her. A little younger than us?"

"Yeah."

"Wild as a buck?"

"That's her."

"What is he saying about me?" asked Ardor.

"That you're pure as fresh snow and a warrior for truth and justice."

"Hee-hee," said Ced.

"Well, that's a lie."

"You don't want to know what he said."

"She's spunky," said Ced.

"Brother, you don't know."

"What?" asked Ardor.

"Nothing."

"Nothing?"

"He thinks he might know you."

"Really?"

"I think she ran with my cousin a few years back."

"Says you ran with his cousin."

"Who's his cousin?"

"Who's your cousin?"

"Kendal. He likes the white stuff."

Lester turned his head to the backseat. "You know a Kendal?"

"Kendal? I don't ... wait, yeah, I know a Kendal. That brother used to get me some kick-ass weed."

"Of course, he did."

"She know him?"

"Uh-huh, said he used to get her some good weed."

"That's him. I remember that girl trippin' one night, just off the planet. She a lot smarter than she lets on. Very, very cocky."

"That's her."

"What the fuck? I'm right here."

Lester noticed a car pulling up behind them.

"What? Where the fuck did they come from?" asked Lester.

"Is it them?" asked Ardor.

"Goddamn it."

"You all right?" asked Ced.

"Those fuckers are right on us. I'm gonna try to lose them."

Lester slammed the car into drive and then quickly drove out of the parking lot with the white car following.

"Where you at?"

"Close to downtown."

"Tell you what to do. Head south on the Parkway, take 'em down about fifteen minutes, maybe twenty, and then come back to that plaza on Oakwood that used to have Big Ed's. You know which one I'm talking about?"

"Yeah, I know the one."

"They probably won't try anything on such a busy road. And that'll give me some time to work something up."

"That sounds good."

"If anything happens, call me. Just stay ahead of them. And do not stop if you can help it."

"Okay, I'll check back with you in a few minutes. Thanks again, Ced." Lester ended the call.

"Now what?" asked Ardor.

"Ced's gonna help us."

"What's he gonna do?

"I don't know, but he'll get us out of this."

"You sure?"

"Yep."

Within ten minutes they made it to the Parkway, the main north-south artery of Huntsville, and turned on a ramp heading south.

"Are they still behind us?"

"Yeah, afraid so."

"Sorry about raising my head."

"You didn't know they were right behind us. How could you know that? Very bad luck."

"How far you gonna go?"

"About fifteen minutes or so."

"I'm so sorry about all this."

"Don't worry, we'll lose these guys."

"I left you some money at the house."

"What?"

"I told you I'd pay you for your help. Now seems like a good time to remind you."

"Where did you leave the money?"

"It's under Lizzy's pillow."

"I don't believe that."

"It's in your bathroom, in your shaving kit."

"How much?"

"A few thousand."

"How much is a few?"

"Less than fifty. That's all I'm gonna tell you."

"You said ten thousand earlier. Is that the amount?"

"Maybe. Let me assure you that you deserve every penny right now."

Lester looked in the rearview again. The sound of the road the only noise in the car. Lester turned to the right and looked back to see what Ardor was doing. The smoky streetlights illuminated Ardor's face; their eyes met. Lester grinned.

"What?" asked Ardor.

"Just checking to see if you're still back there."

"I thought about leaving but decided I'd stay here in the car with you, show some solidarity. No sense in bailing on you. I'm a team player."

"Sure, you're all about the team."

"There's no 'I' in team."

"I bet those dudes back there would give you a ride."

"They look like a couple of really nice guys," said Ardor. "Just a couple of sweethearts."

"I think they just want to give you a hug."

"Probably want to go for a ride, such a nice evening for a spin through the countryside."

"They must like you a whole bunch; they are drafting us, four or five car lengths."

"Fuckers," said Ardor.

Ardor leaned up a second.

"No, no, stay down," said Lester.

"I'm just turning over. They can't see me in the dark that far back. And what the hell, they already know I'm in here. Why else would they be following us?"

"Yeah, I'm just jacked all up. I've never driven a getaway car before."

"Now you tell me. I'm paying good money for someone who's never driven a getaway car?"

"You didn't ask me."

"I thought that was a given."

"Never assume."

"I will say that you seem to be doing a damn good job for someone with no getaway-car experience," said Ardor.

"Hey, you gotta get wet if you want to learn to swim," said Lester.

"Platitudes-R-Us."

"You're funny. So funny."

"How close are they now?" asked Ardor.

"They're a little closer," said Lester.

"Fuck those goons. Maybe I should throw some money out the window."

"I don't think that would work."

Ardor raised her head a few inches from the seat to look at Lester. "Here's what I don't get. You feel good about yourself when you help people, even people looking death right in the eye. But still, seems like that'd be such a downer all the time. Just don't think I could handle it."

"Being around people who are dying is uplifting."

"Uplifting? Cut this guy off, bartender. You been chugging the hospice Kool-Aid."

"You gotta understand that when someone is facing death there tends to be moments of extreme clarity. Having your mortality right in your face melts most of the outside world. Serenity just fills the room. That's what I see."

"Serenity? With death punching you in the face you become calm and peaceful?"

"There's no need for artifice, affectation. Having a persona is for people who have free time to work on their scenes. A buffet of free time. All you can eat free time. Everything is cut to the bone for people facing death. I think you realize that you are in your final scene."

"Do you hear lots of regrets?" asked Ardor.

"Had a guy just weep and weep over an old childhood friend he hadn't seen for years," said Lester. "A falling out over something silly, something to do with a woman. The guy was in his eighties and was crying over a lost friendship from fifty years ago. Most, though, just full of I don't give a damn, just a shame it took death for them to finally realize you gotta stick your chest out and act like you want the biggest and best of whatever they got."

Lester's phone began to ring. He looked at the screen and then swiped the incoming call.

"Hey, Ced."

"How we doing, Mr. Deathinator?"

"They're still hanging tight. I'm about to turn around. You gonna make it?"

"Yeah, we'll make it. This is what I'm thinking."

"Hold on, let me put you on speaker. Ardor needs to hear this."

"Okay."

"You're on," said Lester.

"So, you two go in and make a lap in the parking lot, make sure the Oregon crew is behind you. When you make that final left to turn back out of the plaza, a cement truck will pull out from the side of the building and block them off, which means you gotta make sure you're far enough ahead of them so the truck can get between you. What'cha driving?

"Dark blue Mercedes; it was my mom's car."

"Okay, just want to make sure we see you coming. Now, the cement truck will stop once he cuts them off, which means your gal needs to get out of the car and run to my car that will be parked right there on the right. It's a black El Camino. Once she's in my car, you take off. Then the cement truck will move on and follow you out of the lot. When you get down—"

"Wait, how do you know you'll be able to park right there? What if the parking lot is full?" asked Lester.

"Most of the stores are closed by now. Should be lots of empty spaces. If I can't park right there, then your girl needs to run behind the nearest car and wait until all three vehicles exit the lot. Once everyone is gone, she can find my El Camino."

"Right."

"Now, when you leave the parking lot, Les, make sure you turn right on Oakwood heading toward the Parkway. Right before you reach the Parkway, turn right into that shopping center on the corner. Most of that parking lot should be empty, too. Stop out in the open lot and wait for your Oregon boys to pull up. When they get out of the car, my boy Carlos will pull up flashing his lights on his deputy sheriff's car. He's gonna check out their papers and send you on your way. I'll take the gal back to my place. She can stay here until you come get her."

"Ok, that's a lot of twists and turns. But what the fuck; I'm for it. What about you, Ardor?"

"I don't think I have much of a choice. Looks good on paper; we'll see if we can pull it off."

"Exactly. After I lose the Oregon duo I'll go home and ditch this car, then come to your place in my truck."

Lester found a crossover, made a quick U-turn without looking at the car following them.

"Are you about twenty minutes out now?"

"About that."

"Slow down a little; give us a few more minutes. Now, give me a ring when you're about five minutes out."

"You got it."

"Good luck to you, Les. And you too, Ardor."

"We're good here," said Ardor. "I'm scared shitless, but that'll help me focus."

"I'll give you a call," said Lester.

Lester hung up the call and smiled at Ardor.

"What am I doing?" said Lester.

"I bet you been saying that a lot since you ran into me a few days ago," said Ardor.

"Things are pretty high on the crazy meter right now."

"I knew the Oregon people might show up here," Ardor pointed to the back window, "but I really didn't think it would come to this."

"This whole Jason Bourne thing is a surprise to me, too. And," Lester paused a couple of beats, "you never mentioned hand-to-hand combat."

"I told Wade skimming that weed wasn't a good idea."

"Let's go through the steps again."

"Right. So, I'm gonna pop out of this car, then run over to your friend's black El Camino? That's the car that has a back end like a truck?" asked Ardor.

"That's it."

"This could easily fail," said Ardor.

"Easy-peasy. But you're right, this has failure written all over it," said Lester.

"And then the bad guys will chase you down the street at breakneck speed while the El Camino with the girl gets away."

"Exactly. And that's why you need to keep your head down. They would notice if all of a sudden your head wasn't in the window when they start chasing me back down Oakwood."

"You think of everything, Mr. Bourne."

"Right now, I'm thinking this is no fun."

"Okay, so then, Carlos, a sheriff's deputy, will come to your rescue and provide a diversion for you to escape."

"See how easy that all sounds."

"Except this isn't a movie and the girl in peril is me."

"There is that."

"And our Oregon brothers, now?"

"Still with us. They are good at their job. Actually, they're a little closer since I slowed our pace."

"They are bad-guy certified. Will not stop until the mission is accomplished."

"I'm sure their payday is contingent on bringing that money back, which has to be quite the incentive."

"Fuck those fuckers," said Ardor.

"Fuck those fucking fuckers," said Lester.

"Fuck those fucking fuckers for following us," said Ardor.

"Fuck those fucking fuckers for following for far too long," said Lester.

"You know I was thinking that I could give them most of what I have, but most of what I have is in your house now," said Ardor.

"No way I'm taking them to my house."

"Of course, of course."

Silence filled the car for the next several minutes. Ardor watched Lester from the backseat.

"You keep shaking your head," said Ardor.

Lester let loose with a big sigh.

"Don't want to put a damper on our good time here, pee on your birthday cake and all, but I'm not feeling good about all this. A lot can happen here in just a few minutes."

"Oh, this elaborate plan has holes all through it, but you were just saying that this is easy- peasy. I like it when you say easy-peasy. You're the rock here, not me."

"Work with the fear, not against it," said Lester.

"Exactly. The worst that could happen is that we all die."

"Jesus, really?"

"I think Jesus is with us, dude."

"He's on our team?"

"Yeah, of course. We're part of the righteous."

"How so?"

"Lester, think about it. Wade skimmed a little weed off these guys because they were paying us slave wages. They are greedy. And when you're greedy, you are depriving others. Jesus is a union man."

"How much did they pay you?"

"A shameful amount. Wade made $28,000 and me $23,000."

"So that's low for a grower and helper?"

"I was a budtender most of the time and they average $12 an hour, which is $23,000."

"And he was underpaid, too?"

"This was a small operation. Wade was the only grower, so they paid low compared to the big farms. Wade wouldn't let it go."

"Once people taste the blood of money, they get ravenous," said Lester. "Like fucking vampires."

"Do vampires fuck?"

"Langella's *Dracula* was a pussy hound."

"Are my admirers still following us?"

"Yes, they're so close I can smell their anger."

"Maybe if I just give them about twenty grand they'll go away. They have no idea how much we took."

"That's what I'm saying."

"I think I should save that option for a last resort."

"Okay, listen: when I get back to the house to get the truck should I get all the money, you think?"

"No, no, no. Just grab another ten thousand. No sense in giving them all the damn money."

After a few more minutes Lester exited off the Parkway to the Oakwood intersection. "Okay, we're goin' in." The left-turn light was red. He punched Ced's call-back button.

"Les, where you at?"

"We're at Oakwood and the Parkway, waiting for the light to turn green."

"They still behind you?"

"They're tight, right on our ass."

The left turn-lane light changed to green.

"Here we go. We're on Oakwood now."

"Okay, got the El Camino in position. I decided to duck down and hide when you enter the plaza. Don't give them anything to ponder. Just make sure you tell our gal to be quick about it. She needs to jump in the El Camino as fast as she can."

"Right," said Lester.

"Just don't freak, okay," Ced said.

"I'm freaking. We're both freaking. We're freaking full of freaking. I know that's not good news to hear, but I'm freaking, man."

"You got this. Ain't nothin'. You deal with dying people all the time; this is nothing but candy for you."

"Alright, the candy wagon's comin' at cha."

"Bring it, Cap'n D!"

Lester ended the call.

"Ardor?"

"Yeah?"

"Don't worry; this is gonna work."

"I'm with you, 'to the righteous good shall be repaid,'" replied Ardor.

"Quoting the Bible, are you?"

"Proverbs 13:21. They don't call it the Good Book for nothing."

Lester forgot to look left at the corner plaza to see if a sheriff's deputy was parked close by. He accelerated, increasing his speed enough to make the Oregon men tighten their pursuit. About a minute down the road, he saw the small plaza.

"Hold on, turning left into the plaza."

"Still on us?"

"Oh yeah."

Lester slowly drove down the ramp into the lot and turned left at the end of the row. He looked in the rearview to make sure the Infinity made the turn. He glanced to the left and saw the black El Camino in the exact parking space it needed to be.

"The El Camino is there."

He saw the cement truck idling next to the plaza building.

"And there's the cement truck."

"I think I'm gonna throw up," said Ardor.

"Get ready; I'm turning left again. You need to jump out in just a few seconds."

"Fuck, fuck, fuck, fuck, fuck, fuck, fuck, fuck."

Lester popped the gas to create a gap between them and the Infinity, giving the cement truck enough room to pull out and block the lane. When he turned the final left at the end of the lane, the cement truck drove out right behind him and stopped. Lester stopped the car.

"Go, go, go, go, go."

Ardor quickly opened the right rear passenger door and sprinted toward the El Camino. A few feet from the vehicle, she tripped and crashed into the front left bumper.

"Oh my god," said Lester.

Ardor quickly scrambled to all fours and scurried around the front left corner of the El Camino, opened the door, jumped in, and eased the door closed.

Lester turned right back onto the ramp that led out of the lot, stopped at the top, and turned right back onto Oakwood where they had just driven. The cement truck followed close behind him, stopped at the edge of Oakwood, and waited for the Infinity to blow its horn. After a few seconds, the truck turned left onto Oakwood. The Infinity turned right without stopping and accelerated to close the gap between it and Lester.

"Oh man, oh man, oh man," said Ardor as she turned her head and suddenly came face to face with Ced.

"That went well," said Ced.

"This is ridiculous," said Ardor.

"Those dudes want to talk to you," said Ced.

"They seem to have a problem with a girl saying no. Move on; get a life, right?"

Ced sat up. "Just stay down for a while. I'll let you know when you can sit up."

"Right."

Ced pulled out of their space, drove up the ramp, and turned left onto Oakwood. He drove up Oakwood, then came to an intersection with Pulaski Pike, turned right, and headed north.

"Are we on Pulaski?"

"Yes, my place is a few miles north of town."

"Anybody behind us?"

"I think you're in the clear."

"For now," said Ardor.

"They have no idea where you are right now."

The scene at the next parking lot fell into place as if everyone had rehearsed their roles: Lester pulled in, drove to the empty section at the rear of the lot, waited for the Oregon boys to pull up next to him. He jumped out of his car at the same time as the Oregon duo. Yet before the two men moved toward Lester, a sheriff's deputy car sped to a lights-flashing stop a few feet in front of the Infinity. The young deputy demanded to see ID from all three, looked at Lester's first, then let him go, but called in the other two's IDs and the vehicle registration.

A few minutes after leaving the lot, Lester called Austen to tell him he would be home in a few minutes, without Ardor, that there had been a glitch in their plans. He explained that he needed to switch vehicles and then leave again, not sure if he'd be back later that night or in a few days, as earlier planned. And he told Austen not to wake the kids, that he had to pick up something from the house, then quietly leave.

When Lester walked in his back door, he was met by Austen.

"Let's put the Mercedes away now."

"Okay, I'll go open the garage door."

The two men walked out the back door, Austen walking over to his detached garage he had built a few years before and Lester to his Mercedes. Lester pulled his mom's car back out of his driveway and drove up Austen's driveway, squeezed by Austen's pickup, and into the now- open garage.

When Lester walked out of the garage carrying a small satchel with his clothes and Ardor's duffel bags, Austen pointed the opener at the garage's ceiling. Both men watched the door slowly come down.

"Thank you for doing all this. I owe you, for sure," said Lester.

"You have always been there when I needed help with my son."

"Still, you are being very kind," said Lester.

"We're not keeping score," said Austen.

"I need to go in the house to get something. Are the kids still asleep?"

"They were a few minutes ago. I need to go to my house for a minute. I'll meet you in your kitchen."

"All right," said Lester as he turned back to his back fence. When he walked through the gate, he was met by Georgia. "Hey, girl, what are you doing out here?" he said to the lab. He stopped a second to stroke the dog's head with both hands. "Such a good girl. You stay out here for a few minutes, then we'll let you back in." He walked into the house, went quickly to his bedroom, then to his bathroom where he turned on the light and closed the door. He pulled out the bottom drawer of the vanity where he kept his shaving kit. He pulled open the top zipper and looked inside. "Wow," he whispered. He set the kit next to the sink, then pulled out a bundled stack of twenty-dollar bills. The paper bundle was marked with a handwritten $5,000. There were seven of those bundles that he stacked neatly next to the kit. He took two of the stacks and shoved them into his blue jeans back pockets. He then returned the rest of the money to the kit, zipped it up, and pulled the drawer completely out of the vanity, placed the shaving kit on the drawer's floor, and replaced the drawer. His bladder was full so he peed, rinsed his hands and face, and gave himself a hard stare in the mirror with a towel in his hands. He snickered to himself while shaking his head, turned off the light, opened the door, and quickly bumped into Chuck.

"Whoa, Chuck. I didn't see you," Lester said as he grabbed Chuck by the shoulders, preventing him from falling on the bedroom floor. "Are you okay?"

"I think so," said Chuck. "Hey, what are you doing here, Dad?"

"We had a change of plans. I came back for a few minutes, but I'm about to leave again."

"Where's Ardor?"

"She's at a friend's house waiting for me."

"Are you not going to South Alabama?"

"I think we're still going, but maybe not. Lots of things for Ardor to consider. She'll be fine." Lester stroked Chuck's head. "You need to get back to bed. You have school tomorrow."

"Okay."

Lester followed Chuck to Jase's room where Jase was still asleep in his bed. Chuck crawled into the other twin bed, then looked at his dad. Lester walked to the side of the bed, pulled the covers up to Chuck's shoulders, ruffled his hair, and kissed him on the forehead.

"I'll let y'all know tomorrow what exactly we're doing, okay?" stated Lester as he turned to walk away.

Chuck grabbed Lester's right arm.

"Dad?"

"Yeah, Chuck, are you all right?" Lester turned back to Chuck.

"I just wanted to tell you that I'm sorry about those drawings."

"Apology not needed. You're curious; nothing wrong about that. Just gotta learn how to deal with that curiosity. All about respect, Chuck. Right?"

"Okay. Respect."

"Make sure you help Austen while I'm gone. You're a big man."

"Thanks, Dad."

"Good night, Chuck."

Lester walked out of the bedroom, down the hall, into the den, and stopped in the kitchen. He checked to make sure the two packs of bills were still in his back pockets. He heard Austen open the back door.

"Lester, I've been thinking. Maybe me and the kids should stay at my house, just to be safe," he said as he walked into the kitchen.

Lester opened a cabinet, grabbed a glass, and filled it halfway in the kitchen sink. "That's probably not a bad idea," said Lester, tilting the glass back and drinking all of the water. "Let me think a minute."

"I have the two extra bedrooms, one with twin beds."

"Right."

"Should we do it now?"

"I'd feel better. Let's do it," said Lester.

"I'll get the boys," said Austen.

"Chuck's awake. I just talked to him. I'll get Lizzy. They can just come back over here in the morning to get ready for school," said Lester as he started down the hall. "We'll get them in bed, then I'll take off."

THE BABY BLUE CARDIGAN AND KHAKIS ARE A NICE ENSEMBLE

LESTER DROVE along back roads on the way to Ced's house, the traffic sporadic on these smaller lanes, avoiding the busier streets, even hiding down a side street for ten minutes when he thought someone was following him. Though he had not been to Ced's house in several years, not even able to remember the last time he pulled into Ced's driveway, he knew exactly where the house sat on the rural road five minutes from the Huntsville city limits. Nevertheless, he had to stop in the middle of the road in front of Ced's house to make sure this was the right house. The house was much bigger now, though the design looked familiar. Instead of a two-car garage at the end of the driveway, there was now a large building with two double-car garages, including a second floor. Lester pulled into the driveway, then slowly drove to the back of the home in front of one of the double-car garages. Behind the house itself was a large pool surrounded by a four-foot-high picket fence with a dog-ear cut. The lights around the pool deck shone brightly, including a couple of blue lights in the pool. Lester spied Ardor sitting at a table with Ced and another woman. The woman, as best Lester could remember, looked like Ced's wife, but too many years had passed to be sure. He had a faint memory of someone telling him that Ced had divorced and then meeting the new wife out somewhere, maybe shopping. He stepped out of his truck, pulled the packs of money from his back pockets, and slid them under the front seat before walking across the driveway. He stopped at the gate that opened to the pool.

"Nice pool," said Lester. "The mansion that concrete built."

"Just lucky. Worked at it, but still lucky," said Ced.

"Here's to hoping we're lucky tonight."

"Come on in, Lester. The gate's not locked," said Ced.

Lester walked in and up to the wrought-iron table where the three of them sat. "Hello," said Lester to the woman sitting on the other side of Ced.

"Hi," said the woman.

"This is Denise, my wife."

"Yes, we've met before, right? A few years ago, just can't remember exactly where," said Lester.

"Yes, I believe we met at a park. Some type of festival, perhaps?"

"That sounds right," said Lester. "Sorry to bring all this. I'm a novice in fleeing from villains."

"Sounds like a bad situation."

"Ced pulled it out for us. Owe him everything." Lester looked down at Ardor. "So, you seem to have recovered from the somersault into the grill of Ced's El Camino."

"I don't think I could have hit that car any harder even if I was trying to hit it. There was no give with the bumper. I'm sore."

"No sign of the bad guys?" asked Lester.

"I think my boy Carlos stopped them in their tracks. He called five minutes ago and said one of them had an outstanding misdemeanor assault charge, so he was able to give him a lecture about how he could run him in and have his ass extradited back to Oregon. Which is all bullshit, Carlos said, since they don't extradite misdemeanors with less than a year's sentence. Carlos told him he'd let him go if the man promised to get out of town as soon as possible. I'm sure they're still looking for you, but at least he and his buddy have no idea where you two are sitting right now."

"I do have one fear," said Lester.

"What's that?" asked Ced.

"I'm thinking they can find my address by running my tag number."

"Doesn't take much work for that. Private companies have databases. Is the car registered to you?"

"That car belonged to my mom. I transferred the title after she died."

"Unless they're idiots, they can find your address," said Ced.

"Even though they didn't look too sharp it's not difficult to run a license plate. There're readers, high-speed cameras mounted on cars, poles that companies can use to build databases. Repo people can buy the info, also police departments. A cop friend told me that. They should be able to find my house. I did park that car in my neighbor's garage, so they might think I'm not there if they can't find the car. And I also moved my kids to the neighbor's house just to be safe."

"Austen," said Ardor.

"What they'll probably do is break into the house to see what they can find," said Lester. "They're looking for you, of course," he said pointing at Ardor.

"The ultimate goal is the money," said Ardor.

"Maybe you should go bring your children here. Y'all can sleep in that garage apartment. No way they can find you here," said Denise.

"I might take you up on that offer. That's very kind of you," said Lester.

"Think about it," said Denise. "You need to convince Lester, Ced. Having the kids there, even at a neighbor's house, is dangerous. There's no danger over here."

"She's right, Lester. Staying here is much safer for your kids, and a few days away from your house might throw them off of you," said Ced.

"Yeah. Let me think about it."

"The sooner you bring them over here the better. Anybody want a beer, a glass of wine?" asked Ced. "I need a drink. That whole scene in the plaza rattled me up."

"Bring me a shot of liquor," said Ardor.

"Yeah, I know all about you, gal," said Ced.

"You know that I'm terrified?

"My cousin was right about you," said Ced.

Ardor looked at Ced, glanced over to Lester, then back to Ced. "What did your cousin say about me?"

"He said you are one of the few women he's ever met that thought like a man."

"I've never been the submissive type, but I don't think men are smarter than women."

Ced smiled.

"Some truth in that," Lester said.

"Let me say this to everyone here, thank you, thank you, thank you," Ardor said as she pointed to all three. "And the dude who was driving that cement truck. And, and the sheriff's deputy."

"I'll bring you a shot," said Lester as he stood up. "What you want?"

"Tequila, if you got it."

"What did you do on that marijuana farm?" asked Lester.

"I was a budtender. That's the job title. I already told you that."

"Yeah, you did. My mind is a wreck right now. Give me a little slack here."

"I hear you. Follow me, Cap'n D.," Ced called out while tapping Lester on the shoulder.

"Cap'n D.?" asked Denise.

"Deathinator," said Ced. "Hospice nurse seems about right."

"Hey, who was the guy driving the cement truck?" asked Lester.

"The son of an old friend of my daddy's. DeeDee was like clockwork. Couldn't have been smoother," said Ced.

"He was perfect," said Lester as he put his right arm around Ced's shoulder.

Ced led the way to the back door of the home.

"You got yourself in a jam, didn't you, girl?" said Denise.

Ardor shook her head, scratched the back of her neck with her left hand, and massaged her temples. "My boyfriend thought we were being ripped off. It's about money; like everything else, it's always about money."

"They think you stole money from them?"

"We didn't steal money, but we did skim some of the weed we grew. We were their growers. At least, my boyfriend was. We'd take the weed and sell it for cash to some local dealers."

"No wonder they're after you."

"They were paying us very little for what we were doing. I'm sure that's not exactly how the company sees what we did."

"And you got a hospice nurse to get you out of this jam?"

"Right? I guess he could be a preacher. I ran into Lester a few days ago and asked him if I could hide out at his house for a few weeks. Then I crossed paths with those two guys at a convenience store not far from Lester's house. That was just rotten luck."

The back door opened; out walked Lester carrying two shot glasses filled with an amber liquid. He stopped at the table and gave one of the shots to Ardor.

"A hospice nurse widower with three kids does look like a good cover for you," Denise said.

"Let me tell you, that man right there," Ardor nodded the shot glass at Lester, "is one hell of a hospice nurse."

"That I do not doubt. And from what I've read, you have job security," said Denise.

"Everybody dies," said Lester.

"Also, people are living longer," said Denise. "Diet, exercise, medical technology, which means a greater demand for hospice care."

"A pitiful truth. A grotesque irony: the better you have lived the worse you may die, which leads to a greater demand for hospice nurses," Lester said.

"The worse you may die?" asked Ardor.

"Yeah, for the very old the end can get mighty ugly. One reason is that you have longer to think about your death, which for many people is extremely depressing."

"I guess we're counterbalancing that right here," said Ardor.

"Okay, I have to tell you this. It's bad news."

"Now what?" asked Ardor.

"I just got a call from Austen when I was in the house. He saw two men walking around my backyard. His description of the two men matched the Oregon boys. Looks like they found me from that fucking tag."

Ardor turned up the shot glass and poured the liquid down her throat. She placed the glass on the tabletop, then clapped her hands together.

"Fuck," she shouted. "What are you gonna do?"

"You're staying here. Ced and I are driving over and ending this chase."

"What? Are you gonna get into a gunfight?" asked Ardor.

"No, just give them some money and send them on their way."

"It better be lots of money," said Ardor.

"We're still deciding on the amount."

"I'm coming with you," said Ardor.

"No, you're not," said Lester.

Ced walked out the back door carrying a glass of wine which he gave to Denise.

"Did you tell Ardor about the call?" he asked.

"Yep. Ardor wants to come with us. I said no."

"Look, they're after me to get the money, so I think they'll be more likely to believe the lie if I'm there with you."

"Believe the lie? What lie?" asked Ced.

"That the money I give them is all the money we made from selling that weed."

"You don't want to give them everything?" asked Ced.

"No. They don't have any idea how much weed we took."

"They certainly don't know how much money you made from selling it," said Lester.

"I just need to make sure they believe me."

"My cousin nailed you," said Ced.

"I didn't fuck your cousin."

"I mean he said you're hard."

"I just don't care what people think about me." Ardor turned to Lester. "I'm coming with you."

"Well," said Lester as he looked at Ced, "I guess you're coming with us."

Lester turned his truck around in Ced's driveway with Ardor sitting next to him. They had left their bags sitting on the backseat in the cab. With Ced following in his El Camino, Lester turned right out of the driveway, this time not worrying about taking back roads. Lester pulled out the packets of cash from under his seat and handed them to Ardor, who placed them on her lap along with the money she had pulled from her suitcase.

Lester glanced at the money.

"How much is all that?"

"Including the ten thousand you brought, that's a little over forty-five thousand. I don't understand why you brought that money. That's what I left for you, not them."

"That's too much money. Thirty-five thousand? Come on, that's a lot of money. Too much money."

"Look, first of all, those dudes from Oregon are at your house. I think there's a good chance they've broken in and are trashing it right now looking for the money. Maybe they found that twenty-five thousand in the bathroom. If so, maybe they take that and leave. If not, then I'll give them ten and say that's all I have. I think they'll take it and go back. And what the fuck is the difference between thirty-five thousand," Ardor held up seven packets of $5000, "and twenty-five thousand?" she said dropping two packets in her lap with the rest of the money.

"A little over fifteen thousand."

Ardor smiled at Lester.

"Is this a trick question?" asked Lester.

"You kill me," she said as she tapped his shoulder with one of the packets. "Don't be crazy; use the money for your kids."

"Okay, I'll take back that ten thousand."

"Thank you," said Ardor as she handed the packets to Lester who slid them back under his seat.

"Let's be clear here. You're not gonna give them all the money you have?"

"Nope, and I've got more in my suitcase. And don't ask me how much. Ten thousand should appease them," said Ardor.

"Okay, so they're in the house. What are you gonna do? Just walk in and hand them a bunch of money. Smile and tell them 'Sorry fellas, here's all that money we made from selling the skimmed weed. We felt we were being screwed, so we took matters into our own hands. No hard feelings?'"

"Your friend Ced has a gun, so maybe he should be our point man. He'll help me make my case."

"You expect to just walk in with a gun pulled? That sounds like instant confrontation," said Lester.

"My guess is that these dudes are all about the money. The guys that own the whole operation are mostly just greed heads, not mobsters. I'm thinking I give them this chunk of money, and they'll leave me and Wade alone."

"And Ced. You know, Ced, the one with the gun who saved us?"

"You're right."

"Don't worry about it. I'll give him this ten thousand."

"No, I'll give him twenty of this." She held up four packets.

"I still want to give him this ten. He deserves it."

"It's your money; whatever you feel good about."

They had stopped at a red light. Ced pulled up and stopped right behind them.

Ardor turned and looked back at Ced. She waved. He waved back. "You think I'm this wild woman who burns down everything she comes in contact with, don't you?"

"No, you're just another fire. A patient told me a few days ago that he was tired of living. The guy is dying, and he's telling me that he wants to die right now. My daughter is full of anxiety because her new best friend is as shallow as a kiddie pool. And Chuck, I don't really know what to do about that." The light turned green. "And I found out a couple of days ago that an old friend's son died suddenly. They found him dead in his bed. Just bam, their son is dead. They haven't determined the cause of death yet. Oh, and our dog Georgia, she is covered with tumors. The kids don't know yet, haven't had the heart to tell them. She needs to be put down in the next few weeks."

Ardor looked at Lester but didn't say a word.

They pulled up to another red light.

"Look, sure, you're a free spirit, but being a free spirit is a luxury. Most people have flames licking their feet."

Ardor stood on her knees in the seat, leaned over, and kissed Lester on the cheek.

Lester shook his head. "I'm sorry for going off like that."

"No, you're right; I get that. I'm gonna get you out of this mess."

Lester pushed a few buttons on his phone.

"Hey," he said.

"We good?" asked Ced.

"Yeah, I was just thinking. When we get to my house, why don't we park in front of my next-door neighbor's house, so we don't draw attention to ourselves?"

"That's fine. Are we close now?"

"No more than ten to fifteen minutes away. Just stay behind me."

Ardor reached down and gathered all the cash. She counted out the money for the two men, then placed the rest under her seat. Lester pulled the truck to the side of the road.

"What are you doing? I'm not giving these freaks any more than this."

Lester looked in his rearview mirror.

"Ambulance."

Ardor turned around to see Ced also pull off to the side of the road. A couple hundred yards in the distance, an ambulance sped toward them. The siren's wail slowly worked its way into the truck. After a few more seconds, the ambulance made it past both parked vehicles.

"Maybe we should just grab your kids, then drive back over to Ced's house."

"Or," said Lester, "maybe we should kill those guys and bury them out in the country." He slowly pulled back onto the road.

"I like it. Take the fight to them," said Ardor.

"I had a feeling you'd say that," said Lester.

"No, the truth is I'm not a murdering kind of gal."

"You just break hearts."

"Ohhh, now it comes out, your version of the unvarnished truth."

"Just repeating what I've heard," said Lester. "I'll admit that it's mostly rumor, just grapevine shit and sad tales from dudes whose hearts you've broken."

"Most guys I've dumped deserved it."

"Everybody says that."

"I still don't understand how you deal with the dying."

"It's not as dramatic when you deal with it every day."

"Right, right."

"Let me tell you something, you want to learn how to live? Then live with the dying," said Lester.

He called Ced again, hoping a brief conversation on the speakerphone would help settle their nerves.

"We close?"

"Five minutes. Hey, Ced, we're both beginning to shake here. I don't know, man."

"Pull over at that station."

"The one on the right here?"

"Yeah, I want to talk to you two."

Lester turned into the station and parked to the right of the little store, Ced parking to his right. He popped out of the El Camino, then walked up to the back passenger door.

"Whatcha got?" Lester asked.

"Unlock the door," said Ced. He grabbed the handle of the back door, waited for Lester to flip the switch. When he heard the click Ced opened the door, slid the bags over, and said, "This is one beautiful night" as he entered the truck and sat down with a grin on his face. He leaned forward and patted both of them on the shoulder.

"Hey now, you two look like you're going to your execution. We good here, folks. Ain't nothin' gonna happen. You're gonna give them money; right, pretty girl?" He reached over with both hands and began to massage Ardor's shoulders.

"Yes, I'm giving them some money," said Ardor.

"If you don't mind my askin', how much you givin'em?"

"Ten thousand."

"That's good. That's good. Now if they've broken into the house, you could call the police, Lester. That would solve the problem for tonight."

"But they'd keep comin' for me," said Ardor.

"Yeah, I think that's right. Givin' 'em some money right now might put an end to this chase."

"And we're giving you thirty for all your help." She handed him four packs then Lester reached under the seat for the other two packs.

"Here," he said as he handed the packs to Ced.

Ced looked at the money in his hands. "All right. I didn't work alone. The others will get theirs."

"Let's just end this as fast as we can," said Lester.

"Okay, tell me what you two think of this. You walk up first, Lester, since it's your house. You have a legitimate reason to confront them. Ardor will be behind you. I'll be in the rear with my gun in my jacket pocket and my finger around the trigger."

"What if they pull guns and start shooting?" asked Ardor.

"I don't think they'll want to do that. They want to jack you up for the money; they're not here to commit murder. And they surely don't want the police to be after them, especially after Carlos got into their shit. Give them the money, then tell 'em it's all you got. The key is going to be how you explain that this money is all the cash. They'll have to know you're keeping some for yourself, so the amount you're givin' 'em has to be enough for them not to care. They'll probably skim a little for themselves, give the owners a few thousand. Everybody takes a slice. Just make sure your little speech is the real deal."

"I'll give it every ounce of lying I got. I'll leave it all on the field, coach," said Ardor.

"Look," Ced said as he popped his head upright, "you're trying to convince these two chumps who are strangers. This should be a layup for someone with your skills."

"You got to act like you believe it," said Lester.

"Yeah," said Ardor.

"You got this."

"I got this."

"Do you think she should apologize for stealing the weed?" asked Lester.

"No. They don't give a shit. Just don't give 'em a reason to think you're still holding lots of cash." Ced patted Ardor on the shoulder.

"I need a beer," said Lester.

"Fuck me," yelled Ardor.

"Yeah, Lester, go in and get us three beers," said Ced.

"Tall boys," said Ardor.

"I'll be quick," said Lester.

He exited the truck and walked to the front of the store.

"Listen to me, Ardor. This ain't nothin'. They just need some money to take back to Oregon. The tension will ease down when you start handing out the money."

A few minutes later, Lester walked around the corner of the store and up to the truck carrying a plastic sack. He gave the parking lot a quick scan and noticed five white dogs standing at the back corner of the building. They were small dogs running back and forth at each other. Very playful. Suddenly they stopped, turned, looked at Lester. They didn't move for several seconds, then they quickly ran around the back of the building.

Lester sat back down in the truck and placed the bag on the seat next to Ardor. "Did you see those white dogs over there?" He pointed to the edge of the building.

Ardor and Ced looked over to where he pointed.

"I didn't see anything," said Ardor.

"No, I didn't see any dogs," said Ced.

"Why do I keep seeing white dogs look at me like I'm Satan?"

"The devil is all over you, man," said Ced.

"You have been chosen by the Prince of Darkness. I noticed that right off when we met in that greenhouse," said Ardor.

Ardor pulled out a beer from the bag, opened it, and took several long swallows. She brought the can back down and deeply belched.

"There you go," said Ced.

"God, I needed that."

"I've never heard a woman burp like that," he said.

"Ardor ain't no woman. She's a warrior," said Lester.

"I mean just *like* a man," said Ced.

"Fuck you both," said Ardor, then tipped up the beer nearly finishing it off. She belched again, this time longer and deeper.

"Hell, let's do this," said Lester as he lifted the can to his lips. He tilted his head and poured the beer down his throat. When he finished he crushed the can with both hands and threw it on the floorboard by Ardor's feet.

"No way I can drink beer like that." Ced took long swallows of beer and let out a short, deep burp. "It gets in my nose." When he raised the beer to his lips again, he noticed Lester reach out with his right hand and grab Ardor's left hand.

"Don't worry," Lester whispered to Ardor. She nodded.

Ced finished his beer, dropped the can to the floorboard, and said, "Up my damn nose." He stepped out of the truck and walked to where he stood next to the hood. He looked at them both, then slapped the hood, smiled, and walked back to his El Camino.

After driving ten minutes in silence, Lester and Ardor pulled up and parked in front of Austen's house, the car facing his home. Ced parked directly behind them. Ardor stuck the money in her purse, then stepped out of the truck and walked with Lester back to the front of Ced's El Camino.

Ardor pointed at a car parked in Lester's driveway. "There's the Infinity," she said.

"Showtime," said Ced as he stepped up to where they stood. He pulled a pistol out from behind his back, made sure a round was in the chamber. "Only if needed."

"I'm first but let's change the order. Since you have the gun, why don't you, Ced, follow me. They're after Ardor, so let's give her a buffer for protection. She'll tuck in right behind you."

"A much better plan," said Ardor.

"My first thought was to give you the gun and let you lead," said Lester.

"Only if I had a bazooka," said Ardor.

"Let's make it quick. Give them the money and tell them to leave," said Lester.

Ced and Ardor nodded. They walked down the street until they came to Lester's driveway where they turned and began the walk to the house. As they passed the Infinity, Ardor said, "Fuckers."

Lester looked over to Austen's house. He noticed the light over the side door was on, but inside the home seemed to be completely dark. He stopped when he drew even with his house, the other two stopping behind him. He looked into the side windows, then the backyard. Lights seemed to be on throughout the house, but no one was spotted outside nor inside the home. After a couple of minutes, the three of them walked to the back gate and stopped. The backyard was quiet and motionless. Lester leaned over the fence to have a better view of the back door. Georgia was lying down facing the back door gnawing on a bone. The light above the door was on but no one was in sight.

"We'll go in the back door," he whispered to the other two.

Both nodded. In single file, they slowly walked through the gate and to the back door. When Georgia saw them, she grabbed the bone and quickly trotted to Lester. The door stood open a few inches. Splintered wood littered the doorway. Lester stroked the dog's head and back.

"Now what?" whispered Lester.

"Just walk in and ask them what they're doing in your house," whispered Ced. He pulled the gun from his jacket, looked at it, then crammed it back into the pocket.

Lester nodded, and looked at Ardor who nodded back. "Let's go." He grabbed the doorknob, paused, took a deep breath, then eased the door open and entered the house with the other two following behind him. Ardor blocked Georgia from entering the house and pushed the door to the broken door jamb. They slowly entered the kitchen and stopped. Most of the lights in the kitchen and great room were on, but there was no one in sight. A noise came from the hallway around the left side of the house where the bedrooms were located. Drawers were being pulled open, then closing.

Lester looked at the other two and pulled his hands up to chest level, palms up in a questioning gesture. Ced nodded, then pointed toward the hallway. As they began walking to the hallway, one of the men suddenly appeared from around the corner. He stopped, crouched, and with one fluid motion pulled a pistol from behind him. He pointed the gun at Ardor.

"If any of you have a gun I want it on that table right there," the man said, pointing at the coffee table. The man was short, five foot six at most, and sported a bushy mustache. The three of them stood motionless.

"I said put your fucking guns on the coffee table."

"We don't have any guns," said Ardor.

"I don't believe that."

"We'd have to create guns out of thin air. Who the fuck are you, and what are you doing in my house?" asked Lester.

"I believe Ardor can tell you who we are and what we are doing here. Can't you, Ardor? Give us the money, and we'll leave."

"Leave them out of it. This is between y'all and me."

"Fair enough, let's see the money."

Ardor opened her purse and pulled out the packs of cash. She held it up to the man, then threw the money on the coffee table.

"How much is it?" asked the man.

"Over fifteen thousand."

"That's all you have?"

"That's it."

The man walked up to the coffee table. As he reached for the money Ced pulled the gun out of his jacket pocket and pointed it right at the man's face. The man froze in motion.

"You were right; we did have a gun. Put your gun on the table."

The man, still frozen, looked at Ced.

"I hope you're not thinking that I won't shoot you. That idea will get you shot," said Ced.

The man placed the gun on the table.

"Good choice," said Ced.

Ardor quickly grabbed the gun off the table and pointed it at the man.

"Just take the money and leave," said Ardor. "No one gets hurt; just tell Hale and the rest of those fuckers in Oregon that's all we took. And tell them we skimmed the weed because they fucked us with the slave pay. Hell, we deserve lots more than this."

The man picked up the cash and quickly counted it. "I don't believe this is all you've got." He walked into the kitchen and threw the money on the kitchen table.

"I don't care if you believe me, but that's all I got," said Ardor.

"I don't believe you," said a voice behind them in the kitchen. The other man, also short, wore a baby blue cardigan and khaki pants. He pointed a gun at Ardor's head.

Everyone turned to the man standing in the back of the kitchen. He nodded the gun as he said, "I want to thank you for saving us the trouble of finding you again. You are a slippery girl."

"Where the hell did you come from?" asked Lester.

"In the pantry," said the man. His hair was pulled back into a short ponytail. "You two give my partner your guns." Ced and Ardor handed their guns to the other man.

"Will you please not point that gun at me? The baby blue cardigan and khakis are a nice ensemble, but fuck, man, you need to check your manners," said Ardor.

"They said you probably had at least fifty thousand," said Mustache.

"Are you an idiot? Why did you tell her that?" asked Cardigan.

"I don't have fifty thousand dollars. That's it; that's all I got."

"Where is Wade?" asked Cardigan.

"That is all the money that we have," said Ardor.

"Where is he?" asked Cardigan again.

"I know you won't believe this, but he has cancer. He's dying."

Cardigan and Mustache looked at one another. They shook their heads.

Cardigan looked back at Ardor. "You want us to believe that your boyfriend is dying of cancer. What type of cancer?"

"Nose cancer."

Cardigan laughed. "Nose cancer? Are you sure it's not dick cancer? How about tongue cancer."

"The cancer has spread into his brain. He's dying," said Ardor.

"I don't believe that garbage," said Cardigan. He looked to his partner. "Go get the dog."

"The dog? What are you going to do with my dog?" asked Lester.

Mustache walked by Ardor, Lester, and Ced, then through the kitchen to the back door.

"If your friend here doesn't cough up more money, then we're going to kill your dog," said Cardigan.

"What the fuck? You fucking fuck," said Ardor.

"Does that mean you are going to give us all the money you stole?"

"It's okay, Ardor," said Lester.

"It's not okay," she replied.

Georgia trotted into the kitchen with Mustache following behind her. She stopped next to Lester, her tail wagging wildly.

"No, it's okay, really. Like I told you earlier, Georgia has cancer; she needs to be put down anyway."

"Really?" said Ced. "That's some sad shit."

"The dog has cancer, too?" replied Cardigan. He rolled his eyes. "Who doesn't have cancer?"

"I don't have cancer," said Lester. "You'd have to ask the other two."

"Not that I know of," said Ced.

"The only cancer I have is you two. You're both killing me," said Ardor.

Cardigan looked at the dog. "Just ... take the dog out of here," he told Mustache.

"Come on, girl," said Mustache. "I wasn't looking forward to killing this dog, I can tell you that." He led the dog out the back door and quickly returned.

"Get a knife, a big knife from the kitchen," said Cardigan. "We're going to start cutting fingers off. See if that can persuade you to give us all the money."

"You've seen too many mob movies," said Ardor. "Cutting fingers will get you nowhere since I don't have any more money."

"I'll guess we'll see about that," said Cardigan.

Mustache pulled out a small cleaver from one of the kitchen drawers.

"Bring a dishtowel; this will be a little bloody," said Cardigan.

Mustache draped a black dishtowel across his shoulder from a rack by the sink, stuck one of the pistols in a back pocket, and stepped over carrying the knife and other pistol to where Ardor stood.

"Where should we do this? On the coffee table here?"

"That's fine," said Cardigan. "I want you to hold her hand down," he said to Ced.

"I don't think I can do that," said Ced.

"I'm not asking you. I'm telling you."

"What are you gonna do if I don't?"

"I'll put a bullet in her leg."

"I guess you'll have to do that," said Ced. "I ain't holding the girl's hand down so you can cut a finger off."

"Suit yourself," said Cardigan. He aimed his pistol at Ardor's right leg. "This is going to hurt a little bit."

"If you do that then I'm going to shoot you in the stomach and that's going to hurt a lot," said Marlin, Lester's neighbor, as he walked into the kitchen with a shotgun pointed at Cardigan. Marlin sported a long gray ponytail, a navy-blue baseball cap with an orange AU, blue jeans, a Boston T-shirt with its guitar-shaped spaceship, and a black pair of flip-flops.

"Who are *you*?" asked Cardigan.

"I'm a neighbor. A friendly neighbor."

"That's true; you are friendly," said Lester.

"You, fella, put your weapons on the kitchen table by the money," Marlin said to Mustache.

Mustache placed both guns and the cleaver on the kitchen table.

"Yours, too," he said to Cardigan.

Cardigan walked up and placed the pistol on the table, then stepped back.

"Marlin, you are a sight for sore eyes," said Lester.

"These boys snooping around your backdoor seemed a little fishy. Then I saw 'em break in and I thought, *Hell fire, what in Lord's name is going on here?* I couldn't think of a good reason why they'd be creeping around your house. A good man, a widow man, doing right, raising three children by himself, and these two sorry fellas knocking your backdoor in? That's just rude behavior. I don't have a lot of tolerance for rude people, you know?"

"Did you call the police?" asked Ardor.

"I was about to, almost started pushing buttons on my phone, but I had to take a whiz and when I finished, I walked by the kitchen and grabbed a beer. Then I got caught up in a song, Queen's "Fat Bottomed Girls," and I started telling Mary about how I saw them up in Nashville in '78, right after their *Jazz* album came out, believe it was right before Thanksgiving. That ticket only cost me eight dollars. Can you believe it, eight dollars, to see Queen?! So, one thing leads to another, and I got lost in all that."

"Of course, you did," said Lester.

"When the song finally ended, I made it back to one of the windows in my den to see you three enter the house, so I thought I'd come over to make sure things were in hand. I brought my shotgun to encourage these two cat burglars to apologize for their rude behavior."

"You saw Queen in Nashville? Damn," said Ardor.

"You're a damn good neighbor," said Ced.

"Oh, hell yeah, Freddie, man, that voice booming all over the arena. And that's the night I realized he was a gay fella. He came out wearing shiny black pants with suspenders and no shirt. What the hell, right?"

"We don't have to call the police. We can settle this like civilized people," said Ardor.

"Are ya sure? Sounded like this one here," he pointed at Cardigan, "was about to put a bullet in your leg."

"I was only trying to apply pressure to this young lady. She and her boyfriend stole quite a bit of money from our employer out in Oregon. My partner and I were sent here to bring back the stolen funds."

Marlin looked at Cardigan for a moment, then brought his gaze to Mustache.

"Ain't that a lawyer way to put things, almost like you're in a courtroom. Damn shame we're all standing here in Lester's kitchen where you trying to lawyer-up the situation just don't gain no traction."

"We've crossed paths with these fellas a couple of times tonight, and they've been rude both times," said Lester. "Just ugly dispositions."

Marlin nodded his head. "Why don't y'all each grab a gun there to make sure these two rude gentlemen remain courteous?"

Ced grabbed his gun from the table. Lester lifted the bigger one, and Ardor picked up the other gun and cleaver.

"I should cut your dick off," Ardor said to Cardigan. "His little story about why they're chasing me is a simple tale for simpletons. Anybody here a simpleton?" She looked around the room. "Besides you two." She pointed the gun and knife at both Mustache and Cardigan. "The story is lot more complex than your little Thomas the Tank Engine narrative."

"Do you want me to stay until they leave here?" asked Marlin.

Ardor and Ced looked at Lester.

"No," said Lester, "even though I don't believe we'll be all hugs and kisses when they do leave, I think they'll leave in peace. I'm pretty sure I can speak for all of us when I say your intervention is much appreciated. I agree with Ced: you're a damn fine neighbor, Marlin. I owe you one, my friend."

Ced kept his gun pointed at the two men but turned his head to look at Marlin. "I want to thank you, Queen, and your bladder. And that shotgun. Why don't you two," Ced pointed at the two men, "sit down on the floor and put your hands behind your head? Up against the wall over there. I think everyone would feel safer and happier if you did that."

Lester nodded. "Don't worry, you two; you'll soon be leaving with money in your pockets."

Ardor pointed the knife at Marlin's shirt. "What's your favorite Boston song?"

"'Long Time,' darlin'."

"I knew it. Most Southern dudes love the hell out of that song. Don't worry about us. I'm giving these boys all the money I have. Happy faces all around."

"They hunt you down like a dog, threaten you with a gun, and you're still giving them all the money you have. I don't *even* want to know the details; it's already pissin' me off. I'll leave y'all to it. Mary was loadin' up the bong when I was walking out the door," said Marlin, then turned and walked out of the kitchen.

"Look," Ardor said to the two men, "Wade and I knew they were taking advantage of us, not paying us what we were worth, especially since we were the ones responsible for growing such big plants full of buds. Wade more than me, of course. He's a horticulturist, don't you know? We skimmed a little weed, sold it, then split. And Wade really does have cancer. Things ain't looking too good for him. Just take all that money, leave, and never come back. I can't give you more money because I don't have any more money."

Cardigan looked at the money. "I still think you have more money."

Ced walked over to where the two men sat on the floor. He pointed the gun at Cardigan's face. "Take the money. Walk out the door. Get in your car and drive to Oregon. Or do we need me to call the police?"

Cardigan looked at Ced's gun, then into Ced's eyes. After a couple of moments, he turned to look at Mustache, then looked back to Ardor.

"What the fuck is up with your thumb, man?" Ardor asked as she pointed to Mustache's hands that were laced together on top of his head.

The man didn't respond.

"Your thumb, it's huge. Like circus big. Not trying to be rude, but what the fuck is up with your thumb?"

The man stuck his hand forward almost like a cop signaling to stop traffic, revealing his right thumb that was several times the size of a normal thumb. "I had a problem growing up, couldn't stop sucking my thumb. My mother tried everything: taping it, soaking it with hot sauce, putting a cast on it. I didn't stop sucking on it until I was in high school."

"You were embarrassed?" Ardor asked.

"No, just decided I didn't want to do it anymore. Of course, by then I had deformed it."

"I bet you've pleased a lady or two with that magic thumb," said Ardor.

"My wife likes my thumb," said Mustache. "A lot."

"Oh, for fuck's sake. Okay, we'll take the money and leave," said Cardigan. He stood up, walked over to the table, picked up the packs of cash, and stuffed them in the front pockets of his khaki pants.

Mustache asked, "Can we have our guns back?"

"Hell no," said Ardor. She pointed the gun right at Cardigan's head. "Just fucking leave, ok?"

"Please unload them and give them back," Cardigan said. "Do that and you'll never see us again. I promise you that."

"What do you think, Ced?" asked Lester.

"First, why don't you call the police and tell them someone broke into your house? They'll come over and investigate, probably dust for fingerprints, then file a report. Your prints," he pointed at Cardigan and Mustache, "should motivate you to travel back to Oregon. And if there is any hint that you two have not left, then I'm sure Marlin will talk to the police about seeing you two breakin' in. We have your tag number, so that'll help them track your asses down. Sound good?"

Both men nodded.

Lester unloaded his gun and gave it to Mustache. Ardor gave Lester her gun and watched him unload that one. He gave it to Cardigan.

"You got any duct tape?" asked Ced.

Lester pulled open a drawer, then grabbed a roll of duct tape and handed it to Ced.

"Give me your guns," said Ced. The men gave him their guns, then watched Ced as he wrapped each gun a few dozen times with the tape. He handed the guns back to Cardigan.

"I'll follow you two to your car so I can wave goodbye," said Ced. "Gonna miss you two. While I'm gone, call the police," he told Lester.

"Nice meeting you two gentlemen. Perhaps if I'm ever up in Oregon, I'll look you up so we can grab a beer and catch up," said Lester.

"I hope you two rot in hell," said Ardor.

The two men looked at one another without saying a word. Cardigan tucked the taped guns under the front of his cardigan.

"Come on, boys" said Ced, "The journey of a thousand miles starts with the first step."

"Tootles," said Ardor.

Cardigan and Mustache walked out the back door with Ced a few steps behind.

"Hate to see you rush off, but we understand; you've got to get back home," said Lester.

As the men walked out the back door, Ardor said to Lester, "I think we need to listen to 'Fat Bottomed Girls."

FRESH AIR

"DOES IT HAVE to be tonight?" asked Lester.

"The house is way out in the country, just a few miles past Otis's house. I really need someone to check on him this evening. And you're already out that way," said Jenny Lynn.

"So just check on the patient," Lester said as he drove down the two-lane country road a few minutes from where he would turn onto Otis's driveway.

"Right. A good family, just sweethearts, dealing with their world turned upside down. They opened him up hoping they could cut out most of the cancer in the liver, but it's spread all over his organs, so they closed him up and gave him a few months tops."

"And there's a PITA situation?"

"No, no, I wasn't clear. They *were* a pain in the ass before, at least that's what I heard from Becky, but that was the initial anger. Like many, he reacted to the bad news with unbridled rage, striking out at everyone and everything. Becky said that now they're just numb, trying to figure things out. The man is the patriarch of the family in the truest sense of the word. A venerable old cuss who's suddenly a short-timer. She thinks they're just stunned with what they're gonna do without him."

"When did they find out?"

"The operation was about a week ago. He's in a lot of pain, so he's on morphine. He jokes that he sees a little man flying around the room."

"Okay, I'll go see him," said Lester.

"Now, these are country folks, Lester. So have an open mind. Good people, here, gold, but be prepared for ..." Jenny Lynn paused, "for some simple ways of livin'."

"What do you mean, like an outhouse?" asked Lester.

"No, lord no, can't remember the last time I saw an outhouse."

"They're still out there, saw some a few weeks ago," said Lester.

"Where?"

"Out there around Skyline and, what's that little place north, uh, Hytop. There's lots of land with very few people. Real mountain people up there, just away from everything. Hillbillies, in a good way."

"What were you doing out there?"

"With a friend, we were taking the kids out to look around. Beautiful country, gorgeous, gorgeous, just isolated. We were planning on hiking to the Walls of Jericho, but we lost track of time taking side roads, got too late on us. Quite a few people out there mostly living off the land," said Lester.

"Right, they look at the world a little different from most. I feel like I don't even need to tell you this. You know country folks."

"Yeah, Jenny Lynn, been around country people all my life. Like a lot of people, I got country folks all in my roots. If you're Southern, you got some country in you. How are they with hospice?"

"At first, they hated it, were mad at everything, especially people who were babbling about helping them come to terms with the approaching death. They see it as giving up and giving in. Becky said she was out there a couple days ago, and they seemed to have turned the corner on all that anger, seemed to be open to the idea of welcoming the help. It's the wife, according to Becky, who's realized what's in store down the road. Good people, though. And they're big."

"Big?"

"Big folks. Probably the biggest family you'll ever run across."

"Okay. Well, you know I was all worried about Otis before I met him, but we hit it off from the very first moment we met. I can handle big country people."

"That's what I like to hear. You'll do fine. Good luck, and let me know if you have any problems."

Lester sat in his idling truck that he parked in Otis's driveway, lying on his back in the front seat, his legs straight out facing the passenger door. He had just spent over an hour in the bedroom talking to Otis, Lilly, and Lee Ellen on what to expect when death is near, which seemed to be close for Otis. Lilly and Lee Ellen stood crying on each side of his bed; Lester stood beside Lilly. Otis was stoic. He listened intently as Lester explained the process of dying, nodding at the unvarnished details of what lay ahead. He let his friend and niece cry themselves out for several minutes before he spoke.

"Now we've been through this, you two. This is inevitable, and it's about to happen. Right, Lester?"

"The signs seem to point that way, Otis. It's not absolute, though."

"Right, right, I'm circling the drain here, you two. I need you to be strong, not just for me but for yourselves, for when I'm gone."

"You can't expect us to take this in stride, Uncle Otis. That's just not gonna be possible." Lee Ellen was trying to blink through her tears. "Tell him, Lilly. Tell him we can't pretend this is gonna be like changing a flat tire."

Lilly laughed. "Lee Ellen's right, Otis. We want to be strong for you. We really do. You know that, but this is not gonna be easy. Sure to God you understand that."

Otis looked at the floor, eyes fixed. "I know that," he said.

The two women continued to cry, dabbing at the tears with Kleenex pulled from one of the boxes located all over the house.

Otis drank a few swallows of water from a glass sitting on the bedside table. When he placed the glass back onto the table, he turned to look at Lilly. Lester felt intrusive as he saw the two old friends stare into one another's eyes, now slick as glass. But he didn't look away. He couldn't; he was drawn to the intimate moment, the human moment between two people who deeply care for one another. Otis turned to Lester with what looked like a tiny smile and a few short nods before he looked over at Lee Ellen whose tears now rolled down her cheeks and dripped off her chin.

Otis squeezed Lee Ellen's hand. "Hey, it's okay. I'm gonna be okay. And so will you."

Lester let out a big sigh and draped his right arm across his face. Someone tapped the driver-side door window. Lester quickly popped up to see Lilly looking at him with a blank expression. He rolled down the window.

"Are you okay, Lester?" she asked.

"Yeah, I'm fine. Just wanted to rest for a moment or two before I left. Nothing to worry about, just been a long day. Hope that's okay."

"I certainly understand that. Just wanted to make sure you weren't in any trouble out here. Saw the truck but couldn't see you anywhere. Anyways, thanks for being here. You made this horrid situation much better."

"I know this stage can be very hard on the family, but he's one tough guy. He wants to put y'all at ease."

"Lee Ellen and I are both trying to be strong here, but that's nearly impossible."

Lester noticed her bloodshot eyes, tears on the brink of flowing down her cheeks again.

"Just be with him, follow his lead. And," Lester reached out and squeezed Lilly's arm, "call me for anything you need. Even if you just want to talk. Okay?"

Lilly nodded. "Thank you." She squeezed his arm just above the elbow, then stepped back.

Lester put the truck in reverse and slowly began backing out of the driveway as they waved at one another.

Lester drove down the two-lane country road following the directions of the GPS on his phone. The darkness of the rural landscape seemed endless; the only light besides the occasional passing car and porch lights came from the stars that stretched across the cloudless sky. The dark landscape at once lonely, vacant, chilling, and warm. The mundane giving way to the sublime.

He rounded a curve in the road that was dense with trees, mostly pine and oak. The GPS told him that the address was up ahead on the right. He slowed the truck to a crawl and spotted a driveway and a mailbox to the right. He studied the stuck-on address numbers missing one digit. This was the address. He turned onto the driveway, the gravel slowly crunching beneath his tires as he drove down the narrow road. The drive wound through a copse of trees at least one hundred yards thick. He noticed a light through the trees and brush, then suddenly came to a clearing where a two-story wooden house stood, a front porch stretching from corner to corner to just past the front door. Two cars and two trucks were parked on a large concrete parking pad to the left of the house. Floodlights from the house and a couple of poles lit the parking area and another light shined by the front door, which was in the middle of the large porch. Smoke rose from a chimney standing left of the front door. Lester parked behind one of the pickup trucks, turned off the motor, and sat for a moment. He looked the house over, a farmhouse that seemed to be a hybrid between a Craftsman and a Victorian. He turned on the cab light and read through the text that Jenny Lynn had sent him earlier in the day.

"Ross Pugh," he said to himself. The number "63" sat next to the name. "Farmer," he said out loud.

He turned off the light, grabbed his leather satchel, stepped from the truck, walked over the concrete parking area, and then over grey flat stones that lead to the front steps. He looked around, thinking he'd find fields somewhere, maybe a tractor or two. But all he saw was a house in the middle of a small clearing lit by floodlights pointing out from the corners of the house and a few poles, two acres, maybe three surrounded by trees in all directions. He stepped onto the porch and walked to the front door. There wasn't a doorbell or a doorknocker, so he rapped the front door three times and waited several seconds before he knocked again, this time five knocks instead of three. Still no response, no sound.

He stepped back to see if he could see anyone through the window to the left of the front door. Through a gap in the drawn curtains he spotted four people: a middle-aged man covered with a red and blue patch quilt lying back in a black recliner, asleep, Ross Pugh he assumed; to the man's right sat a middle-aged woman on a sofa wearing navy blue slacks and a red sweater with a stitched brown reindeer topped with a bright red nose, also asleep; on the same sofa sat a young woman, late twenties maybe early thirties, who wore blue jeans, a crimson sweat shirt with "BAMA" written in white letters and a crimson toboggan cap, a white "BAMA" shining from the turned-up bottom flap; and just to the left of Ross Pugh sat a young man, looking a few years younger than the young woman, sitting in a brown leather club chair, also wearing jeans, a red and black plaid lumberjack button-down shirt, his right hand resting on the older man's left arm. The family *was* huge, just like Jenny Lynn had said; "big-boned" came to mind. Barrel trunks and limbs like bears. Most of the lights in the room seemed to be on, but he couldn't see another soul.

Lester stepped back to the front door and knocked once again, this time six hard raps followed by a low shout, "Hello, anybody home? Hello."

He waited a few seconds before returning to the window for another peek. There was no movement from the four. Foul play flashed across Lester's mind as he sought the slightest movement from any of the four, perhaps a chest rising and falling. He thought he saw the daughter's "BAMA" moving, but he couldn't be sure from this distance. He walked back to the door, pushed down the finger lever, and was surprised when the door opened. While holding the handle with his right hand he pushed open the door with his left, at first six inches and then a foot.

"Hello, I'm Lester Gordon, a hospice nurse," he called out. He could see all four of them, but again there was no movement. "Hello, excuse me, hello." Nothing.

Lester pushed the door all the way open and stepped inside. Suddenly, a wave of a pungent sour odor slapped him in the face. He quickly looked around the room searching for the stink's source. The room seemed filled with the detritus of everyday living, coats and shoes, empty glasses and coffee cups, a bowl on the coffee table filled with nuts and citrus. His gaze finally made it back to the four people he had seen through the window. His first observation had not been flawed; these bodies were the only ones in the room. A flat-screen television was on over the mantel where a fire still burned in the fireplace. Lester looked at the screen and immediately recognized a scene. George Clooney was explaining that he's a Dapper Dan man. Lester walked a few steps closer to the four bodies hoping to see any sign of life. He walked up to within just a few feet of the two men, father and son. Much to his relief, he saw their chests rising and falling. He placed the satchel on the floor and then whispered, "Thank god."

The foul odor suddenly gave way to a stench of rotten sewage. He stepped back and placed his left hand over his nose.

"Oh my lord," he said.

Next came a long gurgling from the direction of the son. Lester looked to see if the son had awakened, but while he studied the young man's closed eyes he heard rumbles from the mother and daughter side of the room.

Lester shook his head and gave the four faces a quick glance, looking to see if any of them were crawling out of their slumber. And again, nothing. For the first time, he noticed a dining table in the back of the room next to the kitchen; the overhead room light switched off provided dark cover for the plates and serving dishes containing food. There seemed to be a ham, a bowl of potato salad, a casserole of some sort, and a wicker basket half-filled with rolls. He noticed an undercurrent of aromas from these dishes.

Lester looked at the faces again, still no movement. After a moment, he noticed the father's left hand clasped around the son's right forearm. He considered turning off the television, like it would be the polite thing to do, but he reconsidered, thinking to leave the home as he found it. He grabbed his satchel and scanned the faces one more time, then walked back to the front door, stepped out, locking and gently closing the door behind him. He stood at the edge of the porch next to the guardrail for a couple minutes, surveying the grounds once again. A biting wind swayed the limbs of the surrounding trees. To the left in a clump of pines he heard an animal run through the brush, the distance too far for him to clearly identify the type of animal. A deer most likely, he thought. He then walked to his truck, placed the satchel in the passenger front seat, then cranked the engine. He gave a one-note giggle. Lester sat looking at the trees behind the house as the truck idled, the heater slowly warmed.

He pulled his phone from the satchel and thought about calling Jenny Lynn, but he decided to text her instead.

Hey, just now leaving the Pugh place. Good people.

He backed up the truck, then began a wide sweeping turn to his left, the pad easily wide enough for a U-Turn. He saw a small animal walking at the edge of the woods in back of the house and stopped to shine his lights toward the animal.

"Gotta be a deer," he said to himself.

Jenny Lynn answered the text.

They doing okay?

I think they're fine. Quite a night.

What do you mean?

Nothing bad, everything's fine. Will tell you about it tomorrow.

He watched the silhouette move along the line of trees.

Now I'm curious. Call me first thing.

"What the fuck?" Lester asked himself. The animal emerged and walked into the yard. A white dog, bushy like a poodle, the size of a standard poodle. It stopped, turned its head from the house, then looked right at Lester's truck. Lester put the truck in park, first thinking he'd get out and walk up to the animal. But the longer he waited, the less likely such an act would happen. He looked at the dog without moving, like the two of them were in a staring match, just waiting for the other to blink. For five minutes this stare-down endured, Lester waiting for the dog to do something—run off, walk up to his truck, bark—but the animal almost seemed frozen.

"That's enough of that," Lester whispered to himself. He gave his horn a couple quick pops. The dog didn't move. He opened his door and stood up to look over the cab at the dog. "Get on, now," he hollered at the dog. The dog turned its head and looked at the woods, then back to Lester. "Well, maybe you live here. And if that's the case, then please accept my apology." He sat back down and closed the door. Suddenly, four more white dogs walked out of the woods and stood behind the first dog. "Well, I'll be damned," whispered Lester. The dogs looked like they had been looking for him and finally found him. He frowned, then smiled and shifted the truck into drive, gave the dogs one more look, and finished making the U-turn. As he began the drive back to the main road, he looked in his rearview mirror and spotted what seemed to be all of the white dogs standing on the front porch and looking intently at Lester as he drove away.

IT HAPPENS TO US ALL

"WHERE DID you learn this? Who taught you about gambling?" asked Jase.

"Everybody gambles," said Chuck.

"No, everyone does not gamble," said Jase.

"You're a gambler?" asked Lizzy.

"Lizzy doesn't gamble," said Jase.

"Lizzy gambles all the time. She just doesn't know it's gambling," said Chuck.

"Dad? He's not even in high school," said Jase.

"I understand your concern, Jase, but I think Chuck is just having some fun."

"Dad, he's taking money from kids in the neighborhood from football bets," said Jase.

"Just on Alabama games," said Chuck.

"He's using point spreads, like he's in Las Vegas."

"Well, you *can* become addicted to gambling," said Lester. "I've known a few gambling addicts. Not pretty. They get all crazy in the eyes."

"See, you're gonna turn into an addict," Jase said to Chuck.

"You should try to have some fun, Jase. A little gambling would do you some good."

"He's acting like a ... a ... what are the people call who take your bets?"

"Bookies, they're called bookies," said Lester. He looked over to his left where Lizzy sat at the kitchen table. "How's the burger, Lizzy?"

"It's delicious, Dad," said Lizzy.

"And Lizzy doesn't gamble. Don't drag our little sister into your dark life of gambling," said Jase.

"She bets all the time," said Chuck.

"I do?"

"You bet me all the time that you can hold your breath under water longer than I can."

"That's not gambling," said Jase.

"And she'll bet you right now that she can outstare you. Won't you, Lizzy?"

"He won't bet me anymore."

"That's not true," said Jase.

"I bet you four or five times last weekend and I beat you every time. Now you won't bet me anymore."

Jase looked at Chuck, then across the table to Lizzy. He shook his head and turned to Lester, "That's still not gambling, right, Dad? Gambling is when you take money from people when they lose. Right?"

"Both gambling and betting can involve money. I think. Seems like gambling is when the outcome of the bet is pure chance, like flipping a coin. Betting is when you use skill and knowledge to predict the outcome. If I bet you that the next car that drives down our street will be black, then I'm gambling. If I bet you that one football team will beat another one, then I'm betting because I could use skill and knowledge of the game and teams," said Lester. "A gambling buddy explained that to me one day. Makes sense, but he could be wrong."

"I've heard you bet money on license plate numbers," said Chuck. "You're a gambler, Jase."

"It doesn't matter if it's gambling or betting. You're taking your friends' money. You feel good about that? About taking their money?"

"It's only a dollar or two. That's not much; you have to admit that," said Chuck.

"I saw Brad give you five dollars the other day."

"Brad is different. He hardly ever pays when he loses, so when he does pay he usually owes me more than a couple of dollars. And Brad can be a jerk. You can't be upset about Brad."

"Okay, true, I do hope Brad loses lots of money. But what about David? I've seen him lose more than a dollar."

"Yeah, I felt a little bad about David. To be honest, I gave him his money back."

"Wow, Chuck has a heart," said Jase.

"He started crying," said Chuck.

"You made a friend cry for losing money to you? This can't be good, Dad."

Lester dragged a French fry through a puddle of ketchup on his plate. "Jase has a point. You shouldn't take money from friends, even when it's a friendly bet."

"But they're losing a bet."

"If you take bets from friends, then when they lose there will be hurt feelings," said Lester.

"It's called friendship, Chuck. You care about money more than friendship?" Jase turned to Lester. "See what I'm saying?"

Chuck dropped his forehead into the palms of his hands. "I guess you're right; I shouldn't be taking bets from friends. But strangers are on their own. No hard feelings with them."

Jase shook his head. "I think we have a monster on our hands."

"No hurt feelings when you're not really friends with them, and they get excited about the bet," said Chuck. His head lifted a joyful grin, sparkling eyes.

"Who are you talking about?" he asked his brother.

"Kevin," said Chuck.

"Kevin lives right down the street. You see him all the time," said Jase.

"Kevin's not really a friend. He's just a guy in the neighborhood. Maybe you're friends with him, not me."

"Porn, now gambling. Jail is not a fun place, Chuck."

Lester shook his head. "Why don't you just take a break, Chuck, a little pause from your bookie operation? Give some time for thought; give yourself a little air," he said.

"You're going to cut off my money stream?"

"Money stream?" asked Lester.

"Money can't buy everything, Chuck," said Jase.

"Not everything, but most things," said Chuck.

A few light knocks came from the front door. Lester gazed in the door's direction. "Who could that be?" he asked.

"Maybe it's your non-friend Kevin who's crying because he lost money to you, someone he trusted, almost like a friend," said Jase.

"Both of you, give it a rest," said Lester. He stood up and walked toward the front door.

"Kevin is *your* friend, Jase," said Chuck.

Lester turned back to the kitchen table, "No, no more."

"I'll take a little vacation, don't you worry, Dad," said Chuck.

Jase raised his hands, then shook his head.

"Jase, you want to bet me?" Lizzy asked.

"I don't think anyone in this house can beat you, Lizzy. You're the Queen of the Stare," said Lester.

He turned back and walked to the front door. He looked through the peephole and saw what looked like a middle-aged woman wearing blue jeans and a navy peacoat, sitting on the edge of the porch. She faced left so that Lester could see the left side of her face. He saw no one else on the porch, the steps, walkway, nor sidewalk. He unlocked the door and pulled it open a couple of feet.

"Can I help you?" Lester asked the woman.

She turned to face Lester. Her red eyes were swimming. She gave him a confused smile.

"Hi, I'm sorry to bother you at this time of night, but I'm a little lost."

"What do you mean?"

"I'm not sure where I am. I've been walking down the sidewalk for several minutes and nothing looks familiar. I was with a friend at a house a few blocks from here, I think. We were visiting one of his friends who was having a little party, so I've been drinking most of the afternoon. My friend and I had a little fight, so I decided to take a walk."

"How long have you been walking?"

"I'm not sure, ten minutes, twenty minutes, maybe longer. I do apologize for bothering you but I'm a little scared. Can I borrow a phone so that I can call my friend to come pick me up? For some reason I don't have mine."

Lester opened the door a little wider, then took a couple of steps out on the porch. He looked down at the woman who continued to sit. Her shiny eyes jerked from object to object, a light pink in hue, a muddled focus, a puzzled expression.

"I'm so embarrassed, I just don't know what to do. I guess I drank more than I thought I drank. I mean more than I thought I should have drank," she said.

"It's okay," said Lester. "I understand. We've all had our moments. I'll be right back with the phone."

He walked back into the house, closed the door, then walked into the kitchen where his phone lay on the counter.

"Who was that, Dad?" asked Jase.

"A woman who is lost. She wants to use my phone to call someone to come pick her up."

Chuck quickly left his chair and ran into the foyer to look out the window. "Why is she sitting down?" he called back into the kitchen.

At that, Jase and Lizzy raced into the room so they could see the woman on the porch.

"Is she hurt?" asked Jase. "She looks confused."

"Who is she? Do you know her?" asked Lizzy.

Carrying his cell phone, Lester walked up behind his three children. "Hey now, don't embarrass her."

From the hallway, Ardor walked up behind all four of the Gordons, wet hair, a towel draped around her neck wearing black sweatpants, and a purple T-shirt with "Huskies" written in gold across her chest. "What's going on?" she asked.

"There's a crazy lady on the porch," said Chuck.

"She's not crazy, she's just lost," said Jase.

"She looks crazy to me," said Chuck.

"Okay, okay, show's over. Move along, nothing to see. I want you three back in the kitchen," said Lester as he herded them away from the window.

"What about Ardor?" asked Lizzy.

"She's staying here with me. She's going to help me help the woman."

The three children walked back into the kitchen leaving Ardor and Lester standing by the window.

"She does look confused," Ardor said.

Lester explained the situation. "You want to come out here with me?" he asked.

She nodded her head while continuing to look at the woman. "Sure. Poor thing must be mortified."

Ardor followed Lester out to the porch and closed the door behind her.

"Here's the phone," said Lester. The woman took the phone from Lester's hand. "Do you need any help to dial?" asked Lester.

The woman looked at the phone for a few seconds. "I think I can dial," she quietly spoke.

"Would you like a glass of water?" asked Ardor.

The woman looked up at Ardor. "A little water would be nice. Thank you." She then looked at the phone again, studied it, finally turning to Lester and raising the phone to his face. "Would you dial the numbers for me?"

"Sure, no problem."

When Ardor returned with the glass of water, the woman was talking on the phone. Ardor handed the glass of water to the woman.

"She okay?" asked Ardor.

"I think so," said Lester.

The woman turned and asked for Lester's address. After relaying the address, the woman finished the call, then handed the phone to Lester. She took a couple of sips of water and looked at the street. The night was chilly, but not bitter cold.

"I think it's supposed to be in the twenties tomorrow night," said Lester.

"You know why I stopped at your house?" asked the woman.

"Why is that?" asked Lester.

"That Santa Claus you have on the roof."

"Yeah?" said Lester.

"I knew a family lived here," said the woman.

The woman took a couple more swallows. She smiled at Ardor and handed back the glass of water.

"Thank you so much. Both of you are very kind."

"You're welcome," said Ardor.

"Do you want to wait inside?" asked Lester.

"I need to be out here," she said, "so I can flag down my friend."

"Okay. If you need anything just let us know, okay?" asked Lester.

"Thank you, again. Really sorry to bother you."

Ardor and Lester walked inside the house all the way to the great room where the kids sat on the couch watching television.

"Is that woman okay?" asked Lizzy.

"She's fine, Lizzy. Her friend is on his way to pick her up," said Lester.

"Is she drunk?" asked Chuck.

Jase raised up and looked across Lizzy to stare at Chuck. "Really?" he said to Chuck. He turned to Lester, "Dad, I don't know where we go from here. Porn, gambling, and now drinking."

"What are you, a monk?" asked Chuck.

"What's a monk?" asked Lizzy.

"A person who can never have fun," said Chuck.

"Dad?" said Jase.

"I'm glad you're living with us," Lizzy said to Ardor.

"Me, too, Lizzy," said Ardor. "You guys rock."

Chuck raised his right hand to Ardor. She gave him a high five. "That's what I'm talking about," he said with a big grin on his face.

"No good will come from this," Jase said.

"Says you," said Chuck.

The sun had just cleared the horizon when Lester walked out his back door and stood on the last step next to Georgia who looked up at Lester as if waiting for his permission to move. They both breathed fog into the air. Lester stepped down to the patio, then turned left toward his plum trees with Georgia in tow.

"Hey, good morning, Mr. G."

Lester stopped and turned around to look in the direction of the voice. He knew the voice belonged to Kwame.

"Hey there, Kwame," he answered with a wave. Kwame was wearing his Ali robe and blew fog into the air.

"Do you mind if I come over, Mr. G?"

"No, not at all, take the gate," Lester said as he pointed in the direction of the gate on the other side of the home.

Kwame walked down the fence line toward the street and entered the gate on that side of the house where he was met by Georgia. Kwame stopped and petted Georgia for a few seconds before he continued his walk to where Lester stood in the backyard.

"Georgia doesn't look like he's dying," said Kwame.

"Georgia's female. You know that, Kwame."

"Georgia doesn't act like a girl."

"Well, she is. And her body is ate up with cancer. We're going to have to put her to sleep pretty soon."

"That is sad."

"Sure is. What are you doing outside so early in the morning?"

"My dad took all my electronics away from me, so I'm very bored."

"You must have misbehaved for your dad to take all your electronics away."

"Not really. I made a teacher cry at school. It was nothing. My dad is stupid. He's a Black man, you know."

"Kwame, you shouldn't call your dad stupid."

"He's Black. He's stupid."

"I know for a fact that Willard is not stupid. And calling your dad stupid because he's Black is not only disrespectful but it's racist. And you know that you're Black, so you're basically calling yourself stupid. That's the truth, Kwame." Lester gave Kwame a hard look. "I mean that."

"But he's—"

"No, I don't want to hear it. I'll make you leave if you say that again."

Kwame looked at Lester for several seconds, then turned and looked at his house. When he turned back to Lester he said, "I love my dad."

"I know you do."

"But he's—"

"Kwame, what did I just say?"

"Sorry, Mr. G."

"Look, I need to do something. I'm telling you this because I don't want you to be shocked when I do it. Of course, you can do it with me if you want."

"What?"

"Okay, okay, I'm about to lie down on the grass here for a couple of minutes. Just lie on my back."

Kwame nodded his head.

"I know it's cold, there's frost on the ground, but I just need to lie down on the ground for a couple of minutes."

"Okay, Mr. G. So, I can lie down with you? I've done it before. It makes the world closer."

"Sure, sure. Nothing wrong with feeling closer."

Lester dropped down to sit on the grass, then leaned all the way back. He looked at the sky with his head facing the rear of the house. Kwame quickly dropped to the ground and mimicked Lester's maneuver to his back. They were side-by-side, their arms nearly touching one another. To Lester's left, Georgia rolled to her side with her back next to Lester's left arm. He began rubbing Georgia's head, which was nestled next to Lester's elbow. No one spoke for several seconds.

"Mr. G?" Kwame asked, breaking the silence.

"What?"

"Are you and Ardor having sex now?"

"I've told you before, that's none of your business."

"Okay."

Another minute passed before Kwame spoke again.

"Did you do something to some dogs?"

"What are you talking about?"

"A couple of days ago I was outside early in the morning because I was bored, and I saw a bunch of dogs in your front yard."

"How many?"

"A whole bunch. Maybe eight, maybe ten. And they were all white."

"What were the white dogs doing in my front yard?"

"They weren't doing anything, just looking at your house."

"What did you do?"

"I went inside to get my phone so I could take some pictures of all the white dogs, but my dad didn't believe me. He thought I was making it up so I could get my phone back. He gave me the phone but came outside with me to see for himself. But when we walked outside, the dogs were gone."

Lester didn't say anything, just kept rubbing Georgia's head. A few minutes passed.

"I'm gonna miss Georgia, Mr. G," said Kwame.

"We're all gonna miss Georgia."

"She's a good dog. She shouldn't have to die."

"It's a shame, but death don't work that way."

Lester turned his head and looked at Kwame.

"I'm getting cold. How about you, Kwame?"

"I feel a little cold."

"If I lie here much longer I'll be stiff as a log. I'm going in; you can stay if you want." Lester stood up and looked down at Kwame.

"I just need another minute."

"Okay, man. Come on, Georgia, let's go in. We got people waiting on us to make breakfast."

ACKNOWLEDGEMENTS

This novel owes a large debt of gratitude to Ann Blair Huffman, who provided unlimited access to her knowledge and experiences in the world of hospice care. Ann answered every question I posed, directed me to insightful readings, and critiqued the manuscript with honesty and thoroughness. Thank you.

For help and advice on the manuscript, a big thanks to Sheila Jo Collins, Steve Collins, Kirsten Holt, and Marjorie C. Masterson. The motivation to continue and complete the novel is the result of encouragement, support, and praise from Michael Libling, a friend I first met twenty years ago at Bread Loaf. And a special thanks to Jessica Bell, Amie McCracken, Peter Snell, and Alana King, the fine people at Vine Leaves Press who took a chance on me and made the publishing process an enjoyable experience. And finally, to Trish, Annie, and Jackson, a tripod of love and support that makes my world a joy and blessing. Jackson and I know Lester on an intimate level.

Thanks to the editors of the following journals, where earlier versions of these chapters first appeared as short stories: “Anomaly” was published as “Lester Lies Down” in *RE:AL*, Fall, 2003; “Ruby Sweet” was published as “Ruby Sweet” in *littledeathlit*, Winter, 2018; “We Need to Talk” was published as “Niagra” in *The Wax Paper*, Spring, 2021.

VINE LEAVES PRESS

Enjoyed this book?
Go to *vineleavespress.com* to find more.
Subscribe to our newsletter:

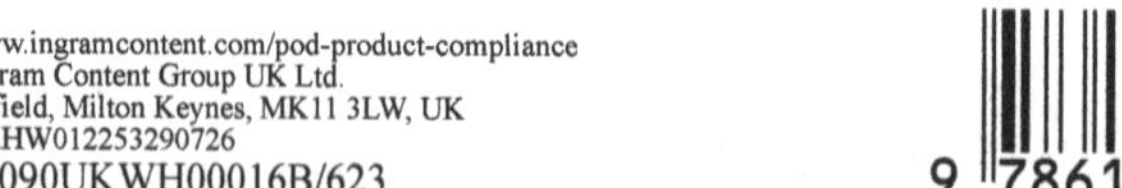
www.ingramcontent.com/pod-product-compliance
Ingram Content Group UK Ltd.
Pitfield, Milton Keynes, MK11 3LW, UK
UKHW012253290726
14090UKWH00016B/623